ROSALIND HEARDER

# KEEP *the* MEN ALIVE

Australian POW doctors in Japanese captivity

ALLEN&UNWIN

First published in 2009

Copyright © Rosalind Hearder 2009

All rights reserved. No part of this book may be reproduced or transmitted in any form or by any means, electronic or mechanical, including photocopying, recording or by any information storage and retrieval system, without prior permission in writing from the publisher. The Australian *Copyright Act 1968* (the Act) allows a maximum of one chapter or 10 per cent of this book, whichever is the greater, to be photocopied by any educational institution for its educational purposes provided that the educational institution (or body that administers it) has given a remuneration notice to Copyright Agency Limited (CAL) under the Act.

Interview extracts from The Australians at War Film Archive are reproduced with permission, courtesy of Mullion Creek Productions Pty Ltd, P.O. Box 2540, Orange, NSW, 2800, Australia.

Allen & Unwin
83 Alexander Street
Crows Nest NSW 2065
Australia
Phone:  (61 2) 8425 0100
Fax:    (61 2) 9906 2218
Email:  info@allenandunwin.com
Web:    www.allenandunwin.com

Cataloguing-in-Publication details are available
from the National Library of Australia
www.librariesaustralia.nla.gov.au

ISBN 978 1 74175 738 5

Internal design by Lisa White
Index by Puddingburn Publishing
Set in 11/16 pt Minion Pro by Bookhouse, Sydney
Printed and bound in Australia by Griffin Press

10 9 8 7 6 5 4 3 2 1

# CONTENTS

| | |
|---|---|
| Author's note | xi |
| Introduction | xiii |
| 1  The road to captivity | 1 |
| 2  Changi: the beginning | 18 |
| 3  Making bricks without straw: the Burma–Thai Railway | 38 |
| 4  Untold stories: the other camps | 68 |
| 5  A complex relationship: doctors and captors | 92 |
| 6  Doctor and officer | 124 |
| 7  Beyond the call: coping in captivity | 155 |
| 8  The long shadow: after the war | 179 |
| Glossary of medical terms | 215 |
| Appendix A   Australian POW doctors | 219 |
| Appendix B   Doctors' deaths in captivity | 225 |
| Endnotes | 227 |
| Bibliography | 263 |
| Acknowledgements | 285 |
| Index | 289 |

*To John Lack*

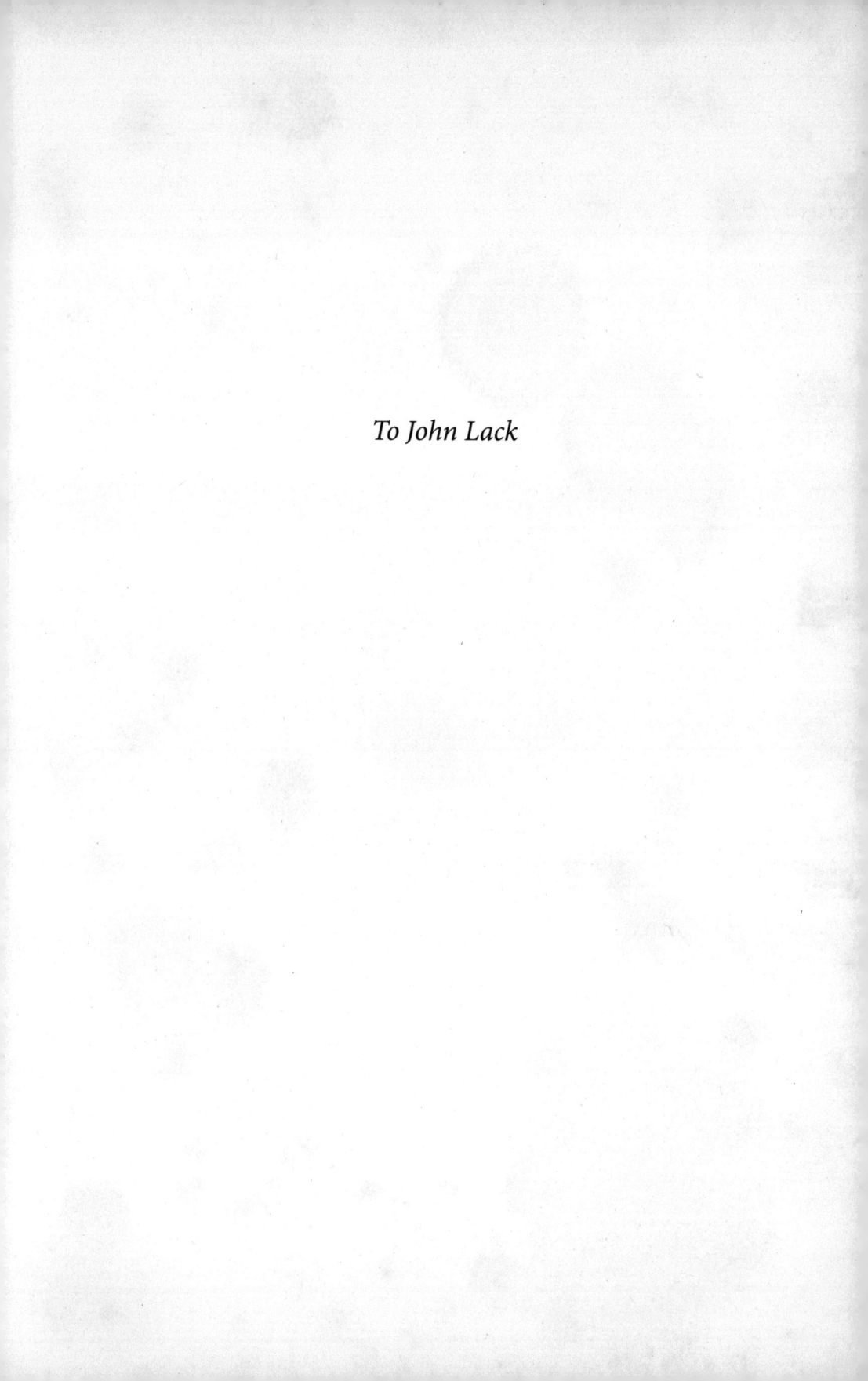

*All wars of any magnitude and duration must be won primarily on the medical front.*

PROFESSOR SIR PETER MACCALLUM

# AUTHOR'S NOTE

Unless otherwise stated, all officers referred to in this book are Australian medical doctors. In each chapter, the first time each doctor is mentioned his rank will be used, and from then on only his surname. Appendix A lists all Australian POW doctors in Japanese captivity in alphabetical order, with their ranks and units for ready reference. Medical or combatant officers of any other nationality are so noted.

All unattributed quotes are from interviews conducted between former POWs and the author.

# INTRODUCTION

*Where would we have been without the doctors? I wonder how many of us would be around today but for them?*[1]

FORMER AUSTRALIAN POW

In 1946 Dr Rowley Richards arrived late to the inaugural postwar meeting of the 2/15th Field Regiment Association, a regiment that had experienced Japanese captivity during World War II. Sitting at the back of the room, he watched as the members began the process of appointing the Association President. Somebody nominated a former POW (Prisoner of War) combatant officer and the response was overwhelmingly negative. To his surprise, Richards then heard himself being nominated. He recalled, 'Now the troops saw me as neither fish nor fowl. I was not . . . one of the officers in authority I suppose, they didn't identify me there. They identified me with somebody who was trying to help them. So I became president and I still am.'[2] That he still holds this position today is a mark of the esteem in which he is held.

Four years earlier, a much younger Captain Rowley Richards, recently graduated in medicine from Sydney University, found himself a prisoner of Japanese forces after the fall of Singapore on 15 February 1942. He was joined by 22,000 fellow Australian servicemen and many thousands more British, Dutch and American troops. For the next three and a half years, Richards would struggle daily to keep men alive in the brutal environment of Japanese imprisonment. But he was not alone in his efforts—another 105 Australian doctors had also been captured, and like Richards, would spend the war working tirelessly for the welfare of fellow POWs.

Despite this group's best efforts, one-third—approximately 8,000—Australian soldiers and sailors died in Japanese captivity. Those who survived would return home with varying degrees of physical and psychological impairment, which some would endure for decades after the war. While imprisonment under other Axis powers was by no means easy, the prisoners of the Japanese were the most unfortunate of an unfortunate lot. Of the 8,000 Australians in POW camps in Europe, 3 per cent died, compared to 36 per cent in the Japanese camps.[3]

Japanese internment was not the same experience for all Australian prisoners. Some spent most of their time as POWs in Changi—a huge, well-organised and comparatively autonomous camp in Singapore. Others were sent with work parties to the primitive conditions and oppressive climate of Burma or Borneo, where they were forced to build their own camps, and were frequently moved from camp to camp under the constant vigilance of their captors. Thousands of Australian POWs, including 44 medical officers, spent almost a year in a horrific 400-kilometre stretch of jungle building the Burma–Thai Railway. A third of the total Australian POW deaths in Japanese imprisonment occurred here. A small number of men, such as those on Ambon and Hainan islands, spent their captivity in total isolation, while others were eventually moved from tropical Singapore and Malaya to the freezing environments of Manchuria (a Japanese-controlled area of China) or the Japanese home islands.

In all these places, Australian doctors accompanied their fellow prisoners and did whatever they could to keep them alive, often at great personal physical and psychological cost. They faced complex demands and pressures, for which there were no precedents, and often assumed positions of importance far outweighing their normal military role.

MAP 1

Japanese military forces held Australian and other Allied POWs in camps all over Asia. Major areas of concentration are identified here.

These doctors ranged in age from Captain Roy Markham Mills, who was just 24 years old when he was captured, to Colonel Edward Rowden White, captured at 58. Mills joined up in 1940 at the age of 22. He had no previous military experience but, like many young men at the time, had a desire to do his bit for his country. White, on the other hand, had decades of surgical experience behind him. He had served in World War I and remained in the militia throughout the inter-war period.

These two men were the youngest and oldest of the Australian POW doctors in World War II, and represented the opposite extremes of experience, both medical and military. At the beginning of the war it would seem that they had little in common; however, as captivity was soon to show, background differences became less marked when the challenges of imprisonment created a shared bond.

Regardless of their previous experience, age or military rank, in Japanese captivity all Australian POW doctors faced an overwhelming combination of factors destined to kill many of their men: debilitating climate, rampant disease, starvation, physical abuse and forced labour. Many Japanese POW camps were without any built infrastructure, and doctors had little or no diagnostic or sterilising equipment, vitamins, or everyday medical supplies such as syringes and bandages. Captivity demanded adaptability, forcing many doctors to be surgeons, dentists, anaesthetists and psychiatrists, whether or not they had specialist knowledge. While in a camp on the Burma–Thai Railway for example, South Australian doctor Captain Colin Juttner, trained as an ophthalmologist, recalled: 'They needed someone to go out with the working parties who was an eye man . . . Well, up on the Railway, I was supposed to be the bloke doing the eyes but I finished up being the bloke doing the amputations—legs and arms.'

In a lighter moment, in Sime Road camp in Singapore, orderly Sergeant John 'Jack' Higgs assisted Australian doctor Captain Frank 'Joe' Vincent to perform some dental surgery. The rudimentary anaesthesia used was ether, dropped onto a cloth mask rigged above the patient's face. Unfortunately Higgs leaned a little too close to the mask and passed out before the patient.[4]

With their unique problems, responsibilities and burdens, the POW doctors faced a series of challenges that no other group of prisoners had to endure, both during and after the war. As well as being vulnerable to the same illnesses as other POWs, they were also often the target of systematic physical and psychological abuse by their Japanese captors, who were constantly dissatisfied with the high levels of illness among the prisoners. Of the doctors themselves, ten never returned, dying alongside their patients.

That this high level of illness was of course a direct result of meagre food, lack of medical supplies and physical brutality was a truth the Japanese never acknowledged. Constant entreaties to their captors for better provisions were mostly met with cold indifference, and the reiteration that the lives of Allied prisoners were worthless. Lieutenant Colonel Albert Coates recorded that men were frequently weighed, as Japanese logic dictated that the less a prisoner weighed, the less food he needed.[5] The food supplied in many camps was often inadequate to sustain survival, let alone the heavy labour which was a part of daily life. Major Howard Eddey recorded an experience at Sandakan, Borneo, where rice polishings (containing much-needed vitamins) were fed to camp pigs designated for the prisoners, but 90 per cent of these pigs were then eaten by the Japanese. He wrote, 'The priority, we considered, was pigs [first] and prisoners next.'[6]

Despite these challenges, in one way doctors were lucky. Unlike other POWs, their role as medical caregivers became *more* important as captivity continued and survival became more difficult. They did not share to the same extent the sense of anger and helplessness that many Australian soldiers, and especially combatant officers, felt upon becoming prisoners of an enemy they had underestimated in battle.

Though their individual experiences were different, common threads connect them. Each doctor worked out strategies to achieve the survival of the greatest possible number based on their training, medical specialties and ingenuity. By trial and error, medical personnel learned to treat illnesses they had never seen before, as well as dealing with familiar conditions complicated by malnutrition and a combination of illnesses.

They made use of whatever skills and resources were available to them to find solutions to the relentless problems they faced. In spite of it all, perhaps most crucially they continued to have faith in the career they had chosen.

Ask an average Australian to name a figure from World War II and, more likely than not, you will hear the name Sir Edward 'Weary' Dunlop. Through his autobiography and in many biographies, the charismatic Dunlop's compelling account of his experiences as an Australian doctor in Japanese imprisonment has been told. But Dunlop's is only one story.

The medical and physical privations of Japanese captivity are widely known, but not the role of those who daily accepted the burden of responsibility for dealing with them. There is a popular perception that Australian POWs were victims of their physical ailments, and that nothing could be done to alleviate their suffering—yet this does not reflect the very high esteem and gratitude that exists towards Australian POW medical officers for their tireless work, and for the lives they *did* save against significant odds. Indeed, ex-POWs 'reserved many of their most heart-felt tributes for the doctors'.[7] Those 14,000 Pacific War POWs who did return to Australia in late 1945 largely attribute their survival to the dedicated work, professional skill and dogged determination of their 'medicos'.

This book tells the story of this small group of extraordinary men who were often the only difference between life and death for Australian prisoners. For almost four years, each of these men was driven by one goal: to do whatever it took to keep men alive. How these doctors adapted to captivity, the ingenuity they showed in creating essential equipment and medicines, the various relationships they forged with different groups of fellow prisoners, their dealings with their unpredictable and brutal captors, and how they ultimately came to terms with their own harrowing experience of Japanese captivity is a fascinating and moving story of Australians in war.

# 1

# THE ROAD TO CAPTIVITY

When they joined up, few Australian doctors considered the possibility of spending the war as prisoners of the Japanese—at that time a largely unknown enemy. World War II saw many Australian doctors eager to enlist, for two main reasons. Those who had previous military experience, either in a medical or non-medical capacity, saw it as a continuation of duty to their nation. For many, this was partly out of loyalty to the British Empire. A sense of duty to their profession as caregivers also influenced their decision to join the war.

The 1933 Australian population census—the last before the outbreak of the war—counted 3,922 medical practitioners. Approximately 2,500 Australian doctors served in the armed forces during World War II—about one-third of the medical profession in Australia at that stage.[1] Of these, 58 per cent were aged 25–44.[2] Among the 106 Australian doctors who became POWs of the Japanese, 86 per cent were under 44, and over half were aged 35 or less.[3] The relative youth of the POW group is also reflected in their rank on enlistment: 86 were captains or majors, the two lowest starting ranks for commissioned medical officers. In fact, over half had no military experience at all before joining up, and only ten had seen service in World War I.[4]

The older group of doctors saw their World War II service as the continuation of a tradition that they had been a part of for many years, while the younger doctors sought to join that tradition themselves. A large component of this sense of duty was the doctors' allegiance, not only to Australia, but to Britain. Most lecturers in Australia's university medical schools were British, students' texts and journals were mostly British, and their 'courses were carefully constructed so that graduates would be eligible for registration by the General Medical Council in London. There was a romantic content in Australian medical attitudes to Britain.'[5] During World War I, medical lecturers at Sydney and Melbourne universities often actively encouraged their students to enlist, usually telling them it was every man's duty to help Britain.[6]

As in World War I, the cultural pressure on Australian men to enlist was intense:

> These were men and women nurtured on tales of empire. They went to school when Empire Day was one of the two great celebratory days in the school calendar, and most believed, in spite of the evidence they could read in the newspapers, that Britannia still ruled the waves.[7]

Many doctors remember the pressure of this legacy. When remembering his childhood during World War I, Dr Leslie Poidevin recalled that 'the relatives and others who came home horrified us with their stories, but at least they had gone to join in with England, which was the thing to do then'. Dr Edward Dunlop, who was seven at the start of World War I, wrote in his *War Diaries* that 'Scores of sturdy, heroic men, including four Dunlops, donned the Anzac garb to seek high adventure or death.'[8] This romantic notion of war service from his childhood spurred him into 'speedily obtain[ing] a commission' in the militia when he qualified in 1934. The outbreak of war saw Dunlop doing further medical training in London, where 'the British spirit was stirring to Churchill's growing bugle call to war'.[9]

Dr Colin Juttner said, 'I suppose I didn't want to do what I did, but that seemed to be the only honourable thing to do.' He was also influenced by the fact that his brother, who had tuberculosis, said to him, 'Well, Col, one or other of us has got to go.' The importance of his role as a doctor in the war became apparent to Juttner later in captivity when he felt 'I was able to *do* something as a doctor'.

A sense of adventure and the chance to experience different types of medicine was also an attraction to young doctors thinking of enlisting. War provided opportunities for them to gain practical skills that they may never have acquired working in a hospital.[10] It also provided an opportunity to work with senior doctors from a variety of specialties, and possibly to secure their patronage to further their future career. Some of the Australian medical officers who served in World War I were 'exceptionally fortunate in being able to use their wartime careers to secure training for peacetime medicine'.[11]

Despite being driven by their sense of duty to enlist, the majority of POW doctors were entirely untrained in the ways of the Australian Army. Dr Des Brennan joined up in 1941 as soon as he had finished his year-long postgraduate training at St Vincent's Hospital in Sydney:

> I came up to Vic Barracks full of joy and happiness because I knew that the Dutch cruiser *Oranje* had been seconded to the Australians as a hospital ship and I could see myself in glorious surroundings out on the open sea patrolling along majestically . . . I got up to Vic Barracks and [his superior] said, 'Captain Brennan, I'm sending you to Malaya . . . to join a motor ambulance convoy.' And I said, 'What on earth's that?'

In 1940, in his second year of residency, Dr Lloyd Cahill recalled the moment when the war began for him: 'Paris fell, and before I knew what had happened, I was called up to go into the army. I knew nothing about the army at all.' He felt lucky that his unit, the 2/19th Battalion, was commanded by Lieutenant Colonel Duncan S. Maxwell, a doctor who also had served in World War I. Cahill was made Regimental Medical

Officer (RMO) and, despite his inexperience and a childhood desire to be in the air force, Cahill soon realised that he loved army life.

Poidevin, who graduated in 1939 and chose to study medicine partly to escape the poverty he and many of his peers had grown up with in 1930s Australia, felt a sense of obligation to join up: 'I felt I had to go to the war and my [medical practice] partner was married, so I was the one who could get away from the partnership and he was prepared to carry on and do the lot.' Interestingly, Poidevin was attracted to army medicine because 'knowing the history of the doctors in the First World War, it was the army doctors that really were the active medical people'.

The men who would become orderlies in captivity—in many ways the backbone of the POW medical services—similarly had a variety of reasons for joining up in a non-combatant role. Bill Flowers, a 'confirmed pacifist', initially refused to join up. When his best friend did, loyalty to his friend overcame his political sensibilities, but he found a compromise by becoming an orderly in the medical corps. His medical work in captivity, along with many other orderlies, would prove crucial.

Gordon Nichols, also destined to become a POW orderly, originally followed his brother's example and joined the artillery. At his training camp, a situation arose where medical volunteers were called for, and Nichols volunteered, primarily 'to get out of doing route marches and rifle drill'. He was so impressed with the medical officer for whom he worked, Captain Des Brennan, that when Brennan asked him to join the medical arm of the 2/3rd Motor Ambulance convoy, 'I got to become very interested in it and I began to think to myself, "Well I joined the army to be trained to kill people, but there's much more fun in trying to save people."'

His father's experiences influenced Dr Philip Millard to join up: 'Well the obvious reasons were I suppose everybody was doing it . . . and my father had played a very big part in World War I. He was a doctor and he was an Anzac.' His father returned from the war 'with the rank of colonel and CMG, CBE and he was really quite somebody. That of course was quite a good reason for joining up.'

The young Roy Mills expected that his father, a banker, would want him to follow his example. However, on a summer evening during the Depression, 'my father said to me, "Would you like to do medicine?" I said yes. He said, "I think we can do it." And that's how it happened. Simple.' His reason for joining the army was equally simple: 'I think I was just stupid that day. I was just plain stupid. And yet there was this sort of mood in the country and you were caught up in it.' Still, Mills had prepared somewhat for the day he joined up:

> It was quite obvious in a short time that Germany was rearming and we were going to see the same sort of period we had gone through in 1914–18. So I was at the university and had completed my medical course, and got a position as RMO at Prince Alfred Hospital in Sydney and I'd also joined the Citizen Military Forces because I felt that there was something happening wrong.

When attached to the 2/10th Field Ambulance, Mills was instantly impressed by the attitude and experience of Colonel Alfred Derham and his deputy, Lieutenant Colonel John 'Glyn' White, both of whom had served in World War I and would prove to be key mentors to young doctors in captivity.

Dr Victor Brand 'just drifted' into studying medicine. 'I didn't have the idea that I wanted to cure the ills of humanity.' Although employment opportunities were few due to the Depression, 'my father found that he could afford to send me to university and we chose medicine'. At the time of the war, Brand was practising as a rural locum, which he was not enjoying, and he wanted a change. Also, being Jewish, Hitler's anti-Semitism naturally disturbed him, and he wanted to do his part to fight Nazism.

Similarly alarmed by the advance of the Nazis across Europe, Dr Michael Woodruff was spurred into enlisting. He was advised that he would be of more use to the army if he had more surgical experience, so he completed a Master of Surgery Degree at the University of Melbourne in early 1941.[12] The more senior Dr Burnett Clarke studied medicine at the University of Melbourne from 1915 to 1920. Medical students were not allowed to join the war partway through their studies—as was the case in World War I.[13] Between the wars, Clarke set up a successful radiology practice, married and started a family. Yet when war broke out in 1939, he immediately left it all behind to join up.

In the period before World War II medicine was taught at only three Australian universities: Sydney, Melbourne and Adelaide. All the doctors who became POWs in 1942 received similar training. Most would have received a basic course in tropical medicine, but this was often regarded as a relatively unimportant subject. Dr Leslie Poidevin recalled: 'we did tropical medicine in Sydney University in our course, and we learnt the rudiments of malaria'. Some did short courses in the army before embarkation, other did not—an omission that would later cause problems in captivity. What Australian doctors were prepared for, however, was 'outback' medicine: living off the land, and hygiene and sanitary measures such as boiling water before drinking it. Such knowledge would prove extremely useful.

British doctors, on the other hand, were all schooled in tropical medicine. For centuries the city of Liverpool had been the world leader in this field, both because of the thousands of immigrants and slaves who arrived there during the height of British imperialism in the nineteenth century, and the need to provide protection for British civil servants who were posted to the colonies.[14] The Liverpool School of Tropical Medicine's first lecturer, Ronald Ross, had a military background, and he was particularly interested in malaria, a real problem for troops in tropical areas. During World War I, the school temporarily became a tropical diseases hospital.[15] As it turned out, however, British medical officers seemed less able than the Australians to cope with the special characteristics of tropical diseases in Japanese captivity, an anomaly that will be discussed later. Dutch doctors, on the other hand, had extensive experience with tropical diseases, many having lived for several years in the Netherlands East Indies.

Despite their differences in age and experience, all the doctors had similar social backgrounds and cultural attitudes. They all trained in the early years of the twentieth century, a period when 'general medicine and military medicine stood on the threshold of remarkable progress in the science of saving lives'.[16] By studying medicine they were implicitly learning 'an introduction to the values of the medical culture',[17] and they expected the responsibility and leadership afforded them by their status in society. In short, the doctors of that era were revered and in many ways considered infallible. As their experiences in captivity would show, this esteem would be both a blessing and a burden.

## The Malaya campaign

Described as 'one of the greatest disasters in British history',[18] the Malaya campaign resulted in the capture of more than 100,000 Allied troops. The many theories about who should be blamed for the failure will not be examined here, but rather the work of doctors during the campaign and how they began to shape and adapt their roles within an environment with limited resources, a process that would continue in captivity.

Set up as a strategic naval base for the British in 1923, Singapore was not the 'impregnable fortress' that it was imagined to be, but was still considered a significant stronghold of the British Empire.[19] Australian deployments from the 8th Division arrived from February 1941 and throughout that year, and further reinforcements landed in January 1942. By the beginning of that fateful year, there were 15,000 Australian troops in Malaya, approximately 3,000 in Java, 1,300 in Timor, 1,100 on Ambon, 1,400 in Rabaul and 1,500 elsewhere in New Guinea. After Japan's attack on Pearl Harbor on 7 December 1941, and the subsequent sinking of the Royal Navy battleships *Repulse* and *Prince of Wales*, it proved impossible to save Singapore and Malaya, despite the thousands of British and Commonwealth troops stationed there.

Before the Japanese invasion, life in Malaya was relatively easy for medical personnel. One Australian nurse commented that Australian doctors 'were mainly from big city hospitals and were used to having everything at their fingertips'.[20] In Malaya, they did. Malacca had a large, modern hospital, which was the main medical base for Australian troops. Lieutenant Colonel Albert Coates described a typical day:

> . . . rise at daylight—a brisk walk up the 'Bukit' [mountain] reading Malay vocabulary, then breakfast at 7.30 . . . work begins at 8.15, the morning being the best time for operating or visiting wards, lunch, a session with a Malay dispenser . . . then tennis or golf (9 holes) or a five mile walk with Col White and then evening rounds and some entertainment or lecture.[21]

Coates took the opportunity to learn as much as he could about tropical medicine, which had been only a small part of his medical training at Melbourne University.[22] Juttner also recalled the relative ease of his lifestyle during this time: 'We didn't do anything much except look after our own members of the unit, the 13th AGH [Australian General Hospital], and moved about and enjoyed ourselves at least as much as we could.'

The Alexandra Military Hospital had been established in Singapore by the British in 1938 to serve the Far East Command troops. Conditions there were similarly relaxed before the Japanese attacks began. British doctor Captain Will Brand of the 32nd Company commented:

> Life in the hospital turned out to be fairly easy going, apart from the irritating militaristic interferences which took precedence over everything else, or so it seemed . . . Much later on when it occurred to Malaya Command that there might be hostilities, we had sessions on the rough ground at the rear of the hospital, dashing about with stretchers and of course revising how to apply field dressings and Thomas' splints. We treated it all as a big joke and nuisance. Still life went on quite peaceably and we learned how to dodge trouble from too officious N.C.O.'s.[23]

Australian doctors were unimpressed with what they saw of Singapore's defences, and with the British troops that were part of 'the society of the residency, long drinks on cane chairs, overhead fans and a hierarchy of servants to cut grass, wash clothes and serve food'.[24] When war broke out in 1939, the '"business as usual" feel to the colony persisted even when the war news from Europe grew gloomy'.[25] Captain Peter Hendry, a young doctor, was shocked by the attitude of the British as the Japanese invasion closed in. When he was sent to a mobile British Field Ambulance across the causeway linking the Malayan peninsula and Singapore, the officers greeted him with a lavish lunch waited upon by Indian servants, complete with a tablecloth and silver. Hendry felt his British hosts behaved as if 'they didn't know there was a war on'.

Medical officers tried to stay as busy as possible before the war reached Singapore: 'it seemed every man's tonsils came out, and every appendix'.[26] They also kept up their medical training, seeking contacts in the local medical community to learn more about tropical disease. Stationed at Kajang, Brennan described his early days:

> Most of my work was simple stuff, checking the boys for venereal disease . . . after days off, and training my own medical orderlies because there was already a hospital there to do the routine stuff. I used to love to go and do a few rounds at the hospital with some of the physicians there because I was always going to do medicine rather than surgery. I used to enjoy that and I got myself included a few times we had anything worthwhile there.

Similarly, medical orderly John Higgs, stationed in Kuala Lumpur with the 8th Divisional Headquarters, recalled:

> At times it seemed that our activities in K. L. were largely a continuation of what we had been doing at Rosebery Racecourse, simply translated into a tropical setting. We went swimming before breakfast, but in the pool at the Selangor Golf Club instead of Maroubra surf beach; we did our target practice shooting at the Selangor Rifle Club's range, just as we had done on the Long Bay range in Suburban Sydney . . . we carried on our administrative duties in much the same fashion as before.[27]

These months of relative ease for the Allied forces in Malaya and Singapore were short-lived. When the Japanese forces landed at Kota Bahru on the north-east coast of the Malayan peninsula on 8 December 1941, the Allies were soon overwhelmed: the capabilities of the Japanese had been grossly underestimated. Not only were they widely portrayed as ineffectual fighters, but racially ignorant views were commonly passed about among the troops, for instance that the Japanese were shortsighted and thus could not aim guns properly, or that they were 'bandy-legged and pigeon-toed and could not march properly'.[28] Only senior officers and a small number of the lower ranks 'were conscious of the efficiency of the Japanese, and of their own vulnerability'.[29]

Numbering 35,000, the Japanese troops swept south through the peninsula with their eyes fixed on the ultimate prize: Singapore. Their 70-day campaign, which pushed the Allied forces down the Malayan peninsula and into Singapore, was 'a triumph of rational planning, considered preparation and brilliant execution' and showed without doubt that 'the island's defence had been poorly planned, was being badly executed, and that its participants were disheartened'.[30] Higgs recalled the unsettling and swirling rumours: 'For the first day or so of warfare, confusion reigned supreme ... The Japanese were being thrown back. The Indians were being routed. The Japanese had suffered immense casualties. No, it was the Indians. The Japanese were streaming down the peninsula. No, they weren't.'[31]

During the campaign, major Australian actions were fought at Gemas, Muar River and Bakri. Captain Victor Brand won the Military Cross for his work at Bakri, where he left the protection of the slit trenches to rescue wounded men while they were being bombed. Although the Australians comprised only 14 per cent of the overall British force, they sustained 73 per cent of the battle casualties.[32] Most Australian troops had received several months of jungle training, but some were so badly resourced during the campaign that they could not live off the land once supplies were exhausted. Hungry and dispirited, many were showing signs of malnutrition, dysentery and malaria within a week.[33] Doctors had to treat the wounded while remaining constantly mobile to keep ahead of the advancing Japanese. Hendry, with the 2/10th Field Ambulance, remembered:

> From then on, we moved back regularly, being told, 'Move back. Move back. Move back.' I was out on a tour of all the advanced posts . . . we were waiting there for casualties to come back and the troops came back and said, 'You'd better go back. We're the front line.'

Captain Rowley Richards also remembered the retreat and the exhaustion it caused: 'Well, frankly by this time we were plain buggered. You know weary, tired and . . . we often withdrew two and three times in a night. Move, move, move, move and we had very little or no rest at all for two weeks.'[34]

Some of the wounded had to be left behind as troops withdrew; some of these men were executed by Japanese soldiers along the way.[35] Mills described feeling 'naked and exposed' during the retreat. His 2/10th Field Ambulance alone evacuated 3,000 men, including non-Australian troops.[36] Brand, with the 2/29th Battalion at Muar on 17 January 1942, wrote of the hopeless circumstances in which he had to minister to patients:

> The night was pitch dark, and I had to find the position and extent of the wounds with my fingers, and dress them while holding my morphia syringe in my mouth, so that it was no wonder that the next morning I found my hands, face and clothes stiff with blood.[37]

Pufflett remembered the chaos as they moved from Johore along the Bukit Timah Road:

> Snipers were shooting around the hospital and in fact shells fell on the hospital and killed some of the people in the wards. I can still remember people working in the wards, around the beds and as a shell would go over, everybody would sort of sway down or bend down with the sound of the shells.

The Australian reinforcements hastily dispatched to Singapore in January arrived to a scene of complete chaos: 'The city was littered

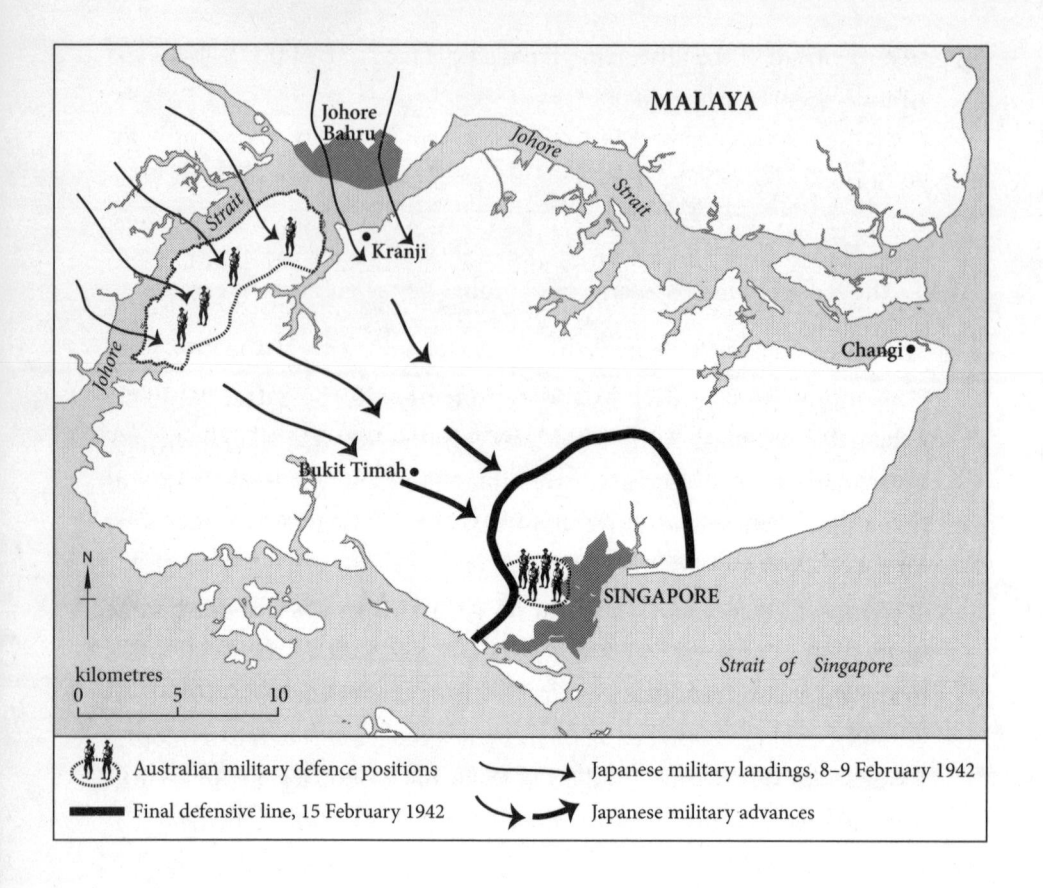

MAP 2

The final positions of the Australian forces leading up to capitulation, showing the path of the Japanese military invasion.

with gutted buildings and smouldering wreckage, and was crowded with refugees who, like everyone else, had nowhere to go when the bombs fell.'[38] Some medical staff felt disillusioned when called upon to do non-medical work, such as digging trenches or driving trucks. The 6th and 7th Divisions were also recalled from the Mediterranean and North Africa to reinforce the Allies and protect Australia. About 3,000 men of the 7th Division were taken prisoner soon after landing in Java in early 1942.

The final retreat of the Allied troops across the causeway from Malaya to Singapore occurred on 31 January. The causeway was then destroyed with set charges, trapping the Allied troops on Singapore Island. The 10th AGH, with 900 patients, was set up at a variety of sites in the city. Alexandra Military Hospital, built to house 550 beds, ended up with 900 patients by 14 February. Makeshift beds were squeezed in between existing beds, and placed in corridors or wherever there was a space.[39]

The Japanese continued to bomb the island and Australian hospital staff braced for the onslaught of casualties, which increased by around 2,000 per day, including civilians. Extra buildings in the city were requisitioned for staff and patients, with the enormous St Andrew's Anglican Cathedral, for example, set up as a makeshift hospital. The Cathedral was bombed, but still the Australian doctors worked around the clock. Brennan, trying to perform as much surgery as he could in the last frantic days before the surrender, recalled, 'I spent half my day giving anaesthetics on the baptismal font.'[40] Pufflett said, 'One operated on anything that was able to crawl down the long corridors of the hospital to reach the operating theatres.' With little water supply, Pufflett had only one bucket of water in which to wash his gloves between surgeries. Despite these terrible conditions, Mills remembered, 'Senior British officers who had had experience at Dunkirk and North Africa said that the treatment of the wounded . . . was the best they'd ever encountered.' During this time, a handful of the doctors and other medical personnel caring for the wounded lost their lives.

Neither their exhaustion nor the dangerous conditions in which they were working affected the doctors' professional ethics. Orderly Bill Flowers remembered that several civilians and Japanese soldiers were taken in and treated at the Cathedral, with no difference in the quality of care they received. Brennan came across a heavily pregnant Singaporean woman in the Cathedral who had been shot in the chest. He said:

> She was obviously dying and this is where I got very brave. I yelled out to some of my soldiers who were there, 'Have you got a knife? I'll get that baby out and do a Caesarean right here.' I'd never done one in my life, had never even seen one done I don't think.

Brennan was too late to save the mother and baby.

The heavy fire continued and the doctors knew they were likely to be taken prisoner. Brennan set about scrounging for supplies in the burning city, an example of the resourcefulness that doctors would demonstrate in captivity. He walked into Singapore's Adelphi Hotel and stole towels—which were to prove extremely valuable—and even buried some top-range whisky, thinking, 'When we come back we'll have something to drink.' Thirty years would pass before he returned for that drink.

Other doctors grabbed what medical supplies they could. Captain Claude Anderson remembered stealing a lumbar puncture needle from a hospital as troops were chased down the peninsula: 'I stole several things just being left there for the Japanese . . . For some reason I carried this lumbar puncture needle and it came in very useful once.'

Seeing the battle casualties all around him and perhaps sensing the inevitability of defeat, Lieutenant Colonel Duncan Maxwell talked to fellow Australian and combatant officer Lieutenant Colonel James H. Thyer on the night of 9 February. Thyer recalled the conversation: 'he was a doctor in civil life and his function was to save life. Maxwell considered that what was going on on Singapore Island was senseless slaughter. Maxwell was going back to Lieutenant-General Arthur Percival [General Officer Commanding, Malaya] to urge him to surrender.'[41] Maxwell was advised not to, but regardless, due to this perceived 'defeatist' attitude, his career in the army was effectively finished.[42]

However, when the Japanese cut off the water supply to Singapore two days later, Brigadier C. H. Stringer, the British commander of the medical services for the Malaya Force, recommended to Percival 'that from a medical standpoint it would be wise to capitulate immediately before the outbreak of malaria and hygiene-related diseases became uncontrollable'.[43]

The 65 Australian nurses in Singapore were ordered to evacuate on 11 February, though none wanted to. One, Betty Jeffrey, said about leaving her patients, 'I have never felt worse about anything.'[44]

With the departure of the nurses and the resulting dearth of medical staff, medical orderlies who had been allotted other jobs were brought back into medical teams. Luckily, due to an initiative by Coates a year earlier, many orderlies had been trained to assist with surgical procedures in case nurses were evacuated—a foresight that proved crucially important in the following years.[45]

During the campaign, the doctors had quickly learned that medical personnel received no special treatment from the Japanese. Cut off with the 2/19th Battalion and many casualties at Muar, Brennan remembered: 'The British had approached the Japanese with a white flag and said, "Can we send an ambulance in and bring out the wounded, the seriously wounded?" and they were refused.' On 14 February a horrific massacre occurred at Alexandra Hospital. British radiologist Major John W. D. Bull was a witness:

> [There were] two Japanese soldiers about two hundred yards away, one with field glasses and the other with a rifle. The Major took up a Red Cross flag and held it up at the window, thinking that there might be some doubt in their minds that [this] was . . . a hospital. The Japanese responded with a shot which missed Major Bull and struck the wall behind him.[46]

A short while later, 50 doctors, nurses and patients lay murdered, with many more wounded. The next day, when Percival officially surrendered, the Japanese military killed a further 200 patients.

In his diary on 16 February 1942, Major Hugh Rayson wrote, 'Everyone is overcome by the fate we are the victims of and very uncertain of the future.'[47] After the surrender of Singapore Island to the Japanese on 15 February 1942, the doctors' immediate concern was treating those injured during the hard and bloody fighting. Nearly 2,000 Australian soldiers died fighting in Malaya and Singapore, and most of the survivors of the Australian forces stationed in Timor, Ambon and Rabaul were captured.

British Prime Minister Winston Churchill had issued a directive in Malaya that 'Commanders and Senior Officers should die with their troops. The honour of the British Empire and of the British Army is at stake.'[48] Clearly, for some officers this edict did not extend to captivity:

the commander of the Australian troops in Malaya, Major-General H. Gordon Bennett, successfully escaped. Bennett's justification for leaving Singapore was that he wanted to return to Australia to 'give first-hand information of Japanese methods and strategy'.[49] Many Australians who became POWs saw Bennett's escape as a betrayal, and time has not dulled the animosity many feel towards him. Pufflett said of Bennett's departure, 'It was pretty crushing after the capitulation when you knew your senior officer had gone.' Bennett's tenure in Malaya, however, had not been a smooth one. Higgs recalled that '8 Div HQ was not, at the most senior level, a very happy unit, largely because of General Bennett, who appeared to disagree with Army HQ in Australia, with Malaya HQ (British) in Singapore, with his own senior staff officers at 8 Div HQ and with several of his senior commanders in the field.'[50]

After the Singapore debacle and a postwar inquiry that found he was at fault for leaving Singapore, Bennett was never given another command position and, rightly or wrongly, his name is now associated with ignominy in the minds of most Australians.

For many doctors, however, escape was never an option. Most medical personnel chose to remain with their sick and wounded patients, knowing that they themselves would surely become prisoners. As carers for the sick, escape was an anathema to their professional and ethical code.

A British doctor, Lieutenant Colonel C. W. Maisey, who decided to stay behind, commented wryly that 'the majority of [combatant] officers in Java were trying to make arrangements to get away and were snatching at the smallest chance of doing so'.[51] Maisey, the Assistant Director of Medical Services for the South-West Pacific Command, wrote, 'I had undertaken to stay behind in Java and care for our sick and wounded . . . no officer could understand that the greatest battle to be fought in the South-West Pacific was disease.'[52] Maisey also wrote about the self-sacrifice of a fellow doctor in the Royal Army Medical Corps who had escaped from Singapore to Tjilitjap on the south coast of Java. Major Beadnell 'offered his services, although he had been offered a place in one of the ships leaving Tjilitjap . . . This officer's devotion to duty at a time when it was so rare was most stimulating to all Brit. Force Headquarters.'[53]

Also in Java, Lieutenant Colonel Edward Dunlop wrote to Brigadier Arthur S. Blackburn, Commanding Officer of the 2/3rd Machine Gun Battalion (known as Blackforce), of the refusal of Dunlop's medical staff to evacuate: 'All ranks promptly notified their intention of remaining with the patients in their care, and expressed their complete willingness to undertake any further services Blackforce might require.'[54] In Rabaul, New Guinea, with the 2/22nd Battalion, Australian medical officer Captain John Finch Akeroyd was equally selfless. When he was asked to join the remaining members of his unit in escaping, Akeroyd 'voluntarily returned to Rabaul into captivity to care for the sick and wounded there'. He received an MBE for this action.

The vast majority of the 106 doctors who would be responsible for the lives of thousands of POWs for almost four years were young and inexperienced in any kind of military environment or conflict. In many ways this would prove an advantage, as youthful enthusiasm and risk-taking would prove very useful in finding solutions to medical problems in captivity.

During the Malaya campaign, the doctors demonstrated characteristics that would be strengthened in captivity: selflessness when it came to patient care, resourcefulness and an implacable belief in the importance of their work. Hendry later wrote, 'And so the campaign was concluded, but this was not the end of the war for our medical troops. Rather it was a pause before the long years of captivity were to bring out the very best of our men and the benefits of their months of medical training.'[55] Despite the exhausting Malaya campaign, the hardest challenges for the medical officers still lay ahead. While they may have felt prepared for war when they joined up, none were prepared for captivity.

# 2

# CHANGI: THE BEGINNING

For most of the 14,972 Australians captured in Singapore, Java, Timor and Ambon their introduction to imprisonment under the Japanese was Changi. This large camp, situated on the east of Singapore Island, housed many thousands of Allied prisoners, and occupied a pivotal place in the Australian POWs' lives over the next three and a half years. It became a 'home' camp, where most Australians started their captivity, and where many witnessed the war's end.

Most doctors who were captured in places other than Singapore were imprisoned at Changi at some stage. During their first months here they began to learn about the reality of practising medicine in captivity, and became aware of the limitations that would hinder their work. Ingenuity and a shared professional determination to find solutions to problems would only go so far. In general however, although the adjustment period was difficult, Changi did not test the doctors' resolve, professional confidence, and personal stamina to the same extent as later camps would. Lessons from Changi became increasingly relevant as POWs were moved from Singapore to other camps where doctors were subjected to much greater challenges. In a sense, Changi was a halfway house between the experience of the Malaya campaign and what was to follow in camps outside Singapore. In Changi doctors began the process of learning POW medicine's language, including the kinds of diseases and conditions that would remain chronic threats for POWs throughout their captivity.

## The move to Changi

The first challenge for the Australian Army leadership and doctors was the physical relocation to Changi. The day after the surrender of the Allied forces, the captured Australian soldiers began the 29-kilometre march to the camp, along with thousands of British, Dutch and Indian troops. The wounded, including 1,100 Australians, required close medical attention. Altogether there were 9,000 Allied sick and injured, including medical personnel caring for them, who would be unable to make the trip on foot.

Previously used as a large accommodation base for British troops, Changi was unusual among POW camps in that it had an established infrastructure including several large barracks, running water and electricity. The area also held the smaller compound known as Changi jail, which Allied civilian internees and POWs would later inhabit. However, Changi was never designed to hold so many thousands of people at once.

The daunting task of transferring the sick and wounded Australian troops to Changi fell to Lieutenant Colonel Glyn White, Assistant Director, Medical Services. His slight build and short stature belied great courage and leadership. White had received an OBE (Order of the British Empire) just ten days earlier for his organisation of the 8th Division medical administration in Australia, and for overseeing the establishment of all Australian Imperial Force (AIF) hospitals and medical services in Malaya during the campaign. General Gordon Bennett wrote of White, 'His untiring efforts under most trying climatic conditions, and his keen sense of duty, combined with a very high standard of efficiency have assured recognition for outstanding services.'[1]

On the day after the surrender, White was told by a group of Japanese officers, including the chief Japanese medical officer, C. L. Sekiguchi, that he had seven days to move the sick and wounded using only five ambulance cars. White began by asking Colonel Hedley Summons, still at the makeshift hospital in St Andrew's Cathedral, to use his own Red Cross vehicles to move as many staff and as much medical equipment as possible and to set up a temporary hospital at Changi. White commented, 'The move was made without any major incident and it was not long before I realised that the Japanese were so disorganised that though they issued orders they did not have the personnel to see that they were carried out.'[2]

Negotiating with Sekiguchi, White established that he would be allowed to use any other vehicles he could procure. By the morning of 17 February, White had found no fewer than 20 three-ton trucks, 55 motor ambulances and a staff car he could use. Sekiguchi then surprised White by organising passes for all the vehicles. White mused about his intentions: 'I wondered at the time whether he was remembering he was a medico and on the previous day he did not want to appear "soft" in front of junior military officers.' Australian officers were already discovering the intricacies of interacting with their captors: 'I was to learn later that if you wanted to request something, it was always wiser to wait for the opportunity when you could speak alone, to the officer concerned.'[3]

The disorganisation of the Japanese administration in the chaos of capitulation worked to the Australians' benefit. White's orderly, John Higgs, described how, by playing one Japanese officer against another, his boss:

> ... managed to secure far more ambulance and other transport than the Japanese had authorised; and he brought into Changi equipment and stores far in excess of what he had the authority for. The result of his enthusiastic initiatives in directing scrounging and pilfering on a grand scale was that it became possible to set up a remarkable standard of hospital accommodation and treatment for prisoners right from the outset.[4]

White was 'determined to take as much equipment as possible'. In an incredible effort, his staff managed to bring in to Changi 4,500 hospital beds, 7,000 mattresses stuffed with hidden medical supplies, 'a couple of pianos', and most importantly arranged transport so efficiently that none of the sick or wounded had to walk.[5] Other measures such as distributing medicines and equipment in small portions among men and officers meant that no large caches could be confiscated by the Japanese. This stockpile acted as an insurance policy for future work parties too, as doctors moving out with men to unknown destinations would have at least some stores to take with them.[6] Despite these efforts, it soon became clear that supplies would not last forever. Allan Walker, the official World War II medical historian, recorded that the end of supplies as basic as surgical gloves marked a clear increase in post-operative infections in captivity.[7]

Though few Australians had really had much direct contact with the Japanese, and what was known about them was a mix of myth and xenophobic stereotype, White was correct to assume they would not provide adequate food and supplies. Nor did he envisage that their captivity would be short, as many Australians hoped. White's cautiousness and strategic hoarding of medical supplies was another sign of the resourcefulness and strength that would sustain doctors throughout their confinement. His foresight and sheer determination to get as many supplies into the camp as possible would help many over the next few years, and secure him lasting respect among Australian POWs.

When they arrived at Changi the Australians were allocated Selarang Barracks as their living quarters, formerly used in peacetime by the 2nd Battalion Gordon Highlanders. Located in the centre of the Changi area, Selarang consisted of seven three-storey concrete barracks and some bungalows. Buildings like these were scattered throughout the camp. Some were uninhabitable because of the bombing, but the mild tropical climate meant that the men could sleep outside. British prisoners were held in Roberts Barracks and Kitchener Barracks, Roberts later becoming the main POW hospital. Dutch POWs were concentrated around India Barracks. The Australians later established their own hospital at Selarang, due to the high numbers of the sick, but major cases and operations continued to go to Roberts Hospital. Most of the Australian doctors initially slept together in one large room.

While conditions in Changi were crowded, rudimentary and by no means easy, it would be the best organised and supplied medical base the doctors would encounter during their captivity. Compared with other camps doctors would face throughout Asia, Changi hospitals were medically well equipped—at least in the beginning. They had operating theatres and equipment such as X-ray machines and laboratory apparatus, and simple but essential supplies like bedpans. Also, because the Japanese commanders allowed each Allied army administration to run its own affairs, the doctors experienced little interference from their captors.

The Japanese ordered the Allied divisions to put barbed wire around each of their perimeters within the camp and before long a routine and a semblance of pre-captivity military order was established.

## Diet, deficiency and disease

After the logistical effort of moving to Changi, medical personnel faced urgent work. There were many men with injuries, from shrapnel wounds to amputated limbs. However, the most critical challenge soon became the lack of food and the resulting malnutrition, a problem that would remain a struggle for all prisoners. Within two weeks of captivity, the radical change in diet—from military rations to mostly rice and a few vegetables given by the Japanese—caused widespread digestive problems.[8] Australian Sergeant Stan Arneil wrote that in these first weeks, 'The rice played havoc with our insides and with our minds.'[9] Gross overcrowding and inadequate sewerage systems led to outbreaks of bacillary dysentery, which would remain endemic in all camps.

Although many men had brought what army rations they still had with them to Changi, these did not last long. Many POWs believed that they would be rescued or somehow released after a few weeks, so at first there was little thought of rationing, and 'many found it hard to make physical and mental preparations for a long internment'.[10] Captain Roy Mills recalled wondering, as others did, whether the American Navy was on its way to rescue them: 'Realists, like Capt Ian McGregor, who proposed and was allowed to initiate a paw-paw orchard, were scorned and regarded as out and out pessimists.'[11] By April 1942 food was so scarce that when Major Alan Hobbs was given a crushed peanut product to use as fertiliser, he ate it although it was 'not pleasant', had 'no peanut flavour' and was full of weevils.[12] As time passed, more concerted efforts were made to conserve the most precious foodstuffs. Cooks eventually learned how to prepare rice properly; their first attempts had resulted in 'a tight ball of grayish, gelatinous substance, nauseous in its lack of flavour and utterly repulsive'.[13]

As early as eight weeks after the fall of Singapore, deficiency diseases began to appear in Changi. This was because the major part of the men's diet was polished rice; that is, rice which had the husks removed, depriving prisoners of the vital vitamin B they contained. Doctors had to quickly learn about the nutrients in the unfamiliar foods and how best to prepare them for maximum effect and digestibility. Terms such as 'vitamins, proteins and carbohydrates . . . became household words.'[14] A report written in June 1942, on the back of an old calendar, described a group of 261 POWs who were all affected by some kind of vitamin deficiency, stomatitis and scrotal dermatitis.[15] Men began experiencing chronic fatigue, muscle weakness, blackouts and massive weight loss. Captain Claude Anderson recalled losing 3 stone (approximately 19 kilograms) in his first few months in Changi. To Allied medical officers these new nutritional challenges 'provoked their protestations and unleashed their energies'.[16]

After repeated requests from the doctors, the Japanese provided the prisoners with bags of rice polishings. However, these were too potent for most weakened men to digest directly, so they had to be processed further. One method was to boil large amounts of rice polishings in calico bags, leave them for 24 hours, and then reboil them. The men were then given the stock from the double boiling.[17]

Lack of familiarity with the different foods also posed problems. From 1943, for example, the Japanese at Changi supplied soybeans, a rich source of protein and vitamin B. However, the POWs did not know how to process them to make them edible and they ate and passed the beans whole.[18] On the advice of some Dutch POWs who were more accustomed to Asian foods, the doctors learned how to make tempeh—by boiling the soybeans and removing their husks, then cultivating them with fungus from hibiscus leaves, leaving them to soak for 36 hours, and deep-frying the result.[19] Captain Rowley Richards commented: 'Our fellows got on quite well with the Dutch. They were pretty smart.'[20]

Dietary deficiencies presented a constant struggle for the doctors. Even if the men could cope with hard labour, physical abuse and starvation, the lack of vitamins meant their immunity to disease and infection was drastically lowered. Without vitamin B, high numbers of men fell victim to a range of deficiency diseases—beri-beri, pellagra and amblyopia (visual defects), to name a few.

Common in Changi from March 1942, beri-beri caused myriad problems, ranging from grossly swollen lower limbs and oedema (an accumulation of water in cavities of the body) to cardiac failure. Manual labour increases the body's need for vitamin B1, but the prisoners' diet was already deficient in this vitamin, which meant they could not properly metabolise their food—all of which contributed to the development of beri-beri. Captain Robert Pufflett recalled the delicate balancing act required to avoid beri-beri: 'If there was too much rice ingested over [and] above a certain ratio to vitamin B1 . . . the symptoms of beri-beri would arrive, and this dilemma of satisfying hunger with rice was frequently complicated by the appearance of beri-beri.' White credited the arrival of the first Red Cross supplies in late 1942 with helping reduce the rates of beri-beri, an indication of how easily many medical problems could have been remedied by better rations.

Another condition that presented in Changi was nicknamed 'happy feet'. This was another effect of vitamin deficiency, in which men experienced burning and itching in the soles of their feet, the ache spreading up their legs until the sensation resembled burning or freezing. To get relief, 'The sufferer ... would have to resort to extreme forms of counter-irritation such as "cooking" his feet against the smouldering fires in the kitchen, or trying to sleep with his feet elevated and exposed to any breeze.'[21]

Scrotal dermatitis (nicknamed 'Changi balls') was another common and extremely painful condition where vitamin deficiency caused men's testicles to swell and the skin to crack. Not sure how to treat it, Dr Stanley Pavillard, a British civilian doctor captured while serving with the Singapore Straits Volunteer Forces, recalled doctors trying a variety of treatments, all 'guaranteed to make the recipient do a spectacular war dance'.[22] Scabies, tinea and lice were also permanent skin complaints, but supplies of medicinal ointments had to be used sparingly.

One of the most menacing diseases throughout captivity was malaria. Ever-present and extremely debilitating, malaria became a constant companion to POWs in tropical areas. Before the war, and as far back as 1927, British troops in Singapore reduced the breeding grounds of malarial mosquitoes by reclaiming surrounding swamplands. Japanese troops did not continue this practice or introduce any other anti-malarial measures. Any attempts to eliminate the disease in the camps—such as draining stagnant pools of water to prevent mosquitoes breeding—had to be organised by Allied officers.

While doctors were often able to obtain quinine, their captors had access to Atebrin, a far more effective treatment for malaria that was almost never distributed. In April 1944 in Changi, British Captain Ben Wheeler of the Indian Medical Service recorded 'an explosive outbreak of bacillary dysentery', but that the medical personnel's 'main preoccupation throughout this period was caused by malaria'.[23] Enormous importance was placed on controlling malaria in Changi. Squads of anti-malarial workers undertook 'field work'—implementing measures to stop mosquitoes breeding—and lab work: identifying mosquitoes, and conducting regular blood, urine and stool examinations of malarial patients.[24] While preventive measures were possible in Changi, in other camps malaria was harder to control and was often the final blow to a man in ailing health. British doctor Lieutenant Colonel John Huston commented that on the Burma–Thai Railway, malaria's presence 'often heralded the end of the struggle'.[25] Frank Robinson, a private in the 2/20th Battalion, described his first brush with the disease:

> I was sitting with three or four friends and we were talking. The next thing I thought they were whispering and talking about me. I just jumped up and abused hell out of them; I had got my first bout of malaria. But after that malaria seemed to come to me about every fourteen or fifteen days.[26]

Without the right kind and amount of medication simple conditions that could have been quickly cured became life-threatening. Pufflett remembered the debilitating effects of dysentery: 'With no medication, the diarrhoea would last up to six days and one has a quite clear recollection of large open bore-hole latrines covered with planks and men lying on the ground around the latrine and crawling or staggering over to defecate.'

The fact that the men sometimes did not pay attention to the medical officers also stymied their efforts. With respect to enforcing hygiene in Changi, White wrote:

> Education of the troops in the simple laws of hygiene was not an easy task and I am afraid it took a couple of hundred deaths in a relatively short space of time, before it was realized that we medicos were not talking a lot of rubbish and guards had to patrol the latrines to enforce proper hygiene.[27]

Similarly, Pufflett laid the blame for the state of some of the men's health squarely at their own feet:

> The Japanese issued pay in the form of paper money and there was a canteen where prisoners could buy tobacco and sometimes fruit.

A large percentage of the men would sacrifice their money and food to get tobacco and this contributed significantly to malnutrition in these people.

Despite these early challenges, and some inevitable tension between the various Allied forces, a routine was soon established in Changi. The Japanese presence was little felt, leaving the individual army administrations to manage their own affairs. Except when receiving rations or written directives, the Australian doctors rarely saw their captors, Hobbs commenting in his diary that 'on the whole we are personally left very much to ourselves and left to run our own hospitals'.[28] Formal medical structures were set up, with Australian, British and Dutch doctors generally caring for their own men. However, while any mixing between forces had to be authorised, doctors of different nationalities visited each other frequently.

The Australian administration functioned smoothly fairly soon after the move to Changi. The aim was to delegate the necessary duties as rescue seemed increasingly unlikely. Concentrated efforts were made to run the camp efficiently, and the breakdown of command that would be a feature of some later camps never occurred here.[29] White noted that while morale remained generally high, he did discern a relationship between physical decline and mental attitude:

> Plain insufficiency in calories was probably the cause of most of the deterioration in mental attitude. The individuals who kept the fittest were those who were able to work hard and keep themselves cheerful and occupied, while those who sat about grumbling and pitying themselves, lost weight and condition rapidly.[30]

In August 1942 senior Allied officers—those with ranks of colonel and above—were transferred from Changi to various camps in north Asia. Command of the remaining troops fell to the British Commanding Officer, Colonel E. B. Holmes, and his Australian counterpart, Lieutenant Colonel F. G. 'Black Jack' Galleghan, both capable and respected leaders.

## Necessity: the mother of invention

Whatever their rank or experience, captivity necessitated a constant process of adaptation for all Australian medical personnel. They had to deal with medical conditions they had rarely come across before, if at all, and they had to learn how to provide treatment without access to normal equipment and medications. They soon found ways to alleviate medical problems and to overcome shortages of food and supplies. The doctors began to practise 'POW medicine' rather than civilian or normal military medicine and this was crucial to their ability to manage what they would later face.

A vital factor in the battle against deficiency diseases was the realisation that self-sufficiency was the key to survival. The Changi gardens that were cultivated from March 1942 provided crucial supplements to the food supply. On 5 March the Australian Quartermaster, Major Alexander N. Thompson, noted in his diary: 'Importance of supplementing rations by own efforts realised. Major Maxwell appointed [in charge of] Gardens. 800 men to commence work on gardens.'[31] By October 1943 about 34 hectares of land around the camp was under cultivation. White later commented on the results of this bolstered food supply:

> I am sure that the comparatively low mortality in Changi was largely due to the type of produce locally purchased and to the careful utilization of these food materials. In addition the local hospital poultry farm produced over 40,000 eggs in the last two and a half years of captivity and the men were encouraged to breed ducks and chickens for their own private consumption and the purchase money to initiate this was provided from their own pay.[32]

A yeast centre was established to conduct research into 'the effect of hops as a bacterial disinfectant, variation of the pH [acidity/alkalinity], and the value of rice and many other substances as a culture medium'.[33] Thousands of gallons of yeast brew were cultivated under the guidance of Allied medical officers. One Australian prisoner remembered that 'Quite a number of remedies were introduced—daily doses of rice polishings and grass extracts which were not very palatable, to say the least, but were however, beneficial.'[34]

Grass contains a valuable vitamin, riboflavin. Lieutenant Colonel Cotter Harvey, aided by a chemist who had worked for a pharmaceutical company, engineered a machine from lawnmowers and motor car pistons that churned out about 230 litres of grass extract a day. While the riboflavin content was small, the 'grass soup' that was then given to the men still provided the much-needed vitamin. Harvey wrote wistfully after the war, 'As I mow my lawn these days, I think sadly how much riboflavin is going to waste.'[35]

Experimentation began in earnest in other areas. Soap was created from various fats and wood ash. Plants were grown in an attempt to produce medications, such as a solution made from derris root which when applied to the skin was effective in combating scabies. An Allied Mobile Bacteriological Unit was set up to monitor malarial parasites in prisoners' blood samples. In 1943 an artificial limb factory was established, and engineers constructed successful replacement limbs from materials such as wood, fire hoses and car parts. Shoes began to wear out over time and Changi's 'Command Rubber Factory', begun in October 1942, made thousands of pairs from rubber.

Despite being in captivity the doctors did not relinquish their scientific commitment to controlled experimentation. In one instance, two Australian medical officers conducted a detailed study of a deficiency disease that causes visual defects—retrobulbar neuritis, or amblyopia—to ascertain the most effective treatment. They trialled no fewer than six regimes using food, drugs or combinations of both.[36] Ethical considerations also remained important: the doctors did not experiment on a prisoner if they thought it would have a detrimental effect on his health.

Another such experiment in September 1942, exploring deficiency diseases, shows the energy with which doctors attempted to find medical solutions with whatever was to hand:

Groups of patients were put on ascorbic acid [vitamin C], salt water, yeast, rice polishings and Pot[assium] Permanganate mouth washes, and controls of equal numbers kept without treatment at all ... Smoking was not a cause, but it certainly did make the mouth more sore.[37]

While it was frowned upon at times by some Australian officers, Changi prisoners were fortunate that a well-established black market operated between the camp and outside locals. POWs who worked in ports and docks also took the opportunity to pilfer whatever they could. This in turn led to the setting up of camp 'canteen facilities' where men could buy supplies to supplement their diet, using the 'pay' that they were entitled to as POWs, and which was sporadically distributed by the Japanese.

A significant difference between Changi and other Japanese camps was that prisoners were rarely short of doctors here. Many Australian doctors recalled not doing any medical work for days at a time, partly because they did not have adequate treatments to employ. Captain Peter Hendry recounted that, 'from a medical point of view I was a washout. There was nothing medical to do.' On the other hand, they were hardly idle: colleagues and specialists formed committees to research specific medical problems related to captivity. The Allied Nutritional Advisory Committee, for example, required doctors and their staff to keep meticulous records of nutrition and experimentation with vitamins and unfamiliar foods. In keeping with their professional attachment to gaining and sharing knowledge, Allied medical officers set up the 'Changi Medical Society', which organised regular lectures on medical topics and panels on various medical issues. British doctor Lieutenant Colonel L. Fernley noted in his diary that Australian doctors were 'mad' about lectures and giving papers.[38]

Doctors occupied their leisure time playing recreational games and reading from Changi's extensive library of pooled books. Richards noted wryly that throughout captivity, 'the Bible was very popular for two reasons. The second reason was that it made wonderful cigarette paper, it was nice and thin and the troops used to be able to split it in two.'[39]

Other doctors attended and taught at 'Changi University', which was established to keep men busy and stimulated. It offered all POWs opportunities to learn from a diverse range of subjects, from a 'Vocational Guidance Scheme' to woodwork, philosophy, public speaking and even Hindustani.[40] Orderly John Higgs recalled that 'anybody who could talk with authority about barging on the canals of England or jackerooing out past Quilpie or how to get a degree at Cambridge without working or indeed about any subject at all could expect quite an attentive audience.'[41] The sheer size of Changi, and the variety of prisoners there was something doctors would rarely see elsewhere. Private Ray Connolly recalled that 'You could march a day and still be in Changi.'

To boost morale, the Australians in Selarang Barracks produced many concerts and variety shows, in which medical personnel sometimes performed. Changi hospital staff even set up a magazine called *Camp Pie*, with intentionally light and cheery articles. Its editorial in late 1942 read: 'Christmas is rapidly approaching ... It will be our first, and, unlike most publishers, we hope our last ... Paper is becoming rarer than a woman in the Camp.'[42] Bill Flowers also recalled a memorable basketball tournament from November 1944 to February 1945 between Australian POWs and Korean guards.

These early days in Changi were the least difficult for Australian medical personnel. When comparing his time in Changi with his later experience on the Burma–Thai Railway, Captain Lloyd Cahill recalled, 'If you were in Changi, you didn't realise it, but you were in heaven. You had light, electric light, and sewerage and God knows what. Could play poker every night and do what you wanted to do and they had a first class entertainment unit there.' When Cahill returned from the Railway a year later, he said, 'I almost wept when I saw the set-up. God, I'm home.'

Yet there is a danger in whitewashing the early experience of the Australian doctors in Changi simply because it was not as difficult as what was to follow for some. Within Changi, mortality rates were worst in their first year of captivity, reflecting the difficulty of the radical change in diet and the resulting constant ill health.[43] Widespread dysentery coupled with malnutrition was responsible for many deaths, as was the lack of medical supplies. Doctors felt a powerlessness that became an important characteristic of their captivity experience, and one that caused them great distress.

In later years Changi had its own moments of crisis—particularly in 1945, when men returning from overseas work parties were very ill and the Changi inmates had their food rations dramatically cut by the Japanese. In March 1945, from a total of 10,213 prisoners, 4,848 presented at sick parades. More than 2,000 of these had deficiency diseases.[44] British orderly Corporal Doug Skippen remembered the struggles in Changi during that year:

> We used to get fed up with people dying. They weren't battle casualties, but they were dying still, and they were dying through illness and lack of real drugs. Instead of having a course of say, emetine, for dysentery, instead of having a full course of fifteen days, you'd be lucky if you had two or three days.

Adding to the crisis was the decision by the Japanese a year earlier to move Allied personnel from the Changi camp area to the much smaller Changi jail, where sanitation and living conditions were harder to manage.

## Movements out of Changi

From late February 1942, along with other Allied prisoners, more than 8,000 Australian POWs left Changi temporarily to work in other areas on Singapore Island and on surrounding islands. They worked in camps such as Adam Park, River Valley Road, Keppel Harbour, the 'Great World' (a former amusement park) and Bukit Timah, performing tasks such as loading and unloading cargo vessels or, unusually, in the case of the latter, building a memorial shrine to Japanese war dead. The size of the work parties varied—sometimes as few as 56 men were employed in a camp, sometimes as many as 2,000. The differences between these camps in some ways foreshadowed the great variations that were to occur between the camps outside Singapore. In some, such as River Valley Road and Adam Park, where respectively 550 and 1,957 men worked, the men suffered less illness than in Changi. With a smaller population, the doctors were able to control conditions more rigorously. At River Valley Road camp there was not one case of dysentery in four months. This was credited to the strictly enforced practice of emptying bedpans onto the surrounding gardens.[45] Although relations with the Japanese at Adam Park were described as 'rather difficult', and the incidence of deficiency disease 'rather alarming', the medical and hygiene teams were praised for having few serious cases of dysentery or malaria.[46] At Serangoon camp in late 1942, ever-present medical conditions were met with humour. Higgs recalled:

> There was a phantom Melbourne Cup race call full of topical allusions—'Tinea has been scratched', 'Diarrhoea has done a lot of running lately', 'Hernia is well supported' and so on—and simple entertainments like these were of immense value in allowing us to forget, even if only for an hour or so, uncertainty and fear about what may lie ahead.[47]

The situation at Bukit Timah No. 5 Camp, however, was quite different. Only kilometres away from the other camps in Singapore, Major Ernest Marsden recorded that the men were overcrowded in brick buildings and tents, and that malaria was causing serious problems: 'There are no nets or mosquito cream available. The anti-malarial measures beyond the camp boundaries are desultory and infrequent.' There were many cases of skin diseases and painful feet, leading to some patients being sent back to Changi.[48]

The Japanese army soon began to view its unexpectedly large prisoner population as a ready source of labour that could be used outside Singapore. The transportation of thousands of Allied POWs to various areas in Japanese-occupied Asia began in earnest in mid 1942. The

Japanese formed work party 'forces' for the construction of the Burma–Thai Railway. Each work party was usually multi-national, and each included a medical team. Half the doctors in the team were Regimental Medical Officers and the other half surgeons and specialists, whose intended role was to establish and run base hospitals along the line. The forces were named using letters. 'A' Force, comprising 3,000 men, left Changi first in May 1942. The force was chosen by Allied officers, and most of the men were volunteers hoping for a change of scenery and better living conditions. Australian orderly Gordon Nichols was one such hopeful: 'My name was on the list and I was very thankful, "I'll be out of here and where it's going to be much better." The Japs said that the food was more plentiful and it was getting short in Singapore—they didn't have to tell us that.' The knowledge that some of the camps around Singapore in 1942 had quite good conditions—and importantly, better rations—added to expectations that leaving Changi meant going to a better place.

Japanese command conveyed to 'A' Force's officers that they were travelling to other camps where they could rest, and advised them to bring musical instruments, sports equipment and other recreational aids. Inexplicably, they were also told that they should bring sick men. The prisoners had no idea that their destinations would be isolated, forced-labour camps, and the doctors had little idea of the medical challenges that lay ahead.

The pattern was similar for the following forces. When 'B' Force was assembled in June 1942, the Commanding Officer of the 2/10th Field Ambulance, Colonel Edmund M. Sheppard, asked his medical unit whether they wanted to go or stay in Changi. The vote to leave was unanimous—the men were bored.[49] Luckily for him, Bob Wilson, a unit orderly, contracted dengue fever and remained behind: of an original Allied force of over 2,000 men, all but six died on the subsequent Sandakan death marches in Borneo. Even a year later, Wilson recalled: 'Conditions generally at Changi, by this time, were reasonably good, in as much as all aspects of our lifestyle as prisoners had been organised in the best way possible in the circumstances.'[50]

Other forces that went to the Railway were 'D' Force (5,000 men including 2,200 Australians), which was later split into smaller parties, 'F' (3,662 Australians), 'H' (666 Australians), 'K' (55 Australians) and 'L' (75 Australians). 'K' and 'L' Forces were composed exclusively of medical personnel, sent as relief teams for their Railway colleagues. 'Dunlop' Force, a group of 878 men captured in Java and headed by Lieutenant Colonel Edward Dunlop, were incorporated into 'D' and 'H' Forces at the Hintok area of the Railway, which became known after the war as 'Hellfire Pass'. Railway parties were also supplemented by men from other camps in Java, Sumatra and Timor. Some forces were sent to labour camps in Japan: 'C' Force (2,200, including 551 Australians) departed in November 1942 and 'G' Force (200 Australians) and 'J' Force (299 Australians) were sent in 1943.

By mid-1943, the Japanese were still telling the Allied officers who were assembling 'J' Force that, 'Climate at destination good, mosquito nets not essential. Hospital facilities at destination better than those at Changi.' 'K' Force, an exclusively medical party, was told, 'An established hospital exists at destination, NOT necessary to take instruments and drugs.'[51] As Sergeant Stan Arneil commented, when the full reality of arriving at the Railway hit home after a hellish journey, 'many of the prisoners never regained their strength and succumbed quickly to the diseases which swept down upon us'. When he returned to Changi in December 1943, he saw the place so differently: 'Ah Changi! You were heaven to us then!'[52]

As those who were there are quick to point out, it is puzzling that myths about Changi persist. It is almost always described as a 'hell camp', but this is not how the POWs themselves recall it. It is a common misconception that Changi epitomised the horror and deprivation of the Australian POW experience. The most recent example of this was the 2002 ABC mini-series *Changi*, written by John Doyle. It was riddled with inaccuracies and perpetuated several myths about the life of Australian POWs there. These self-replicating cliches overlook the suffering of POWs in other camps and add to the misinformation about the POW experience.

In reality, the Australians at Changi were well organised, with a complex and efficient military administration and the closest thing to a normal military hierarchy. It was a camp where a prisoner could go weeks without seeing his captors, and where food and medical supplies were strictly regulated. Even after experiencing nine months in other relatively comfortable camps around Singapore Island, Arneil knew only too well how good Changi conditions were. He wrote at the time, 'I am thoroughly content now to stop here, if possible for the rest of my P.O.W. days'.[53] In popular understanding, however, Changi continues to stand out as 'the one place-name likely to evoke associations of emaciation and atrocity in the minds of most people'.[54] Captain Victor Brand commented: 'They talk about the "infamous Changi Hospital"—well that's nonsense. Changi was a very pleasant spot. The only trouble of course was the lack of food. But compared to other places it was a tremendous place.' Areas such as Ambon and Borneo, where conditions and death rates of Allied POWs were much worse, remain less familiar.[55]

There are some explanations for why Changi has such a high profile. Almost all Australian POWs passed through Changi at one time or another between 1942 and 1945. Most were in Changi or on Singapore Island when the war ended, when the conditions there were the worst they had ever been in terms of food supplies and chronic disease. Perhaps these were the experiences that were thus more widely remembered, compounded by the fact that repatriation teams and war correspondents first came to Changi before other POW areas.

Changi was a key stepping-stone for doctors learning to practise military medicine in captivity. While they began to cope with the limitations of imprisonment, unfamiliar medical conditions and the lack of the tools of their trade, they did so within a comparatively less challenging environment than other prison camps, surrounded by medical colleagues and other officers, and with leisure time. When the enormity of what leaving Changi meant dawned on them, doctors realised that Changi represented a midway point between war and extreme hardship in captivity.

In the camps that were to come, the doctors' ingenuity and improvisation would be pursued on a scale and with a passion commensurate with the desperation of these environments. Their feelings of helplessness and despair would also increase, as they would become aware that despite their efforts, men would not only die, but in higher numbers. Captivity for medical personnel would prove a consistently profound paradox: an experience encompassing optimism and sadness, influence and powerlessness, satisfaction and despair.

# 3

# MAKING BRICKS WITHOUT STRAW: THE BURMA–THAI RAILWAY

———⟐———

*Very soon our men were reduced to the status of a malarious, dysenteric, underfed and overworked slave gang.*

MAJOR KEVIN FAGAN[1]

Allied prisoners were held in many different camps, but it is those on the Burma–Thai Railway from 1942 to 1943 that remain most resonant. Although only about 12,000 of the 22,000 Australian POWs were sent to the Railway camps, the images and stories of these camps are frequently used to encapsulate the entire Australian POW experience, to the exclusion of other sites of captivity.

Of the 106 Australian POW doctors, 44 spent time on the Railway. In their memories of captivity, this experience weighs heavily. The Railway project accounted for one-third of the total Australian POW deaths in the Pacific War, and a quarter of *all* Allied deaths at Japanese hands during the war. British doctor Lieutenant Colonel S. W. Harris wrote: 'Here was no heat and excitement of war, and yet the hardships and privations endured by all were as bad as any likely to be met with on active service and the casualties were unfortunately at least as great.'[2] The Railway experience is also well documented, disproportionately so compared to those areas where only one or two doctors may have spent time.

There are many reasons why the Railway continues to be the source of many painful memories for medical officers and men alike. Going from Changi to the dire conditions on the Railway arguably caused the greatest shock any of them experienced during captivity, and for the doctors, it marked a significant change to their roles and responsibilities. In his War Crimes Statement of 10 April 1947, Lieutenant Colonel Albert Coates reported that until early 1943 he saw his captors' attitude as 'easy-going neglect'. He then compared it with the conditions of 1943: 'Deliberate neglect, deprivation, starvation, denial of drugs, denial of all equipment, and denial of facilities.'[3]

The physical harshness of the Railway jungle camps, the malnutrition and disease, and the heavy labour demanded of the men presented the doctors with a much greater set of challenges than they had ever faced. It was where many doctors were most tested and where their responses as a group truly set them apart.

The Burma–Thai Railway was planned to stretch for 415 kilometres, from Ban Pong in southern Thailand to Thanbyuzayat in Burma. The aim was to provide the Japanese with a land route to supply their troops in Burma. Japanese engineers' initial surveys estimated that the construction would take five to six years, with thousands of workers needed to lay track through jungle and mountain.[4] Instead, using 61,000 Allied POWs as slave labour, it took under a year.

Australian, British, American and Dutch POWs (as well as many thousands of Asian indentured labourers) were spread along the line between the two points, setting up makeshift camps and building there before moving further along the line. Captain Lloyd Cahill described arriving at one area on the Railway: 'The so-called camp was just a clearing in the jungle with a notice up: "Staging camp for coolies and prisoners of war." We were the lowest of the low.' Few campsites had any existing infrastructure such as electricity, running water or latrine systems. The most basic facilities had to be established by the POWs themselves after arriving at each site.

MAP 3

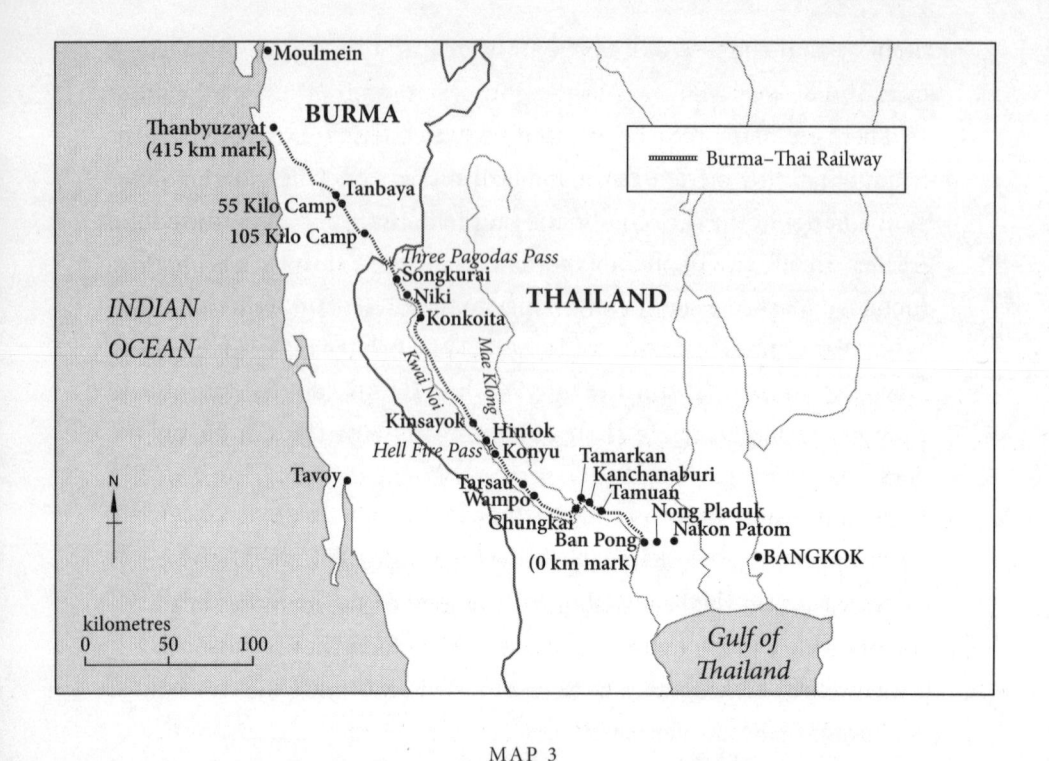

The main Allied POW working camps on the Burma–Thai Railway.

The men of 'A' Force, the first to leave Changi, were sent to Thanbyuzayat, Burma, to begin the end-point of the Railway heading south to Thailand. They first travelled for several days by boat and by foot to the nearby town of Tavoy to build a Japanese aerodrome. Packed into the holds of the Japanese transport ship *Celebes Maru*, Major Alan Hobbs reflected: 'This hold made a perfect picture of an old galley with slaves.' He added wryly, 'Except no oars.'[5] Yet they were the lucky ones. Hundreds of Allied prisoners drowned at sea during World War II, killed by Allied submarines or aircraft. Their crews were unaware of the human cargo in the Japanese transports' holds because the Japanese refused to mark ships carrying prisoners.[6] Approximately 1,500 Allied POWs died in this way, including three Australian doctors.

When 'A' Force arrived at Thanbyuzayat in May 1942 doctors were forced to hand over half the medical supplies they had brought with them to the Japanese. Coates had a handful of instruments which he managed to keep and he continued to hide supplies from the Japanese as much as possible: 'We improvised and carefully husbanded every little bit of stuff we got.'[7] Reaching Thanbyuzayat, the full horror of the prisoners' living conditions became apparent. In the middle of the humid and oppressive jungle, the prisoners were forced to construct *atap* huts to live in. The 'hospital' was one such hut—rows of bamboo slats along two sides with men packed in like sardines. Within only two weeks of leaving Changi, there were 147 dysentery cases among the Australians. Lieutenant Colonel Thomas Hamilton described the dysentery ward:

> Men lay in the stench of their own excreta as the ordinary means of cleaning them—soap, shovels, lime, washing cloths and towels— were not available. One Medical Orderly, rendered desperate by the appalling conditions, used his spare stocks of pocket handkerchiefs. The Jap Commander was indifferent and the Jap Doctor, when asked if he had ever seen anything worse (with the misnomer 'Hospital') said shamefacedly, 'perhaps not'.[8]

By January 1943 one man a day was dying from dysentery. The doctors hoped for supplies of drugs from the Red Cross, but these never came. The men who survived began to starve, dropping dramatically in weight. The worst cases fell to below 50 kilograms.

When other forces arrived at various points along the Railway, they met similarly unenviable fates. Despite 'the general state of exhaustion of the men, the presence of cholera epidemics in all camps and practically universal malaria, diarrhoea and dysentery, the men were put to work by the engineers at once'.[9] After setting up camp, they began clearing dense jungle, carting logs, laying railway tracks and roads, building bridges, and often cutting through bare rock with few tools. The length of Railway line to be laid was stipulated daily by the Japanese, increasing as 1943 progressed.

At certain points along the Railway, base hospitals were established which periodically received thousands of seriously ill men. At large Thai hospital camps such as Nakon Patom and Chungkai at the southern end of the Railway, which had access to black market traders, doctors were better equipped to treat the thousands of men who flooded through from the up-country Railway camps. Other camps further up the line towards Burma, however, were isolated and in crisis.

Allied POWs were frequently moved between points on the Railway, and sometimes they would find themselves at a previously inhabited camp. If the camp had been occupied by a crowded group of Asian labourers, it would usually be in such a filthy state that the entire camp and its environs would have to be exhaustively cleaned to prevent the transmission of diseases, particularly cholera. With no leadership infrastructure and no medical aid, the Asian labourers died in horrifying numbers. Australian medical officers gave them medical assistance when they could. One doctor described one of these camps:

> We went into a camp which we rapidly recognised had been a cholera camp. There were a lot of open graves, literally dozens if not hundreds in this area . . . We had to build ourselves some huts out of what material we could find. There were what had been cattle yards and we were allocated that as our isolation ward.[10]

After a long journey a group of 1,200 Allied POWs reached a staging camp at Kanchanaburi, Thailand, where they found only one latrine pit. Eighty per cent of the prisoners had dysentery, and were so exhausted and weak that they could only move a few feet from where they were lying. British doctor Major Eugene Rogers wrote that as a result, 'the camp was little less than a sea of liquid faeces'.[11] By instigating the extensive building of extra latrines and rigorous hygiene measures, Rogers was able to prevent even more sickness.

Doctors in all the camps along the Railway battled a range of conditions: malaria, dysentery, pellagra, beri-beri, dengue fever, tropical ulcers, starvation and physical abuse. Cahill reflected on the devastating nature of these diseases:

> Fellows who I would have thought were the fittest and the toughest to survive didn't, whereas the others that you'd have thought would

be lucky to survive, they did . . . But then up there once you got up into the jungle, the mosquitoes didn't care who they bit. So that you couldn't tell who was going to get malaria. You couldn't really protect yourself completely against malaria. Cholera, well, that was just sheer luck.

In the huts at Chungkai, men lay packed on long bamboo platforms and, as they were almost always touching, they all often suffered from skin infections.[12] British doctor Major A. L. Dunlop wrote despairingly:

> All wards were grossly over-crowded and in the skin and ulcer ward, in which there was almost 1,000 patients, conditions beggar description. Owing to the almost total lack of dressings and disinfectant the stench was appalling and the inadequate staff had a well nigh impossible task in caring for the comfort of these helpless and miserable patients. The avitaminosis ward was also grossly over-crowded and in the absence of specific drugs for Beri-beri and Pellagra [staff] could only look helplessly on while men died . . . in ever increasing numbers from deficiency diseases.[13]

The ratio of medical personnel to workers in Railway camps was grossly inadequate. There was usually one doctor for every 100 men in the Railway camps, and four doctors for every 100 men in the hospital base camps. At 55 Kilo[metre] camp, Burma, as one of only three doctors, Coates was trying to minister to 2,000 men, 500 of whom had severe tropical ulcers that needed daily dressing. Many of the orderlies had been taken to other camps, and Coates wrote that, 'The spectacle of hundreds of men in pain and misery nursing their ulcerated leg on the ground, many infected with maggots, waiting day after day for treatment was revolting even to a surgeon of 20 years' experience.' He described working in this camp from July to December 1943 as 'the worst experience I had'.[14]

For the medical officers and other Australian officers in the Railway forces, negotiation with the Japanese command and engineers proved largely fruitless. Doctors were forced to hold sick parades twice daily, and to pronounce at least 80 per cent of the men fit for work. The doctors were caught in a terrible dilemma. If they argued with the Japanese, they and the men might be beaten, and sick men would usually be dragged out to work anyway. If doctors provided the quota, they had to find a way to minimise further deterioration of the men's health. Evidence of malingering in Railway work parties was unusual as 'most men preferred to work rather than to receive the treatment meted out to the sick by the Japanese.'[15]

Every day on the Railway would see conflict between doctors and their captors, and doctors had to accept this as part of their role. 'Unfortunately I overdid it once and paid the price with broken teeth,' Captain Rowley Richards remembered. 'And that was not unusual. Every now and then they'd lose their block and bang me around the back and the neck.'[16] Likewise, Cahill remembered:

> Oh you had to fight like mad . . . I used to just get up at daylight and start seeing [patients] at about four in the morning. Poor devils. And then they'd go to work and come back about 10 o'clock at night. All exhausted. All sick. All terrible. Some of them would have died out there, occasionally . . . they'd be screaming, the Nips, for the 400 for the next day and you'd have to have a fight. This was going on all the time. Constant fighting and you knew you were sending sick guys out, but you had to send someone out.

Sometimes medical personnel, often sick themselves, were forced to join work parties in order to fill the quotas. Sergeant Stan Arneil described being with men who were too sick to work but were nonetheless forced onto work parties:

> If the beriberi was excessive, you might have to lie some of them down on their backs with their feet against the side of the embankment to keep the fluid flowing down their legs into their bodies so that their legs wouldn't burst. They couldn't work at all. We'd feed them at lunch time. They were looked after, hats placed over their faces to keep the rain out, and they were talked to and joked

to. They understood the position. We would carry them back at night. Usually one would die during the day.[17]

By mid 1943 the Japanese, under increasing pressure to complete the project, demanded the men work longer—often 14 hours daily, with no days off, never seeing their camps in daylight—and for less food. There was no recreation, and as Lieutenant Colonel Edward Dunlop noted, there was little need for it: 'the men were too exhausted to enjoy anything'.[18] They were being fed 250–300 grams of rice and a few beans per day, and rarely any meat. Coates wrote of his frustration:

> The exhortation by Jap generals to forget the frailties of the body and concentrate on the work, that sickness was a sign of lowered morale and cowardice, that our duty to the 'Emperor' demanded the last ounce—all these things goaded the medical men to extreme exasperation.[19]

The physical brutality meted out by the Japanese command and their guards towards all prisoners was both a daily reality for many medical personnel and a source of constant tension. When Colonel Bruce Anderson, Commanding Officer of 'K' Force, protested about camp conditions to a Japanese commander, Colonel Hayakawa, the latter 'said that all the engineering achievements of the world had been carried out in the face of great medical problems'.[20] Threats did not work either. When confronting the Japanese officer in charge of medical arrangements at Chungkai, Dunlop recalled: 'I invited Nakazawa to name the person responsible for his actions and he refused to do so and I told him I would hold him responsible, to which he replied, "Good".'[21] Doctors treated numerous broken teeth, jaws, ribs, arms and legs. POWs could be beaten unconscious while working and would have to be carried back to camp by their friends. The doctors themselves were also frequent targets of brutality in their efforts to protect their patients from further harm.

Another source of conflict and continual worry for the doctors was the lack of medical supplies, a feature of every Japanese camp. Malaria, for example, was rampant, but drugs to treat it were scarce. Orderly Gordon Nichols commented:

> There wasn't enough to give everybody suppressive treatment for malaria, with the result that everybody had malaria pretty well all the time. It was just commonplace. You'd spend a couple of days [in bed] if you were just too sick to do anything, but then you'd be up and about when you should have still been in bed.

Supplies were occasionally supplemented by Red Cross parcels of food, toiletries or medical supplies—when the Japanese did not raid them first. The prisoners were supposed to receive one parcel each, but Captain Philip Millard remembered an instance when two parcels had to be shared by thirteen men. The infrequent distribution of medical supplies by the Japanese generally meant there was 'too little, too late', a situation compounded by the lack of diagnostic tools. Captain Robert Pufflett recalled being confounded by many illnesses:

> We had these chronic cases that we couldn't cure and we didn't know what was wrong. We didn't have the pathology to tell and I can remember losing a lot of men over long illnesses and doing autopsies on them. I can remember a fellow who died of cancer of the lung and another young boy who had chronic diarrhoea for months and he was such a nice country lad, and he died of amoebic dysentery. We couldn't have cured it anyhow. We had no emetine or anything.

On the Railway, medical officers had to practise a type of medicine few had encountered before: without medical supplies, operating theatres, diagnostic or sterilising equipment, or even everyday items such as syringes or bandages. They were forced, as Coates commented, like the Israelites in Egypt, 'to make bricks without straw'.[22]

Often all the doctors could do to prevent the spread of disease was enforce a strict adherence to hygiene. They saw that latrines were kept as clean as possible, utensils were boiled in water before eating, and they conducted regular health checks on cookhouse staff. Their worst memories of the Railway are often of cholera, the most infectious and feared of diseases. The speed with which the disease took hold was frightening. After contracting cholera, men could lose between a half to three-quarters of their body weight in only a few hours through continuous vomiting and diarrhoea. Once a man began to vomit uncontrollably or have 'rice water' pale, mucus-like stools, it was akin to a death sentence. Cahill recalled, 'You couldn't recognise anybody in twelve hours. The first thing . . . was to get a bit of bamboo and tie it round their wrists with their name on, so you'd know who you were going to cremate the next day. It was just unbelievable.'

Cholera could spread through a camp in a matter of days, and many of those who contracted it died—usually between 60 and 80 per cent, depending on the camp. There was little the medical personnel could do to stop it. Even the most innocent touch could spell disaster: a handshake between a cholera carrier who moved camps and was reunited with an old friend was believed to be responsible for an outbreak among the British troops at Takanun Camp.[23] Nichols remembered:

> You used to have to sterilise all your eating equipment before you could put anything into your mouth and then there was a great fear . . . you might find something itchy on your lip, and scratch your lip and, 'Oh boy, where have I had that hand? What have I touched?'

Cholera patients were immediately isolated in an attempt to prevent the disease spreading further. At first the Japanese gave no assistance, but their attitude soon changed, as noted by the British doctor Major A. L. Dunlop when writing about a June 1943 cholera outbreak in Chungkai camp, Thailand:

> At first the Japanese would not admit that this disease was present and refused to take any special precautions. Circumstances soon forced them to alter their view and they provided anti-cholera inoculations. They ordered the cases to be isolated in an area

chosen by them and provided tents for the purpose. There were no beds.[24]

There are many stories of the dread produced by news of the spread of cholera along the Railway. Japanese soldiers became 'hysterical and panicky when confronted with an outbreak', in one instance shooting a cholera patient.[25] When the disease broke out in his own camp, a British doctor wrote: 'Cholera panic all over camp. Max [Pemberton] as jumpy as a kitten, Col. Williamson a trembling jelly. Three deaths today and one late at night—all Choleras.'[26] In mid 1943, Dr Stanley Pavillard, a civilian doctor with the Singapore Straits Volunteer Rifles, recalled warning some Allied doctors with 'F' and 'H' forces heading through Tonchan South to expect cholera: 'when I told them they were passing through a cholera area, they were completely shattered by the news; they were quite plainly in no state to cope with an epidemic'.[27]

After only two days in Shimo Songkurai camp, orderly John Higgs was called by Cahill, who said to him:

We may well be facing disaster. I'm almost certain that one, and possibly up to three, of the men has cholera. Whatever happens, we have to set up an isolation camp. I'm asking you to take charge of the cholera ward—not that you'll be able to do a great deal, because we've nothing to offer as treatment. We'll have to recruit a nursing staff as soon as all the men are in from outside work. If cholera really takes hold here, then God help us.[28]

On taking charge of the isolated ward on 'Cholera Hill', Higgs succinctly summed up the desperation and urgency of a cholera outbreak:

There was, as I have said, steady soaking rain falling unceasingly; we were doing our best to erect the bell tents in almost complete darkness; the doctors were in constant demand to distinguish between acute dysentery cases and further cholera victims; they were also briefing the men recruited to join me in the nursing operation; I was working with Doctors Bruce Hunt and Lloyd Cahill on such matters as how to maintain strict isolation between the main camp and the cholera ward, what to do with the bodies of those who died, how to recruit and roster the staff and how to have food delivered from the main camp; and, while all this was going on, fresh victims were being brought in for such attention as we could give.[29]

This outbreak lasted five weeks, and 109 out of 210 affected men died.

Many doctors felt helpless in the face of such a swift and terrifying disease. Captain Harry Silman, a British doctor, described in his diary an epidemic at Tanbaya Camp where 135 men died in a matter of days:

> There is a long, damp atap hut, with over a hundred thin skeleton-like beings, writhing on the long platform, vomiting and passing motions where they lie. Groans and cries are the only noises to break the silence. Two or three orderlies with masks over their mouths were giving intravenous injections of saline, using Heath Robinson contraptions. About nine corpses lay outside covered with blankets and groundsheets, and a little distance away, the smoke of the pyre where the corpses are burning could be seen.[30]

One Australian prisoner remembered a greeting he received when moving from Niki to Songkurai camp, which was battling cholera. As he walked in, a few British prisoners said, 'Welcome to the Death Camp'.[31]

As more and more men died, the protocol for disposing of bodies became increasingly dispassionate. Cremation parties simply dumped corpses on pyres, and did not wait to watch them burn. The quick disposal of bodies was vital to prevent further spread of the infection.

Besides cholera, malaria and the vitamin deficiency diseases that dogged the prisoners, there were other distressing medical conditions particular to the Railway environment. One of these was tropical ulcers, chronic sores that could start as a scratch and spread until they covered large areas of the leg or foot, sometimes resulting in amputation. Nichols spent much of his time there dressing ulcers: 'I've seen them stretching from the knee right down to the ankle with all the tibia, or the shinbone, exposed so much so that you could push a pencil in one side and out the other . . . It was dreadful.' Captain Colin Juttner described the hopeless dilemma the doctors were caught in: 'You had no option—either they died of toxaemia or you amputated, and if you amputated, of course your chances of survival were not great under those conditions either.'

Another Australian doctor who experienced the horror of this condition was Captain Leslie Poidevin:

> Fellows in the work parties would be in the bush and scratch their legs . . . the smallest scratch which you take no notice of today—you might even put a Band-Aid on it, but you mightn't even do that—up there in that climate . . . osteomyelitis [inflammation of the bone] would spread up the whole tibia and the fellow would have to have his leg chopped off all because of a scratch. We never had any microscopes. We never had any way of knowing whether there was a special organism there at all. You had no idea.

In such conditions, the doctors of course became sick themselves. Sometimes they were so ill they had to leave it to the orderlies to diagnose and care for the men. When he first arrived at the Railway, Captain Victor Brand contracted malaria: 'I was really conked out for I don't know how many days, lying on the ground aching like mad . . . eventually I got up and staggered round the camp and inspected them all.' The doctors struggled to manage their own recovery while continuing to care for their patients. Captain Roy Mills recalled, 'That worst day I had . . . vomiting all night, not able to walk in the morning, couldn't walk, get your legs by lunchtime, and work for the rest of the day. But that's what the men were doing all the time.'

## 'F' Force—a case study

'I didn't have to go on the Burma railway; I volunteered for it. It's sort of like, the grass is greener on the other side of the fence. You think "It can't be worse." But it could be. It was.'[32]

These rueful words were spoken by Private John 'Jack' Barclay, a survivor of the 7,000-strong 'F' Force, half-British, half-Australian, which departed Changi for Thailand in April 1943. Of all the forces sent to the Railway, 'F' Force arguably suffered more than any other with the highest mortality rate of any of the Railway forces. Cholera alone killed 700 men, and the combination of various diseases, physical abuse and forced labour was responsible for the deaths of many more.

By 20 June 1943, just two months after leaving Changi, 'only 700 men of the Force were out at work and most of these were sick, while the remainder, except for the small administrative and medical parties, were lying in improvised hospitals in each of the labour camps'.[33] By the end of December, when 'F' Force returned to Changi after months of starvation and heavy labour, the toll was horrific: 3,000 men were dead, and hundreds more had to be left behind until they were well enough to be moved.

Allied officers on 'F' Force were told by the Japanese in Changi that prisoners would be transported by train to a new location where food would be more plentiful. The officers charged with forming work parties were directed to include 30 per cent sick men, so that they 'would have a better chance of recovery with better food and in the pleasant, hilly country with good facilities for recreation'.[34] What the men experienced, however, could not have been more different. As Juttner put it, 'They told us a lot of lies.'

On the four-day train journey from Singapore to Thailand men were packed into hot, unventilated carriages, with no provisions for rest or sanitation, and no room even to lie down. During the infrequent stops, doctors had to run from carriage to carriage to try to attend to all those in need.

When they arrived in Thailand the prisoners were marched 300 kilometres north to Shimo Songkurai camp, mostly at night, a trek that took more than two weeks. 'Fit' men had to carry and support the sick, and everyone's health deteriorated. Food was scarce and the staging camps provided practically no rest, food or water. Higgs was on this march:

> In the complete blackness of the jungle we simply stumbled along, hoping in the early stages to dodge trouble and in the later stages not caring greatly what happened . . . Some men were so exhausted that they fell asleep without food, and this told heavily during the next night's march.[35]

The sickest were a particularly problematic consideration for medical personnel. British doctor Lieutenant Colonel Andrew Dillon wrote:

> . . . no proper arrangements existed for the retaining of sick at these camps and the men were absolutely unfit to march, owing to disease and sickness. We were beaten and driven from camp to camp, officers—including medical officers—who begged and prayed for sick men to be left behind were themselves beaten at many camps. In one particular case, a Japanese medical officer lieutenant ordered the IJA [Imperial Japanese Army] Cpl. in charge of Taso camp to leave thirty-six men behind, as they were too ill to move. The Cpl. refused to obey this order, although it was repeated in writing and a British officer, a Major, interpreter and an Australian doctor major, Maj. Bruce Hunt of Perth, were severely beaten when they protested.[36]

Although some sick POWs were allowed temporarily to drop out of the march, many of those who were forced to continue died en route.[37]

Medical supplies were exhausted by the march's end, and dysentery, diarrhoea, exhaustion and leg and foot ulceration were widespread. Worse, men were placed in staging camps along with Asian labourers who had cholera, so that by the time they reached their destinations, the disease was present in every 'F' Force work party and spread rapidly in their camps. While the Japanese were generally liberal with their dispensing of quinine and cholera vaccinations, the latter was often given too late to be of any practical use. The Japanese supplied little or nothing for other conditions and the 'F' Force doctors could only take what they could carry, sometimes forced to leave valuable supplies behind.

Officers and doctors continually protested about the treatment of their men, but with little effect in the face of the Japanese belief that depriving them of pay and rations would drive the men out of hospital:

> The Japanese seemed to regard sickness in general as shameful. To them sickness was a matter of will and those who fell ill showed a lack of willpower and were to be despised. It was the doctors who were blamed and punished regularly if the men were found to be sick.[38]

Sick and weak men were forced to carry heavy logs daily, and could be beaten while doing so. The Japanese would often allow two or three times as many Asian labourers to perform the same tasks as the POWs.[39] Doctors also had to contend with Japanese engineers bursting into hospital huts and forcing patients out to work. Lieutenant Colonel Edward Dunlop described one of the engineers at the Hintok Pass, Lieutenant Hirota, as 'a man killer pure and simple'.[40]

Of the 'F' Force men who returned to Changi at the end of 1943, 95 per cent had recurrent malaria, 80 per cent were classed as 'very sick', and 50 per cent required immediate hospital treatment.[41] Some did not make it at all, with 232 men dying on the trip back. Lieutenant Colonel Glyn White remembered:

> I was there to see them off when they left us in April 1943—at 3 am on a lovely tropical morning. I was also there to welcome them back at 2 am some 8 months later. What I saw has left a permanent scar on my memory, many of my mates were missing, and those who had returned had so altered physically, that I did not recognize them. You can imagine the problem this sudden influx of 3,500 men was for the unwarned medical services. Such devastation was brought about by the ruthlessness, cruelty, lack of administrative ability and/or the ignorance of the members of the Jap army . . . gradually most of those animated skeletons improved, but many were left with permanent scars.[42]

Australian orderly Osmund Vickers-Bush recalled, 'I was very weak and weighed only 4½ stone [28.5 kilograms]. Although only a featherweight himself, Colonel Glyn White lifted me off the truck and carried me into the hut.'[43] Upon seeing 'F' Force return, Major Burnett Clarke remarked: 'The loss of weight was simply appalling . . . in the neighbourhood of 70–80 lbs. [32–36 kilograms] per individual.'[44]

Another Australian doctor in Changi, Captain Charles Huxtable, wrote in his diary, 'the fate of F and H Forces, whose fate all these months had been shrouded in mystery, has begun to take shape in grim outlines'. Having served as a doctor in World War I, the return of these 'lean, emaciated, gaunt' figures reminded him of '25 years ago, of exhausted men coming from the trenches after a battle'.[45]

One Australian POW wrote that after seeing these men, many of the prisoners who had been left in Changi realised how lucky they were. The 'F' Force men had 'Open wounds, skinny, pus—the whole lot of us just broke down and sobbed'.[46] Juttner described his sheer elation on returning to Changi: 'They just piled this good food into us, which was terrific. Yes, they did. They treated us like heroes. And they looked so marvellous themselves. They looked so pink and white, it was like coming home.'

Over 12,000 Allied prisoners died on the Railway, including 2,800 Australians. Yet this Railway, which weighed so heavily upon those who did manage to survive it, was barely used once completed. Due to Allied bombing of several sections, and changes in the Japanese war strategy, it soon lay unused and rotting. Today only small sections of it exist.

## Making the best of it

While the death toll on the Railway was appalling, it would undoubtedly have been much higher if not for the ingenuity of the medical officers in recreating the basic essentials that would help their situation—medical tools and diagnostic equipment, disinfectants and anaesthetics for operations.

Doctors also harnessed the skills of their fellow prisoners in making medical tools. Captain Ian Duncan remembered: 'At Hintok a complete water system was made from bamboo. Water was drawn from a dam several hundred metres away to a system of showers, dixi-washing points and to cool a still in a water distillery.'[47]

British doctor A. L. Dunlop described his time at Chungkai in October 1943 as a 'black period', in which there were 257 deaths—but he acknowledged there would have been more without the teamwork of Canadian surgeon Captain Jacob Markowitz and Acting Sergeant Vaughan, 'whose ingenuity and skill as a tradesman enabled him to make useful instruments out of the most unpromising material'.[48]

Captain Michael Woodruff, who trained as an electrical engineer at the University of Melbourne, was credited with many important discoveries that mitigated the impact of vitamin deficiencies. His engineering and mathematics background gave him unique skills during captivity 'in his planning and evaluation of experiments'.[49]

At Nakon Patom Hospital camp in southern Thailand, ophthalmologist Major Alan Hazelton was confronted with many eye-related problems in Allied POWs. Malnutrition and the resulting avitaminosis created many visual defects, which lingered into the postwar years. Conjunctivitis was widespread, due to the heat and dust of the environment, as well as other complaints such as granular cornea, corneal ulceration (which often required surgery), and nutritional amblyopia. The last was difficult to treat, and 'as the patient's general condition appeared fair, it was impossible to convince the I.J.A. [Imperial Japanese Army] of the seriousness of this complaint'.[50]

Hazelton and his staff did what they could to alleviate visual problems by creating substitutions. Spectacles were remade from the glasses of men who had died. To protect patients from further visual damage by the harsh sun, sunglasses were manufactured by inserting blue cellophane paper between thin pieces of glass and a microscope slide. To aid diagnosis, Hazelton also built testing equipment, from colour-vision testing charts to special forceps used for meibomian cysts, where glands in the eyelids become inflamed and swollen. He even devised a makeshift ophthalmoscope 'using an oil lamp burning coconut oil, parts of a Rolls razor, a metal concave mirror and some lenses'.[51]

The range and inventiveness of the tools devised by POW doctors can be seen in this modest statement by Duncan:

> Proctoscopes were made from tin, the edges being turned in, and using a mirror and the sun were effective . . . sigmoidoscopes which could be inflated were built, ileostomy bags were made from Dutch aluminium water bottles and worked well. Silver haemostatic clips and retractors were made from forks, tenon saws were used for amputations and soldering irons were used for cautery.[52]

Like many of his colleagues, Hazelton never lost his sense of professional identity as a prisoner. He continually researched the effects food had on certain medical conditions: 'Experimental work was also done on diseases of the eye. The value of eggs in the diet and also one of the effects of lack of Vitamin B1 was demonstrated.' While sporadic supplies of drugs were available to him, including cocaine, he bemoaned the lack of requisite paper to keep records of his findings: 'records of eye diseases particularly nutritional amblyopia made at the time of first examination would be invaluable'.[53]

Any foods that could provide any of the lacking vitamins and minerals were treated like gold. Marmite in particular—a potent and concentrated source of vitamin B—was jealously guarded by medical personnel. At Tarsau Hospital camp in December 1943, Lieutenant Colonel Edward Dunlop wrote that doctors 'are forced to rely more and more upon dietetic measures—in fact foodstuffs such as eggs and milk are regarded as drugs and not "eats"'.[54] Richards too declared, 'We're all going to be dieticians'.[55]

Despite the lack of paper and writing implements, doctors did whatever they could to record their observations. Medical notes were written on scraps of Japanese paper, old military records, and even toilet paper. Because they had so little space to record notes, shortcuts were taken in medical diaries: 'Each patient is shown as suffering from the disease which was considered to be the most important. For this reason these statistics give a very conservative view of the number of cases of any one particular disease occurring.'[56] Some doctors only held medical notes for a short time before erasing them all and starting again on the same paper.

## An environment of resourcefulness

Where doctors could not recreate their tools of trade on the Railway, they were forced to find other solutions. This led to a reappraisal of their immediate environment, and a changing focus on its possible potential instead of its limitations. It is in this area that they truly began to practise 'POW medicine'.

The necessity for improvisation was clear considering the scant supplies given by the Japanese. For example, at the base hospital at Kanchanaburi, British doctor Lieutenant Colonel J. W. Malcolm recalled:

> ... occasionally one bandage would be given [by the Japanese] and with strict orders that it was to suffice for 1,000 men for one month. This kind of humour was not appreciated as Officers and men had long since given up sheets, handkerchiefs, pyjamas and mosquito nets to be torn up for dressings.[57]

In a letter to a Japanese doctor at Nakon Patom Hospital in 1944, Coates protested about the lack of hot water, soap, medical instruments and poor lighting. He pointed to the fact that 'One quarter of the whole camp population was under treatment for skin disease last month. This figure is too high and speaks for itself.'[58]

The inspirational influence of the Dutch medical personnel on medical improvisation cannot be overstated, from teaching Australian doctors how to experiment with unfamiliar foods, to using hypnosis in lieu of anaesthetic for operations.[59] As members of the occupying colonial power, many Dutch POWs had previously been stationed in the Dutch East Indies or indeed had been born and raised there. As the American POW officer Huddleston Wright noted, the Dutch 'knew the trees or herbs and things that would cure this, that, and the other'.[60] The American POW doctor Hugh Lumpkin was heard to remark that, in his opinion, 'any experienced Dutch doctor ... knew more about tropical diseases than the combined knowledge of the American Medical Association'.[61] The depth of ignorance of tropical disease is demonstrated by the fact that when Lumpkin saw malaria for the first time, he did not recognise it, having never seen a case before.[62] Sadly, Lumpkin died of disease on the Railway in August 1943, the only American doctor in his camp.

In 'A' Force, Captain Christoffel van Boxtel, a Dutch chemist, won much admiration from Australian POWs for his ingenious experiments and treatments. Lack of anaesthetics had become a serious problem. Supplies of Stovain, Procain and Novocain had run out quickly due to massive surgical demands, so ways were devised to eke out existing supplies, such as distilling a small stock of Novocain by evaporating it, and adding purified water, to obtain a four-per-cent Novocain solution. This produced enough anaesthetic for fourteen lumbar anaesthetic doses. Once this ran out, Coates and van Boxtel turned their attention to cocaine tablets, of which they had a small amount. After various trials, they concluded that ¾ c.c. of lumbar cocaine was successful, and patients were administered the anaesthetic 20 minutes before their procedures.[63] Van Boxtel was also renowned for his egg nog—made from rice alcohol and raw eggs.[64]

These extraordinary examples of medical trial and error were not without complications. In this period within 'A' Force, 150 lumbar anaesthetics were given, 80 per cent for amputation cases. However, it was soon observed that patients had severe postoperative headaches when cocaine anaesthetic was used, and doctors discovered it was due to the methyl alcohol solution used for sterilising the syringe.[65]

Other instances abound of the doctors' resourceful improvisations. After supplies of disinfectant had been exhausted, a solution nicknamed 'Dutch Ointment' by Coates was made from sulphur and salicylic acid from a base of candle grease, mixed with sodium bicarbonate. Pork or bullock fat was sometimes added to change the consistency. This ointment was initially used in the treatment of tropical ulcers, but was soon found to be more effective with widespread skin infections such as scabies and tinea.[66]

In one Railway camp, Australian orderly Bevan Warland-Browne recalled clever experimentation with rubber trees. By tapping the trees, collecting the rubber sap and adding formalin (a chemical solution including formaldehyde), they created a latex bandage of sorts that could be put over tropical ulcers and other wounds.[67]

The lack of adequate disinfectants was a significant problem for medical staff on the Railway, particularly in trying to keep tropical ulcers clean, and to prevent postoperative sepsis after amputations. Doctors were worried about the level of methyl alcohol in some purloined Japanese brandy, but were cheered by the knowledge that 'Japanese soldiers are drinking it without any apparent harm'.[68] Disinfectant was also obtained by stealing Japanese supplies of liquor.

Collecting, filtering and evaporating the juice of 80 limes produced a solution of sodium citrate, an anti-clotting agent in blood transfusions. Surgical gut was created from pig or cattle intestines, and in the absence of needles, cannulae were crafted from thin reeds of bamboo. Bamboo was also used for splints, bowls, tablet containers, bedpans, specimen bottles and crutches. As saline, needles and tubing were usually non-existent, the doctors were again forced to improvise in their treatment of cholera. Most doctors tried to flood the affected men's bodies with fluid, in an attempt to prevent complete dehydration caused by vomiting and diarrhoea. Brand recalled constructing an intravenous unit, using bamboo tips as cannulae, the rubber of his stethoscope as tubing, and a saline solution of boiled and strained river water and rock salt. He described the procedure:

> [Boiling water] took off the impurities and we made up a kind of solution which we hoped was about the right strength and we gave it through this way into the vein, and of course it was full of impurities and it caused the most dreadful rigors.

Duncan further explained how the saline was delivered through the tubing, by hanging up a bottomless Japanese wine or beer bottle and closing the neck with a wooden cork. Bamboo was inserted through this cork and connected with the stethoscope tube, which then ran down to the cannula.[69]

Sometimes doctors did not have the luxury of time to experiment and create their own solutions. They were forced to rely on their wits and whatever lay in their immediate environment as their only tools. In just one example, a man in a camp a quarter of a mile away needed an emergency operation for a ruptured gastric ulcer. Millard and a fellow doctor had no appropriate equipment to perform it:

> This was late afternoon and I said, 'What are we going to do about lights?' Well we'd had some oil lamps fixed up for this concert party which consisted of fruit tins from the cookhouse ... So we cut the bottom out of them and put oil inside that and cut out one side so they reflected the light, and he said, 'We'll see if we can borrow a torch from the Nips'. So we did this. So that night we opened him up, we found him fairly easy to do, closed him up, and he did very well. I still get letters from him.

Other ranks also experimented with whatever they saw around them, especially when it came to food. One man recalled:

> There was one thing particularly vile. It was lily root, and when you ate it, your tongue turned purple ... we found by cutting it into very thin slices and putting it on the corrugated iron roof of the cook house where it was exposed to the direct heat of the sun, that this stuff actually improved a bit. There was another thing—swamp cabbage. We discovered by trial and error that the optimum results arrived if you cut this every 13 days. Not 12, not 14 but each 13 days. Apparently it was then it got to its maximum. Consequently, we developed tables knowing which bed had to be cut and which bed had to be left alone.[70]

Captain Peter Hendry was impressed with the ingenuity he saw around him in his men, such as the collection and use of urine as fertilizer. Documents detail meticulous recipes for yeast, grass soup, and various other extracts made from plants found in and around the camps.[71] As well, any animals that were unfortunate enough to stray in the path of prisoners were soon meals. Rats, monkeys, cats and snakes were a few of the meats that Australian soldiers ate for the first time.

In many camps, extra supplies and medicines were gained through illegal outside trading with local populations. Thais, Malays and especially Chinese were particularly helpful to Railway camps. At great risk to both groups, doctors or their representatives would meet outside the camps, trading POWs' personal possessions such as watches and clothing, or using money collected through a central camp fund, in exchange for a variety of food and medical supplies. Brand recalled one instance where he was offered a new taste experience by these traders:

> ... now and then we got contact with Thais, and one day a group of—kind of a little travelling market of—Thais came through. Amongst other things they were selling little bowls of milk with a frangipani flower in the centre, for a couple of cents, and I had one of these bowls, very sweet thick milk. It was human [breast] milk.

A Thai businessman, Boon Pong, was of great help to doctors. Based near Kanchanaburi POW camp, he 'at great personal risk to himself since he was laying himself open to torture and death at the hands of the Japanese military police smuggled in supplies of emetine, Vitamin preparations and other essential drugs'.[72] Similarly, Duncan recalled that supplies of raw opium gained from 'friendly Thais' were a great help in treating the painful cramps and diarrhoea of amoebic dysentery.[73]

Most of the money collected in a camp fund came from the already heavily decreased pay of POW officers. The Japanese sporadically distributed the pay that the officers and men were entitled to as POWs, but often withheld most of it, ostensibly keeping it in trust for them. These occasional contributions augmented food rations for the sick, with purchased eggs or milk sometimes being the difference between recovery and death. In Chungkai camp, in March 1944, 1,937 patients were suffering from severe malnutrition and avitaminosis. From officers' contributions alone, substantial funds were collected to spend on food from local traders.[74]

## Individual approaches

Differences in age, experience and knowledge played a key part in how individual Australian POW medical officers approached the problems they faced in the camps. They often treated the same condition in very different ways. While the treatments they used were greatly affected by what they could create or substitute from the environment around them, the treatments they naturally turned to first, their adaptability and their willingness to take risks owed much to these personal factors. Those doctors who were known for their high numbers of amputations (mostly as a result of tropical ulcers that failed to heal), for example, were trained and experienced surgeons, like Coates and Lieutenant Colonel Edward Dunlop.

There were obvious deterrents to conducting surgery in captivity. Sometimes operations had to be done without so many requisite instruments and medications that it was almost a foreign experience to doctors. However, many continued to choose surgical solutions, even in circumstances where surgery was not a common treatment. When treating chronic dysentery, for example, Dunlop performed ileostomies (a surgical procedure where the small intestine is attached to an opening in the abdominal wall and then to a bag outside the body connected to the opening)—a practice that may today seem to medical professionals strange and ineffective, particularly given the primitive medical circumstances in which Dunlop was operating.

Like many of his young medical cohort, Richards is proud that he never performed an amputation during captivity. In the case of tropical ulcers, he directed his orderlies to gently scrape away dead skin daily from around the ulcers with a sharpened spoon. By this method, they 'meticulously took out the dead tissue, piece by piece, making sure not to damage the granulating tissue coming up which is very delicate, as distinct from the more routine treatment which was to spoon it out.'[75]

Other doctors relied on similarly non-surgical measures, such as wrapping ulcers in banana leaves, thus encouraging maggots to develop and eat the diseased skin.[76] Another common technique involved standing men in nearby rivers, where fish would eat away the dead flesh. American doctors often tried soaking ulcers in hot water for long periods, and even pouring tannic acid distilled from tea over the affected areas. All these methods succeeded to varying degrees.

Surgery was not of course uniformly successful among patients on the Railway due to their already poorer levels of health and immunity.[77] Coates, commenting on the 114 cases of ulcer amputation he performed in Burma (after trying various other methods), noted that '50% so treated ultimately died, mostly of a disease other than the ulcers'.[78] This would certainly seem to suggest that undergoing surgery led to higher mortality rates than for patients under doctors who chose not to operate. However, men treated by different methods may have died anyway from a variety of causes.

This highlights an interesting difference of approach among medical officers. While few openly criticise each other, each believes that his method was the most effective. Richards commented: 'it's literally only in the last couple of years that I've talked about this because this appears to be criticism of some well-known doctors. But the facts are we didn't have a single amputation.'[79]

There is rarely only one solution to a medical problem, making it difficult to determine which doctors' styles were the most appropriate in the abnormal circumstances of captivity. Captain J. J. Woodward of the Indian Medical Service, for example, recorded listed the variety of treatments he encountered for blurred vision due to avitaminosis: Allied doctors used riboflavin, American doctors used nicotinic acid, and POW doctors in Hong Kong camps (of which he was one) used vitamin B1 injections.[80]

In Railway camps, doctors also had different ways of making the daily work party choices. Some worked on a sickness basis—whoever was most sick stayed. Others, such as Richards, used a roster basis, rotating men every couple of days where possible, so as to give the less sick men some rest, and hopefully prevent them deteriorating further. Every night he and the second in command officer would sit down and review the lists of who had been working that day:

> . . . they'd be shown as 'Duty' or 'No duty' or 'Light duty' or 'Hospital' or whatever and we'd go through and we'd say, 'Oh, there's Joe, he's been out six days in a row uncomplaining, we'll give him a day off.' So we'd mark him as 'No duty' the next day and 'Duty' the day after. But then to make up that leeway, we'd go through and find somebody that had had 'No duty' or 'Light duty' for several days and we'd mark him for duty just for a day.

Similarly, Pavillard rotated men on work parties to give them rest by adding fifteen men per day on the sick list who were comparatively well.[81]

## Orderlies: towers of strength

Special mention must be made of the invaluable assistance given to POW doctors by their orderlies—a contribution that was eloquently expressed by Lieutenant Colonel Hedley Summons:

> Firstly let me speak to the nursing orderlies—you have done a magnificent job—working for long periods under difficult conditions both night and day—you have saved many lives of your comrades and your work will never be forgotten. You have carried out your duties in the realm of Nursing Sisters in a way that I did not think was possible for mere men to perform.[82]

The doctors themselves are the first to point out the contribution of orderlies, and many feel this group remains unrecognised. As Richards explained, 'I'm absolutely dedicated to recognition of medical orderlies. I have said many times we as the doctors got a lot of kudos, but the kudos should go to the medical orderlies.'[83]

In many ways, orderlies were lumbered with the thankless but vital tasks of POW nursing. They changed bedpans and dressings, assisted in medical procedures and operations, and cremated the dead. While performing these tasks, orderlies dispensed care, compassion and conversation. They sat with patients when time permitted, talking to them, willing them to hold on, and keeping them as clean and comfortable as possible.

They also provided crucial relief when doctors themselves were too exhausted or sick to function. In 1944, as the sole medical officer of the Wampoy–Tavoy Road working party, British doctor Captain C. S. Pitt was overwhelmed by the numbers of sick. He appealed to the Japanese for another doctor to join the camp, but his 'request was refused and I was told that if I could not do the work, I would be sent upcountry where I would have to do manual labour'. In a camp of great hardship, and where there were frequent daily beatings, Pitt made special mention of his orderlies' work: 'All medical orderlies worked extremely hard and well. Those attached to parties frequently had to take the place of an M. O. [medical officer] and use a great deal of initiative.'[84]

Some doctors remembered times when they were so ill that orderlies were forced to take over their duties, as well as nurse them back to health. When asked whether he worried about his own health as a POW, British doctor Captain Bill Hetreed replied: 'Yes, I suppose so, but after all it was a useless bit of thinking . . . we all knew the situation and somebody would cope.' When Pavillard nearly died from contracting typhus in 1944 on the Railway, he credited the care of an orderly, 'Pinky' Riley, with saving his life.[85]

Many of the POW orderlies often had little or no medical training. On the Railway, many were older men or prisoners who were too sick to work, but were able to perform hospital duties. However, there was a price to pay for not being on work parties—orderlies were exposed to sickness and death, putting their own lives in jeopardy and, like the doctors, having to cope with considerable psychological distress. Orderlies had the unenviable task of watching friends and patients die, and then having to dispose of the bodies. Nursing cholera patients, Ray Connolly 'spent many lonely nights out in the jungle all by myself with only the sick and dying men, many of them only lasting two or three hours after being brought out there on stretchers.'[86] Also nursing cholera victims, Higgs was told by Hunt that though they may not be able to do much medically, 'he asked each of us to do whatever was in our power to see that no man was left to face death alone ... the memory of nursing staff sitting by and talking quietly to a man whose life was ebbing away has never left me nor is it likely to.'[87]

Disposal of bodies usually took the form of cremation, as corpses buried in the shallow soil under monsoonal rains could quickly resurface. Orderly Ken Astill recalled a time when he had to cremate a friend, whose body was so swollen with fluid from beri-beri that it exploded, putting out the flames.

The POWs knew that nursing cholera victims was dangerous work, yet when Hunt gathered his men and asked for volunteers to work as orderlies on 'Cholera Hill', he had his staff within minutes. Juttner also recalled:

> In eight months out of our 6998 ... 3089 were dead. We were just burning 9, 10, or 11 bodies every morning and the blokes who were looking after those cholera patients were really marvellous ... trying to keep them clean, risking their own lives.

The risk of infection was a real one, and several orderlies—Australian, British, and American—paid the ultimate price.

Dunlop recalled the generosity of spirit of his medical staff, as exemplified by Staff Sergeant Alan Gibson,

> who was himself reduced to a near-naked skeleton, shivering with chronic malaria and racked with dysentery, yet when confronted with a man naked and tormented with cholera, dropped his last shred of comfort in the world—his blanket—over the dying man.[88]

The important contributions of the thirteen Australian dentists in Japanese captivity must also be acknowledged, demonstrating great ingenuity in replacing men's teeth as these fell out due to malnutrition. Dentures were created from materials such as rubber, aluminium and scrap metal. They also helped medical officers to find ways around lack of supplies, such as producing a local substitute for Marmite.[89] Of the two with him on the Railway, Richards recalled 'they did a magnificent job'.

## The final toll

By the time the two ends of the Railway eventually met in October 1943, nearly 3,000 Australian prisoners working on it had died. That the building of the Railway exacted such a brutal toll is no surprise, considering the terrible state of the workers' health, the terrain in which they had to build, the torrential monsoon rain and extreme heat, the paucity of adequate engineering tools and supplies, and the unrealistic deadline set for completion.

Having initially adapted to the relative comforts of Changi, Australian medical officers had to then acclimatise to the physical and psychological conditions of remote jungle camps. They were forced to treat conditions with which many were unfamiliar—often in patients who were already starving and exhausted. They watched men wasting away before their eyes, and often could do little to help. As well, they were under the control of captors who cared little about the welfare of their POWs except as a source of labour.

Although many prisoners died in the Railway camps, and others died weeks or months later of disease due to that experience, the doctors' contribution ensured the majority survived. If they had not found supplies of food and nutrients other than the meagre diet provided by their captors, more men would have starved to death. If they had not devised innovative medical treatments, more men would have died of disease. In a variety of future camps, lessons learned during the months on the Railway would prove equally useful.

# 4

# UNTOLD STORIES: THE OTHER CAMPS

Most accounts of Australians in Japanese captivity continue to focus on Changi and the Burma–Thai Railway camps, 'to the exclusion of all the other places and circumstances where Australian troops were held captive'.[1] Yet Australian personnel were also prisoners in several other countries, with different attendant circumstances. Some doctors saw out the war in Java, Sumatra, Japan, Borneo, Manchuria, Formosa (now Taiwan) or Ambon and Hainan Islands. In terms of mortality rates, Borneo and Ambon represented the highest proportional loss of Australian lives of all Japanese camps. Across these many locations the differences in climate, degree of geographical isolation, varied access to supplies, the treatment meted out by their captors, the types of physical labour and the stage of the war created extra medical complications the doctors had to manage.

As there were only a handful of doctors (or in some cases only one) in some of these remote camps, constructing a comprehensive picture of medical conditions in those areas is difficult. While an exhaustive description of every camp is impractical, this chapter will outline the characteristics of a key group of these other camps, and explore some of the factors negotiated by Australian medical officers.

Many Australian prisoners were taken to other camps even before the building of the Burma–Thai Railway commenced. The defence of Timor, Ambon and New Britain was seen as a priority by Australian authorities but, as with Singapore, the attempt to keep these key strategic areas out of Japanese hands was too little too late. Lark Force, comprising 1,400 men mostly from the 2/22nd Battalion, was sent to defend New Britain from April 1941. Sparrow Force, a group of 1,400 men primarily from the 2/40th Battalion, was despatched to Timor in December 1941, with reinforcements arriving the following February.

Even at this early stage, medical officers had to deal with high numbers of patients with malaria, tropical ulcers and diarrhoea. When the Japanese troops arrived, they captured both areas within a few weeks. By this stage, medical supplies were already exhausted or had been confiscated, and the men's health continued to deteriorate.

In December 1941 Gull Force, primarily made up of 1,090 men from the 2/21st Battalion, was shipped to Ambon, a small eastern island in the Netherlands East Indies. They were quickly overtaken by Japanese troops, and it was their medical officer, Captain William Aitken, who eventually negotiated the terms of surrender, by the authority of his commanding officer. Prisoners were housed in Tan Tui camp, the former site of their wartime barracks.

In November 1942, 263 Australian prisoners, including Aitken, and a similar number of Dutch POWs were sent from Ambon to Hainan, a large island south of the Chinese mainland, where they remained until the end of the war. The POW camps on Ambon and Hainan were among the very worst experienced by Allied prisoners: 407 of the 528 Australian prisoners died, most from slow starvation.[2]

By the time reinforcements from the 6th and 7th Divisions arrived in Java in early 1942, the Japanese were already in control of much of the island. Hundreds of Australians were imprisoned in Bandoeng camp, originally the site of an Allied General Hospital. Almost a thousand Bandoeng prisoners, including Australian medical officers, were then sent to the Railway from late 1942 to early 1943.

In October 1942 Captain Des Brennan was sent to Mukden in Manchuria, the Japanese-controlled province of China, where he lived in a camp comprising mostly British and American soldiers. Manchuria was seen as Japan's *lebensraum*, its lifeline to raw materials and to more territory for the expansion of the Japanese population. Brennan and Colonel Douglas C. Pigdon were the only Australian doctors in Mukden. Brennan considered himself fortunate that his camp was one of a few declared to the Red Cross. However, food and medical supplies were still inadequate and, despite his best efforts, many prisoners died. Pigdon himself died of illness in July 1945, just a few weeks before liberation.

Almost 3,000 Australian POWs were held in camps on the Japanese home islands during the war. While the first Allied POWs were transported to Japan in late 1942, the majority arrived a year later, after the Railway had been completed. May 1943 also saw 900 Allied POWs leave Changi, bound directly for Japan. One hundred and fifty (100 British, 50 Australian) members of 'J' force were taken to Hakensho Camp on Kyushu Island for two and a half years. Another 250 Australians went to Kobe, and a camp at Zentsuji held a group of senior Australian officers. Like many others, these camps have received comparatively little attention from historians. As Joan Beaumont writes:

> The experiences of Australian prisoners of war on the Burma–Thailand Railway in 1942 and 1943 were so horrific that they have almost eclipsed in popular memory the sufferings of those 2700 Australians who spent some years of captivity in Japan itself.[3]

When men were chosen in Changi for 'J' Force, the Japanese repeated the lies they had told the forces that were sent to the Railway. Medical officer and 'J' Force Captain Clive Boyce was informed that the POWs were bound for a 'rest camp', and that the force should be made up of convalescent men. Twenty-three men chosen to join 'J' Force were so sick that among them they shared eleven cases of dysentery, one case of tonsillitis, one of septic tinea, four cases of malaria, six cases of dengue, five cases of anxiety neurosis, one case of scrub typhus, twelve cases of eye problems, twenty cases of dietary deficiencies, and fourteen cases of dermatitis.[4]

Some POWs who worked on the Railway were transported to other camps after its completion in late 1943. They were either moved to Thai base camps such as Chungkai or Nakon Patom or relocated to other camps throughout Japan-controlled Asia. The influx of so many more prisoners to these camps had serious ramifications for medical officers.

While the base hospital at Changi continued to operate until the end of the war, in 1944 the entire camp shifted to another location at nearby Sime Road—a large camp where hundreds of Dutch, Indonesian and British civilian internees were already held, resulting in overcrowding and increased competition for food and supplies. After repeated appeals to the Japanese by Allied officers and doctors, a hospital camp was established in 1944 at Kranji, on the north-east side of Singapore. Work parties continued to be employed on various projects around the island.

Smaller camps had their own sets of problems. When he was with a working party of 300 men at Woodlands camp on the Straits of Johore in 1942, Captain Robert Pufflett found that his major medical challenges were skin diseases and widespread worm infestations—including hookworm, strongyloides and ascaris—from which he suffered himself. Treatment of these conditions was made more difficult by the practice of 'using excreta for fertiliser. Most of the gardens were receptacles for faeces and trenches were filled with these and covered, and tomatoes and potatoes were planted in over them.'

These other camps had particular characteristics that were often absent in Singapore and Railway camps, and which placed unique demands on medical officers.

# Isolation

A common feature of many of these camps was their geographical isolation. In Changi, doctors had access to black market trade and they were surrounded by colleagues with whom they could consult, share techniques and divide the burden of decision-making. Even on the Railway, doctors who were alone with a work party moved so often that they would come across other work parties and colleagues, or they would periodically be able to visit base hospitals. In places such as Ambon, Manchuria and the smaller camps in Japan, however, while some black market trading was possible, it was sporadic and infrequent. In such places, finding extra food and medical supplies was difficult or impossible.

The remoteness of these camps put an extra strain on doctors, who had to treat a variety of conditions knowing they had almost no way of acquiring supplies. Doctors and prisoners were at the complete whim of their captors. An increased sense of loss of control accompanied all their decisions. In June 1945, for example, prisoners in Haito, Formosa, were moved to a camp at the top of a mountain—a treacherous journey in itself—cutting through forests and building *atap* camps. British prisoner of war Harry Leslie told how, with supplies hard to procure, 'Rations became less and less and we were beaten continually, becoming sick with no medical supplies. Treatment by the Japanese became more severe, with death occurring continually.'[5]

Medical officers were also professionally isolated. At Paisho camp near Osaka, Captain John Akeroyd served as the sole doctor from October 1943 to March 1944. Major Robert V. Glasgow, Akeroyd's Commanding Officer, said 'He arrived when we were desperately in need of [a] Medical Officer. He was responsible for the saving of many lives during the first winter in Japan 1943–44.'[6]

On Ambon, the Australian POWs had a dentist but no doctor. After their force was separated in November 1942, the prisoners left on Ambon were singularly unfortunate when their only Australian medical officer, Captain Peter M. Davidson, was killed in February 1943 during an Allied air raid. Their medical care fell to an Australian dentist, Captain Gordon C. Marshall, and Captain J. H. Ehlhart, a Dutch doctor in the Royal East Medical Services. The demands on these two men were immense, and conditions so dire that Marshall felt that despite their best efforts, 'the hospital was only a staging post to the cemetery'.[7] Ehlhart was a specialist in tropical disease but had little surgical experience. When one Australian POW's leg had to be amputated because of an ulcer that extended from his knee to his ankle, Ehlhart admitted his anxiety to Sapper Les Hohl:

> I'm not a surgeon. In fact I've never even watched an amputation let alone done one myself... I've done everything I possibly can to find out all about it. I've dug up a couple of books on amputations and read them up to see how to do it.[8]

Psychologically, the isolation of these camps had a profound impact upon morale. There was also little or no news of how the war was progressing, or whether friends in other camps were even alive.

## Other burdens

Malnutrition and lack of supplies resulted in similar medical conditions in most Japanese POW camps, and for those medical officers still in Thailand and Singapore after 1943, these continued to be the biggest problems for men's health. In June 1945 Lieutenant Colonel John C. Collins, a British doctor, wrote an all too familiar memo to the Japanese pleading with them for more drugs and better accommodation at Kranji. This followed the arrival of a nineteen-man sick party from a camp at Keppel Harbour, who were all in dire health. Several had large bedsores caused by lying on concrete floors for long periods of time.[9]

During that same month, eighteen Kranji hospital staff members were admitted for treatment, and their weight decreased dramatically from an August 1944 average of 140 lb (64 kilograms) to 124 lb (56 kilograms).[10] While some Red Cross supplies were distributed in Kranji, they were of limited use. Major Burnett Clarke recalled how a Red Cross parcel that weighed about 3 kilograms was divided among 28 men. By the time the food from the parcel was distributed among all the men and added to their Japanese ration, it 'really only acted as a flavour'.[11]

In July 1945 many patients with severe avitaminosis were shown to the Japanese medical officer at Chungkai. While the sight of these men suffering from paralysis, tremors and greatly exaggerated tendon reflexes must have had an impact on Dr Nebuzawa, and despite the many warnings that continued withholding of vitamins could cause permanent paralysis to the POWs, the Japanese took no action.[12]

The Australian medical officers also had to contend with the difference in climate between tropical South-East Asia with its high humidity and warm temperatures and cold areas such as Taiwan, Manchuria and Japan. Here the winters were harsh and temperatures often fell to below freezing, causing yet another shock to the POWs' already wasted bodies. The men were ill equipped for such intense cold, and the Japanese did not issue sufficient warm clothing or blankets.

Captain Ian Duncan was sent to Fukuoka Camp No. 17 in Omuta, Japan, in August 1943. His patients were mostly American and Dutch POWs who had come from other camps in Japan, Thailand and the Philippines. At its peak, this camp held 1,859 prisoners, housed in crude and crowded Japanese barracks. Duncan recalled that the health of the various groups of new arrivals varied: some were in reasonably good physical condition while others were very ill. In one group of 97 Americans prisoners, every man was extremely emaciated and Duncan judged that at least a third of them were dying. Heating was provided by coal fires, which created terrible fumes, and 'the inadequate heat produced by such fires in cold, drafty buildings rendered them absolutely unsatisfactory as a means of heating a barracks'.[13]

Some of the health problems in Duncan's camp, such as deficiency diseases, bacillary dysentery and gastroenteritis, were familiar to him. However, the most common was one that had rarely been experienced in the tropics: pneumonia, which he came to call 'our most dreaded killer'. This condition caused the most deaths among POWs in Japan, particularly among the Australians and Dutch.[14] The combination of inadequate heating in winter, a poor diet and widespread upper respiratory tract infections among the men working in mines (caused by exposure to mining gases) created ideal conditions for contracting pneumonia. It afflicted 250 men in total, with 60–80 POWs succumbing during the winter of 1944 to spring 1945. Over two years, 122 prisoners in Fukuoka camp died—most from pneumonia (48) and deficiency diseases (35).[15]

While the Japanese did give the Allied doctors small quantities of antibiotic sulphonamides (15 grams per patient) to treat pneumonia, Duncan noted that the medication was not always effective with malnourished men and could sometimes have debilitating side effects. One such treatment, Trianon, distributed during the winter of 1944–45, caused 'mental symptoms' in patients.[16]

Surgeon-Lieutenant Samuel Stening, an Australian naval doctor who survived the sinking of *HMAS Perth*, was the sole medical officer in another camp in Japan, where he described a similar situation: when given in normal doses, sulpha drugs distributed by the Japanese could produce a toxic effect, increasing oedema and precipitating renal failure, due to the inability of the patient's kidneys to process the chemicals.[17]

Other conditions occurred in prisoners who were sent to work in the mines in Japan. Doctors encountered bronchitis and relapsing fevers, but they did not know what caused the latter as they did not have the tools to carry out microbiological investigations. Like dengue in the tropics, such fevers at times occurred in 60–70 per cent of the prisoners, with patients exhibiting symptoms of a high fever, aches and a loss of appetite.[18] When medical officers asked the Japanese for advice, they received no help.

In one respect, the cold camps were a relief to the prisoners who had arrived from the tropics with malaria. Although 88 per cent of Australian POWs arrived with the disease, in many men it seemed to disappear within a few months. Others welcomed the first anti-malarial treatment they had received thus far—in Japan, doctors were given Atebrin for the first time.[19]

Just as in the tropics, however, leg ulceration was common, the result of injuries received in the mines that became infected because of the poor physical condition of the prisoners and their low immunity. The doctors in Fukuoka camp sought mostly surgical solutions, such as curettage and skin grafts. Surgery in captivity was, as ever, a difficult prospect, and in Japan major cases were initially sent to Japanese-run mine hospitals. This proved disastrous: no anaesthetic was used prior to surgery and patients returned in a state of shock. Duncan and his colleagues thus found themselves in the bizarre position of having to treat their patients as best they could in an effort to prevent them being sent to hospital.[20]

In Manchuria, Brennan also faced conditions caused by the freezing climate. Frostbite and chilblains were widespread, and pneumonia, tuberculosis and diphtheria were killers. Deficiency diseases led to other problems such as burning feet and beri-beri, which were thought to be worsened by the cold.[21] In one period in 1942, diphtheria caused the deaths of '22 men in 24 days'.[22] Despite the efforts of Brennan and his medical colleagues, 300 men in his camp died:

> One night we lost six, several nights four or five, and could do nothing for them. If I ever learnt about compassion for the sick and dying, and encouragement or urging to stay alive through sheer will-power, this was the time.[23]

With night-time temperatures of −40°C in the months of December and January, bodies could not be buried as the ground was frozen solid: 'It was too cold to bury them, so they just stored them in an unheated barracks till the thaw.' Brennan, from Sydney, had never experienced such weather: 'It was something I'd never done before, practise cold country medicine.'[24]

On Hainan, Aitken found vitamin B deficiencies and beri-beri to be the main health issues. He was able to obtain some vitamin B from the local market, and some was scrounged by men working on the docks, but it was never enough.[25] Twenty men died from complications of avitaminosis, and lack of vitamin C was also a common problem, leading to widespread skin infections. In August 1943 the Japanese issued some supplies of food, such as unpolished rice, beans, barley and vitamin B powder, but for many men it was too late:

> The hospital was full of men with ataxia, paralysis and oedema—some able to stagger around and others could not. Every bed held

a man with complete oedema of the body and gasping for breath. Others in the same condition were being nursed on the floor, propped up against the wall and boxes with kit bags, etc.[26]

British doctor Colonel C. W. Maisey was shocked at the state of the men who were transferred to Batavian hospital camps from Ambon in November 1943. His description is very moving:

> It is difficult to describe one's reactions when one sees four or five hundred men who are so ill and have been so badly treated that they resemble nothing more than ugly, misshapen slugs. Their bodies were the most fantastic shapes, and their limbs were twisted in the most abnormal manner, and above all there was the most hopeless look of misery and utter dejection in their eyes. It was obvious to all who saw them that those men did not fear death. They had got beyond that stage. When the first draft arrived in St Vincentius Hospital many members of staff wept openly, and there certainly was not a single member, British, Dutch, or even Japanese, who was dry eyed. At the time, I was asked by the Japanese doctor what I thought of their condition. I said that we had no words in the English language to describe it. He did not reply.[27]

Maisey discovered an unfamiliar medical condition among these POWs, which was thought to be a side effect of malnutrition. Many of the men had lost their memory; one man 'was quite unable to read for six or seven months although his vision was quite good, the reason being that he was unable to remember a sufficient number of words at a time to make sense'.[28]

## An impossible workload

In all these camps, the most dangerous reality for all the prisoners was their treatment by their captors. As in every Japanese camp, this varied greatly, with individuals capable of being both callous and sympathetic at different times. While the climate and nature of the labour may have been different from Changi and the Railway, their captors' harshness was unfortunately all too familiar.

On Hainan, 80 men died, eighteen of these from starvation alone. In his postwar medical report, Aitken wrote: 'It is stated at the outset that our treatment by the Japanese and their attitude towards us was so disgraceful and inhumane as to merit the severest condemnation of any civilised person.'[29]

Australians there carried out hard manual labour daily, and were subject to constant physical abuse from the Japanese, imposing a 'great deal of mental strain on all men'. Sick men were dragged out to work, with the typical result that 'This retarded recovery from disease and after some men had been treated in this fashion they never went to work again and were even set so far back as to go rapidly downhill and die.'[30]

On Ambon, troops 'were simply worked to death. In what was called the "longcarry", they carried bombs and bags of cement from one part of Ambon to another for no practical advantage to anyone.'[31] George Williamson recalled his duties in the burial party towards the end of the war, burying up to ten men per day. He remembered:

> We'd go out and dig the graves, and then bury them. And by the time we got back from one there'd be another one ready to go out, and so we'd just have to start again. You couldn't keep up with it. You'd wake up during the night and you'd hear them, you'd hear the death rattles going on ... The next morning you'd find out who it was.[32]

Though some POWs attempted escape and were successful, it became an increasingly unrealistic option. As Aitken remarked, the state of their health made escape from Ambon impossible: 'We were all extremely weak, and I don't think a single man was capable of running 100 yards and it took the greatest effort to carry out the normal functions of life, let alone any necessary duties.'[33]

At Fukuoka, Duncan worked closely alongside another Australian doctor, a Dutch doctor and three American doctors. Each continued to focus on their professional specialties, and took turns meeting working parties at each day's end to establish which men were unable to go the next day. As usual, the Japanese classification system for determining which men were able to work deliberately ignored illness. Lieutenant Fukahara, camp commandant of Fukuoka, would sometimes perform inspections of the sick and classify them himself, invariably sending them out to work.[34]

Cold climates could also affect the types of punishments doled out by the Japanese. Private Mick Ryan remembered how two Australians were simply told to stand in snow as punishment for scrounging for food. They both subsequently died.[35] Brennan witnessed another instance during the 1944 winter in Manchuria where men suffering from frostbite were forced to run a distance without shoes. A Japanese officer then told them that 'frostbite did not exist in this country'. Brennan noted that this was the same man who a year earlier had issued a circular to POWs warning them of the condition.[36]

In Java, the Japanese treated POW doctors as unsympathetically as their colleagues on the Railway. Maisey commented: 'One can appreciate a surgeon's feelings when he has a patient's life in his hands and he is being beaten and kicked about by the Japanese.' He recorded that a Dutch medical officer, Dr ter Laag, 'stuck to his work exceedingly well and maintained his very high standard, although it was obvious to all that he was slowly breaking under the terrific nervous strain'.[37] Other Dutch doctors were in similar states, which Maisey attributed to the constant abuse from the Japanese:

> ... some of the Japanese on the staff were of the worst sadistic type. They poured insults on the doctors from morning till night regarding their work. They jeered, laughed and sneered and bashed the doctors whenever they appealed for help for dying men. They harried and bullied the doctors continuously.[38]

As well as confiscating all drugs and supplies, the Japanese forced them to 'hand in all red cross [sic] brassards and erase all red crosses from equipment of any sort', thereby denying them any identification as non-combatant medical personnel.[39]

At Ofuna Camp in Yokohama, Stening was held for a time in a camp populated mostly by Allied officers, where they were subjected to violent and systematic interrogations by the Japanese. Periods of additional torture and solitary confinement caused psychological strain among the inhabitants.[40]

Similarly, as the only doctor in his Osaka camp, Akeroyd was constantly treated cruelly by his captors, and lost half his body weight during captivity. However, although he was 'repeatedly beaten and knocked about because of the strong stand he took regarding sick and ailing men, he never weakened, and a great deal of credit goes to him for the few deaths recorded in this particular camp'.[41]

In Borneo, many hundreds of Allied POWs from 'B' and 'E' Forces, including 1,800 Australians, died from starvation and mistreatment. In Labuan, a cemetery commemorates 2,327 of these POWs, including three Australian doctors.[42] Of the Japanese camps in Borneo, the most notorious is Sandakan, where 2,771 Australian and British POWs were interned.

Throughout early to mid 1945, prisoners who had endured thus far were sent on a series of forced marches from Sandakan to Ranau—a distance of 260 kilometres through jungle and over mountain, with ever decreasing food supplies. Many who actually survived these marches died once reaching Ranau. By the end, of an original force of over 2,000, only six prisoners had survived Sandakan by escaping during the march— all of them Australians. As so little knowledge of this camp has survived, it is difficult to ascertain how medical care was carried out or how it differed from other camps.

In New Britain, apart from those who had escaped or been sent elsewhere, Lark Force had no survivors. In two separate tragic events, 180 of its POWs were massacred by the Japanese at the Tol Plantation, and the remainder drowned when their transport, the *Montevideo Maru*, was sunk by Allied torpedoes in July 1942. More than three-quarters of the original Lark Force died as prisoners.

In 1944, Allied POWs in Sumatra commenced work on a railway

extending from Muara to Pekanbaru, a distance of 230 kilometres. Five hundred POWs died during its construction, including 40 Australians. They had little medication, and even resorted to crushing the raw bark from which quinine was extracted and mixing it with rice to alleviate malaria. Private Frank Robinson of the 2/20th Battalion recalled the precariousness of experimenting with dosages:

> We didn't know exactly how much to take and I remember when you did take a rice ball with quinine bark in it, it was almost as bad as the malaria. Your ears would really buzz and you would almost become unconscious.[43]

Formosa was the destination for many senior Allied POW officers. Several had been transported to Haito in 1942 from Changi and were accompanied by working parties and housed in separate areas from other ranks. Private Harry Leslie, a British POW, went to Haito in September 1942, and along with other prisoners was forced to do exhausting work—loading stones from river beds and carrying them in two baskets resting on a pole across his shoulders. These stones were carried onto ships for use as ballast.[44]

In 1944 several Allied officers were also held in Mukden. Manchurian camps varied in their conditions—the Allied officers' camp was considered fairly good, but other camps where Allied working parties were sent could be very harsh. Captain Bill Hammon, an Australian officer from the 2/3rd Machine Gun Battalion, was one of those transported to Manchuria via Japan, where he remained until the end of the war labouring in coal mines: 'a long and arduous incarceration, working for over two years in cruel conditions'.[45]

Regardless of their poor health and the protestations of doctors, the Japanese continued demanding men daily for work parties. On Hainan,

> The Japanese still insisted on the 120 men going to work each day and to make up this figure, ataxic and oedematous men had to be included in the work party. These men were hardly able to stagger

to work, let alone stand up to the brutal treatment meted out by the guards.[46]

In his postwar report, Aitken bitterly recorded that all his protests to the Japanese were met with laughter or beatings. He was even told he would not be allowed to record 'starvation' on his men's death certificates. When he initially refused, Aitken was warned that they 'would show us what was really meant by starvation unless it was altered'. He concluded, 'Japanese policy during this period was plain murder.'[47]

At Fukuoka camp in Japan, 75 per cent of POWs were put to work in the surrounding coal mines, and another 20 per cent in zinc foundries. POWs had to learn how to mine with little training, were under constant and usually harsh supervision, were not allowed to rest, and were exposed to constant hazards. As on the Railway, tools were inadequate and conditions dangerous, but for different reasons: 'Cave-ins and the falling of large rocks were frequent enough to keep the men in constant fear of death.'[48] Shifts lasted 12–14 hours, often in freezing conditions. Men worked underground in four-foot spaces and would sometimes be immersed in water the whole time. They could be working in 'hot spots' underground where temperatures were over 38°C, only to be met with freezing temperatures upon leaving the mine. Why they were not supplied with adequate tools is puzzling, as unlike on the Railway they were close to populated, industrialised areas.

A significant change for these POWs was that their overseers were not prison guards but Japanese civilians. Yet their treatment remained mostly harsh. They were, wrote Duncan, 'for the most part sadistic monsters, and beatings, often severe, were an everyday occurrence'. If prisoners stopped to stretch for a moment, they could face 'a savage beating with a heavy metre stick an inch and a half in diameter'. Doctors recorded many fractures, and even a few deaths.[49] While used to mistreatment by their military captors, it was difficult for POWs to understand the equally harsh behaviour of ordinary Japanese civilians. Duncan noted that they seemed frightened all the time, and 'From the beginning various psychological problems presented themselves to the already bewildered prisoners of war.'[50] At Fukuoka, Private Ken Collins twice lost all his hair 'because of the traumatic stresses'.[51] Such distress also created among a few POWs a malingering attitude, and some even broke their own bones in an attempt to avoid being sent to the mines and foundries.[52]

Living in a strange land and overseeing foreign prisoners was certainly one factor that may have helped explain the harsh treatment by the Japanese on the Burma–Thai Railway. Yet there was no softening in their approach back on their home soil: the treatment meted out to Australian prisoners in Japan was not appreciably different from any of the other camps. In Japan, Australian doctor Captain Alex Barrett described a familiar instance of Japanese cruelty: 'I saw Tagouchi, while these men were sick in camp with diarrhoea and beri-beri, beat them insensible and kick them whilst they were unconscious on the floor.'[53]

## The passage of time

A significant enemy of all POWs during the last two years of captivity was simply time. Many camps underwent their most difficult periods in the last months of the war, and POWs had no idea when their ordeal would end. The mortality rate increased over time, and the doctors' feelings of desperation intensified. On Ambon, for example, the death rate increased alarmingly in the war's final months. In May, 42 men died; in July, 94.[54] On Hainan, rations were reduced from 2,662 calories per day per prisoner in 1944 to 1,063 in May 1945, with a subsequent decline in prisoners' body weight and overall health.[55]

Major Hugh Rayson, a prisoner in Kuching in Borneo—a camp of around 3,000 mixed nationality military personnel and civilian internees—wrote wearily in his diary, 'As time went on, it was found that the more energetic of the workers eventually broke down and seldom were fit for heavy work again. It became harder and harder to carry out the necessary chores for our survival.'[56] Men's bodies simply could not withstand the accumulated damage—many POWs survived the Malaya campaign and the Burma–Thai Railway only to die in 1945. In the last twelve months of the war, six Australian medical officers died, two tragically dying in Borneo only days before the end of the war: Captain John Bernard Oakeshott died on 1 August, and his colleague Captain Domenic George Picone five days later. They were 44 and 36 respectively.

Base hospitals in Singapore and along the Railway continued to function right until the end. In 1944 the Japanese also established a large base hospital at Nakon Patom in Thailand for those prisoners who were too sick to make the trip back to Singapore or who continued to work in Thailand.

At Chungkai base hospital in Thailand, starvation was widespread. By March 1944, nearly 2,000 patients were suffering from malnutrition and avitaminosis, yet less than half could be accommodated in the hospital.[57] Prisoners were on a diet of approximately 2,886 calories, and while this was comparatively good compared to other camps, Lieutenant Colonel Edward Dunlop calculated that they needed at least 4,000 calories daily given the heavy labour duties. Calories alone, however, did not necessarily include any lasting dietary value. It is hard to see what nutritional benefits the Japanese ration contained when Dunlop commented that 'the I. J. A. [Imperial Japanese Army] ration supplied is deficient in protein, fat, calcium, iron, salt and Vitamin E', and made the point that calculating calorie amounts was somewhat meaningless when men were practically dead to begin with. Despite his continuous protests, Dunlop added in handwriting at the end of a medical report: 'Note: No action was taken by the Japanese and these heavy expenses for the feeding of the sick remained a burden on the Ps.O.W.'[58]

At Kranji in the second half of 1944, rates of dysentery actually decreased, and due to the cultivation of gardens, green vegetables in the POWs' diet meant that although their general rations were reduced, their diet was generally healthier. Lieutenant Colonel Cotter Harvey noted that at this point, the medical officers had little to do.[59] Six months later, however, the Japanese were still decreasing rations, and many medical personnel became so sick they could not look after patients. Malaria also increased as the Japanese forbade any anti-malarial measures.[60]

In many ways, the behaviour of the Japanese during the last two years of the war was attributable to the turning tide of their military situation. They knew the war in Europe was not going well for their Axis comrades, and were aware of the increasingly threatening presence of the large American force in the Pacific. In addition to the logistical burdens of looking after so many Allied POWs, there was a growing realisation that their countrymen were not conquering the people for whom they had so much contempt. This knowledge had two consequences for Allied POWs. Firstly, in some camps, the mistreatment of prisoners became more pronounced—food rations were decreased further, and even greater levels of cruelty were displayed. This was certainly the case in Ambon, Hainan and camps in Japan. As well, Australians in these camps were told (and many believed it) that they would all be executed at the end of the war. Duncan recalled, 'If it wasn't for the [Hiroshima and Nagasaki] bombs, I have no doubt that every last one of us would be dead.'[61] At Kuching, documents were found prescribing the same end for that camp's prisoners.

However as the end of the Pacific War approached, in other camps, the opposite occurred. Captors began distributing Red Cross parcels and mail more frequently. In 1945 doctors at Kranji began to receive large amounts of precious vitamins which were immediately given to the men. Harvey noted that considering the state of the prisoners' health after three years of mistreatment, the efficacy of these last-minute supplies 'would be very severely tested'. In a few cases, even large doses of thiamine injected into beri-beri sufferers had no effect.[62] The vitamins' effectiveness was also negated by concurrent reduction of rice rations in June 1945, which forced Colonel Robert Webster to include hospital staff on 'Light Duty' rations for the first time, presumably to conserve food.

Major Walter Fisher, an Australian doctor who had been on the Railway in Burma, saw one Japanese officer change remarkably towards the end of the war. Fisher's colleagues who had not witnessed the officer's cruelty to POWs on the Railway found it hard to believe that 'the now obsequious Higuchi was the same man who had reviewed 900 sick men in ninety minutes at a work parade and had been unmoved by his visit to the dysentery hut at Thanbyuzayat.'[63]

Kuching also provides a good case study of changes in Japanese attitudes. In early 1943 Major Howard Eddey, the senior medical officer in 'E' Force, spent his first six weeks as a POW on the island of Berhala, Sumatra, which he found relatively pleasant. POWs were comparatively well, food was plentiful, and there was no forced labour.[64] When he moved to Kuching in October 1943, the doctors were given a supply of anti-dysenteric serum and, as a result, the men in their care had a comparatively low rate of dysentery throughout captivity.[65] Despite this promising beginning, conditions rapidly deteriorated. In the last year of captivity, rations were decreased by the Japanese, and some men lost up to 32 kilograms in weight. It was estimated that 50 per cent of the British troops at Kuching died from starvation.[66]

In 1945, however, the Japanese at Kuching underwent yet another change in behaviour. They handed control of the nearby civilian hospital to the POW doctors who, with access to proper equipment and supplies, were now able to save many of the sick. In August 1945 they also gave out gauze bandages and sulpha drugs. Rayson, one of the doctors there, wrote: 'It is extremely harrowing that this drug has been so long withheld.'[67] That same month Eddey was given supplies of vitamins by the Japanese: 'We had never had them before. They gave out a tremendous amount. We treated our protein deficiency diseases. These were American supplies, which were dated 1943.'[68] Window-dressing of Kuching hospital began too—suddenly, 'Chairs, beds, sheets were supplied to the camp hospital and a cane chair was even sent to me as S.M.O. [senior medical officer].'[69] This last-minute generosity was bittersweet. Eddey wrote:

> This final episode of my life as a prisoner of war showed forcibly how, given a little cooperation from our captors earlier in our

captivity, many more lives of prisoners would have been saved. This lack of cooperation was the main difficulty with which we, as medical officers, had to contend during our incarceration.[70]

Towards the end of the war, some Australian prisoners faced a new danger—Allied air raids. Bomb attacks added another element to their already fearful lives, and for medical personnel complicated an already desperate situation. In July 1945 an Allied air raid destroyed eleven barracks and five hospital wards at Fukuoka. When the Allies bombed Nong Pladuk camp in Thailand on 6 September 1944, 100 POWs were killed and 400 injured. Orderly Ray Connolly remembered, 'an additional 400 [wounded] really caused chaos. We already had been busy with ulcer cases, amputations, dysentery, malaria and all the other diseases.'[71] When American planes bombed Haito camp, British POW Private Harry Leslie had to hold down another prisoner while Australian doctor Captain Patrick O'Donnell amputated the injured man's leg without anaesthetic.[72] On the Railway at Kinsayok in Thailand, Dr Stanley Pavillard remembered with despair seeing POWs killed by Allied aircraft in 1944. He wrote poignantly that these men 'who had survived disease and deprivation for years, died in the jungle at the hands of their friends, beside the railway which they had built for their enemies'.[73]

The POWs on Ambon experienced air raids in February 1943 and August 1944, killing many. The first bombing raid on Tan Tui devastated the camp, destroying most of the buildings and killing several officers. Australian Corporal Arthur Deakin recalled, 'For days we were too frightened to look up into the sky.'[74]

Japanese transports remained as dangerous as ever for POWs, particularly as the threat of Allied torpedoes increased in the final stages of the war. In November 1944, along with 2,200 other Allied POWs, Connolly boarded a Japanese transport in Singapore bound for Japan. He ended up in Saigon. Starving and dehydrated, many POWs died in transit and the Japanese unceremoniously threw their bodies overboard. During the journey, a Chinese guard told the prisoners that he had heard their ship was to be targeted by Allied torpedoes the next day. Connolly recalled thinking, 'Yeah we hope so!'[75]

## Brilliant solutions

As in Changi and on the Railway, doctors in other camps worked hard to overcome the lack of medical equipment and to compensate for the nutritional deficiencies in the prisoners' diet. Like their countrymen elsewhere, the Dutch medical personnel in these camps proved crucial. At St Vincentius Hospital in Java, a Dutch doctor, Major Zaadnordijk, developed an ingenious way of recycling barium sulphate for X-rays. Maisey wrote: 'The patient swallowed his barium sulphate, the X-ray was taken, and we confined him to a room until it was returned, passed to Major Zaadnordijk, who passed it back to us as pure barium sulphate.'[76] Duncan recalled a Dutch doctor in Omuta camp who constructed a microscope using bamboo and lenses from field glasses, sophisticated enough to enable blood to be typed for transfusions, which were then used to treat pneumonia.[77]

Maisey was equally full of praise for Australian doctor Captain Leslie Poidevin for his food experimentation with cookhouse staff in Java: 'Some of the sambals [a strongly spiced chilli-based condiment] were most nutritious as they contained protein from various sources of which I did not enquire too much (rats, cats, etc.), but the strong flavouring of chillie [sic] and other spices completely masked whatever else was in it.'[78] Unused to Asian flavours, Australian soldiers had some trouble adjusting to this delicious occasional addition to their rice. Captain Rowley Richards recalled that the men nicknamed these dishes 'ring burners'.[79]

On Ambon, dentist Gordon Marshall proved similarly inventive. He made aluminium dentures from aeroplane scrap and water bottles, a dental tool from a bicycle wheel, sunglasses from anti-gas goggles darkened with bacteriological stain, a curette from bike spokes, a clock spring and various other ingenious instruments.[80]

At Kuching, Eddey noticed that tropical ulcers improved after the men contracted malaria. Hoping that this was because the fever that accompanied malaria was an immunity booster, artificial fevers were induced in some patients, with positive results.[81] Also at Kuching, Rayson employed a clandestine strategy to help a POW who had been put in the 'cage'—a small box measuring approximately 1.6 × 1.5 × 1.5 metres, in which prisoners were interned for several days as punishment. The POW, who had hit a guard, was beaten severely and placed in the cage with only water. Rayson gave him some relief by secretly dissolving in the water half a gram of morphia.[82]

Surrounded by tuberculosis patients in Mukden, Brennan and a British pharmacist managed to construct an artificial pneumothorax from some bottles, pipes and glass tubing.[83] Brennan was completely inexperienced in this area: 'Now I'd never done one, I'd never seen one done, but I knew in theory how you worked it.' Like his colleagues in other camps, he kept many secret medical records, hidden in patients' mattresses.[84]

In some of these camps, doctors received critical help from outsiders. At Sandakan a civilian doctor, Dr James P. Taylor, went to great lengths to give his imprisoned colleagues food, money and medical supplies, acts of kindness that led eventually to his arrest and imprisonment.[85] Many others who chose to help Allied POWs at great personal risk remain unknown and unrecognised. Historian Hank Nelson noted that these spontaneous acts of kindness left a lasting impression on Australian prisoners. In many of his interview subjects he found 'a sympathetic perceptiveness about the urban and rural people of southeast Asia', such as the interest among ex-POWs in helping the local population during the 1975 Indonesian invasion of East Timor.[86] Likewise, on Ambon in 1967, the Gull Force Association began a medical aid program for the local people, and an Anzac Day service is held there annually.

In Japan, some of the camps were located in or near populous or industrial areas such as Zentsuji, Yokohama and Osaka. Some POWs were put to work on cargo docks. This proved useful to doctors and officers as food and medical supplies could often be pilfered from cargoes by the prisoners and smuggled back into the camps.

Dunlop spent his first months of captivity administering a large POW hospital in Bandoeng, where he believed maintaining high morale was as important as finding medical solutions. In the beginning, 'the prisoners carried on highly organized educational and recreational activity in the teeth of difficulties and misunderstandings'. As in Changi, educational courses were set up for the men—and even a mock 'Commonwealth Parliament'. With its minutes written on toilet paper, the parliament 'was as great and therapeutic an attraction as the rest of the prison educational and cultural activities, and it did a great deal to maintain a feeling of continuity'.[87]

As in all Japanese camps, the orderlies provided dedicated service and support. Brennan felt 'lucky' that in Mukden there were ten trained British orderlies who were 'superb men. I would raise my hat to any of them. They were really marvellous. The way they looked after those guys. We were all in it. They saved many lives.'

With only one doctor on Hainan, orderlies there took over many medical responsibilities. In praising their work, Aitken noted that two in particular had taken sole charge of 30-men wards during a severe dysentery outbreak and a paratyphoid epidemic. He wrote, 'They earned the gratitude of most of the camp and in particular that of a number of very serious cases, who owe their recovery almost solely to the care and attention given them by these two men.'[88]

There are broad similarities between the camps described above and previous camps in Singapore, Thailand and Burma. All Allied prisoners held in Japanese camps during World War II endured inadequate food and medical supplies and periods of hard labour. All, including the medical officers, were victims of their captors' cruelty and disregard for human life. In each camp, doctors did the best they could with whatever was to hand to try to save as many men as possible, aided by officers and other ranks and, if they were lucky enough to have them, by fellow medical colleagues.

However, just as moving to a new camp meant developing strategies to cope with its particular medical and environmental idiosyncrasies, the turning tide of Japan's war fortunes added another layer of difficulty to the doctors' work as their captors' behaviour became even less predictable.

While the doctors did all they could to keep POWs alive, they knew that with the passing of time they were fighting a losing battle: the men died in higher numbers, their bodies unable to cope any longer with starvation and disease. Supplies continued to dwindle, and medical officers had to find the energy to maintain the unremitting struggle. In late 1945, Rayson wrote in his diary: 'weary worried and fed up with these difficult days'.[89] Yet keeping men alive continued to be the doctors' driving force through a very long war.

# 5

# A COMPLEX RELATIONSHIP: DOCTORS AND CAPTORS

*Oh the cursed Japanese—how I hate them.*

MAJOR HUGH RAYSON[1]

In the early days of captivity in Changi, Australian POW medical personnel had very little to do with their captors. This soon changed. From the early 1942 Singaporean work party camps, to those in Thailand, Japan and various other islands, contact between Australian doctors and the Japanese became a grim part of daily life.

In many camps, it was the Australian combatant officers who initially dealt with the Japanese in daily negotiations over food and work parties and to protest about treatment. As time wore on, and captivity took a greater toll on the men's bodies, this burden increasingly fell to the medical officers. While other ranks were seen as a nebulous mass by their captors, the doctors stood out because of their actions, and became known personally to many Japanese camp staff.

In Australian cultural memory, the Japanese captors of Australian prisoners are usually portrayed as barbaric, with little respect for human life. Unlike many representations of the Australian war experience, this one is largely accurate. Evidence of their apathy, negligence and outright brutality towards Allied POWs during World War II is extensive. While one-third of Australian POWs died under the Japanese, many more returned home physically and mentally scarred for the rest of their lives. While there were exceptions, the majority of captors made the experience a terrible existence for POWs, and one of great personal and professional frustration for medical officers.

Yet this does not mean that Japanese captors were a homogeneous group, nor can their relationship with prisoners be easily understood or stereotyped. Like any military hierarchy, Japanese camp staff consisted of various entities: camp command and administration, camp guards and Japanese medical personnel. No single group held a monopoly on mistreatment.

Many medical officers were themselves victims of physical violence meted out by a succession of Japanese commandants and guards. Yet any thought of their own welfare was overtaken by concern for their sick men. Bashing patients, forcing seriously ill men into work parties, withholding essential food, medical supplies and Red Cross parcels—these to the doctors were their captors' worst crimes.

## Japanese camp command

'You are unfortunate in being prisoners of a country whose living standards are much lower than yours. You will often consider yourselves mistreated, while we will think of you as being treated well,' remarked one unidentified Japanese officer in 1942.[2]

The harsh reality remains that Japanese commanders of the POW camps were generally indifferent to the health of their workforce. To them, POWs were expendable—a nearly inexhaustible supply of slave labour for projects such as railways and bridges and for mines and factories. When Japanese officials inspected the daily sick parades, they invariably declared most of them fit to work, despite the protestations of Allied medical personnel. On the Railway, Major Bruce Hunt recalled that:

> ... withholding of quinine supplies was held over any O. C.s [Officers Commanding] Camps as a constant threat for any trivial imaginary complaint. Mock inspection of sick personnel by Jap medical officers, who after merely walking through camps gave opinions that many more men were fit to work.[3]

A common problem for doctors was that the Japanese accepted as real only conditions they could actually see. For example, a man with terrible tropical ulcers was more likely to be relieved of work than another man suffering a severe bout of malaria. However, this also could work to the disadvantage of a prisoner. Captain Ian Duncan recalled instances where Camp Commander Fukahara of Camp 17, Omuta, Japan, would send men to work suffering swollen legs from beri-beri because they looked 'fat'.[4]

As a rule, the Japanese reserved their most severe treatment for the sickest prisoners. They were only given half rations (supplemented by canteens or black market supplies where possible), and if a daily work quota could not be filled because there were too many sick, hospital patients would be turned out and forced to join a work party. British doctor Lieutenant Colonel S. W. Harris recorded that the Japanese allowed sick prisoners to reach 'starvation point in the expressed belief that this would compel them to go out to work. The inevitable result was that hundreds of men died in a condition of extreme emaciation and complete despair.'[5] With 'Dunlop' Force on the Railway in 1943, Lieutenant Colonel Edward Dunlop wrote that not only did Japanese sick parade inspections ignore illness, they actually made a point of punishing the afflicted men:

> Sickness was regarded as a crime and the sick were singled out for specific treatment, so that men with appalling inflamed feet were required to do things which caused the utmost discomfort, such as walking on rough places after dynamiting and log hauling in the jungle ... a feature of the morning parade was men with

so-called light sickness, propped up on sticks with horribly inflamed feet and reeling with [dysentery] who were given sometimes harder work than other men, just to discourage them.[6]

In Java, Dutch medical officer Dr Schmidt encountered a similar attitude towards the sick when he asked the Japanese for some materials to make beds. The Japanese supplied the beds but allowed only working men to sleep on them, punishing anyone who gave the beds to patients.[7]

The most important concern for medical officers remained the most basic—food. Accordingly, their biggest frustration lay in trying to impress upon their captors the importance of a balanced diet in maintaining an efficient workforce. Japanese logic dictated that the more weight prisoners lost, the less food they needed—yet the basic subsistence level in many camps was not sufficient to sustain survival, let alone heavy physical work.

Medical supplies were the second most needed item. From basics such as disinfectant, bandages and bedpans, to drugs such as Atebrin and quinine for malaria, supplies were always lacking. Entreaties to Japanese command to supply medications were usually ignored.

Captain Newton Lee, Australian adjutant of the hospital sections of Tamarkan, Chungkai and Tamuang POW camps from January 1944 to August 1945, recorded a typical incident. In June 1944, rare Red Cross drugs were distributed, after which the Japanese felt justified in cutting back the POW doctors' meagre supplies, including quinine:

> During this period the issue of quinine had to be limited to the severe malaria cases, slight attacks going untreated. When Col. [Thomas] Hamilton asked the Japanese doctor for quinine he smilingly answered: 'Ask Mr. Churchill for some'. Col. Hamilton replied 'If I were allowed to write to Mr. Churchill and ask for quinine we would certainly receive some'.[8]

Red Cross representatives were the only outsiders who ever visited the camps, assuming they knew where they were. From Red Cross Far East reports it is clear they often had only vague ideas about the locations of camps, and because the prisoners frequently moved, it was difficult to keep track of them. In addition, camp names and variations in spelling and pronunciation rarely corresponded to places on maps.

Before Red Cross personnel could visit a camp they had to make an appointment with Japanese command, giving the latter plenty of time to make the camps look presentable. It is not surprising, therefore, that they often went away with an inaccurate picture of what life was like in the camps. As British doctor Lieutenant Colonel Andrew Dillon noted, 'We know from letters received from England and Australia that it is believed there that prisoners of war are being well treated by the Japanese. If the actual facts regarding Thailand were known abroad, the news would be greeted with indignation and amazement.'[9]

Allied medical reports document many instances where whitewashes were conducted prior to Red Cross inspections. In the 'A' Force War Diary, written on the Railway, the entry for 29 April 1943 reads:

> Japanese doing propaganda film of camp have brought in band and members of a concert party from various jungle camps and call on patients when ever they need an audience. They put up shelves in the operating theatre, stock them with empty tins and bottled coloured water labelled with names of drugs. These were immediately removed after filming... Patients are taken down the town and filmed as just arriving in as sick patients from jungle camps.[10]

In one Railway camp, a Japanese medical sergeant ordered 50 hospital patients to hide among some bamboo until a hospital inspection was over. These men were then forced into doing eight to ten hours heavy work.[11]

British doctor Captain C. S. Pitt recorded a similar charade which took place in Kinsayok camp in Thailand in mid 1943:

> On one occasion a high official came to inspect the cholera hospital. Although not recovered from their illness, half the patients were

sent back to the camp in order that the hospital should not appear over-crowded. White gowns, basins, saline infusion apparati, tubing, needles and a host of medical supplies were arranged on a table and stood at the entrance. When the inspection was finished all these medical supplies were taken away.[12]

Such camp 'inspections' were clearly a farce—but Red Cross representatives were often denied entry to camps altogether. Those who tried to visit St Vincentius Hospital in Batavia, for example, were refused entry by the Japanese who accused them of being spies. Of course many Red Cross people were sceptical of what they saw and what they were told when they visited Japanese POW camps. One who saw a camp in Osaka described interviews with POWs as:

> . . . few and very difficult, always closely watched by army officers and expert translators who wrote down every word being exchanged. The prisoners were reluctant to speak, probably fearing possible consequences . . . The actual visits through the camps were rushed and timed to the minute.[13]

Even if they had seen a more realistic picture, there was little the Red Cross representatives could have done. Their main mission in the Far East was to find missing soldiers (practically impossible in Japanese camps because of the incomplete lists and the frequent movement of prisoners) and to send Red Cross parcels. These parcels, which contained food, toiletries and medical supplies, are often credited as playing a part in the high survival rates of Allied POWs in German camps. Yet if they were distributed at all in the Japanese camps, they were frequently first ransacked by Japanese camp staff. Even if they did not receive such supplies, doctors or other officers were sometimes forced to sign a document stating they had.

Some Japanese commanders even directly prevented doctors' performing any medical duties. In a report on Bicycle Camp in Java during 1943, British doctor Colonel C. W. Maisey began dryly:

During this period I held a somewhat anomalous position, as I was considered by the Japanese to be in medical charge of the camp but I was not allowed to visit the hospital or control it in any way. I spent most of my time making string.[14]

In some cases, Japanese camp commanders requested reports on the medical conditions of their prisoners. In Thailand during 1943, Australian POW Private Albert Casey wrote such a report stating, 'It is our firm belief that our recent experiences have not been in accordance with the policy or intentions of the Imperial Japanese Government or the Japanese Red Cross who cannot have been aware of the actual state of affairs in Thailand.'[15] He then outlined many instances in which medical officers had been beaten for protesting about the movement of sick men. In April 1944 Lieutenant Colonel Albert Coates was asked by a Japanese doctor to write a report on the Nakon Patom POW hospital. He began by thanking Dr Higuchi 'for the opportunity of putting on record my impressions of the hospital at this juncture'. He went on to make several requests, such as to allow Red Cross representatives to visit and to repatriate the very sick and incapacitated as a 'gesture of goodwill' so that returning POWs:

> . . . may carry with them happy memories, and that they may, as the result of their association with the IJA [Imperial Japanese Army] and the humane treatment they will have received, be the messenger of peace, goodwill and mutual understanding, and respect among the people of the Pacific seaboard.[16]

Higuchi was annoyed by the report and through an interpreter responded, 'Well, you state the thing very fairly, but you have to remember, of course, that we are a "have-not" nation and you are one of the "haves".'[17]

It is peculiar that the Japanese requested such reports as they rarely acceded to any requests or took any action to improve the situation. Even if doctors were asked to compile specific lists of the supplies they needed, the items would rarely be produced.

## Physical abuse

Corporal abuse by the Japanese took many forms. In Takunun camp in Thailand in 1943, at the height of the building of the Railway, a Japanese officer wrote to an Allied doctor that 'From this morning I order to you the working number because the work is very very hurry. Therefore of course you must select and collect this number from the some sick party. Today—soldier 130 men, the officer 8 men.'[18] British doctor Lieutenant Colonel John Huston wrote that the 'high death rate and the medical situation generally in this camp is causing me the gravest anxiety, and unless stringent and immediate steps are taken to remedy existing conditions, the death rate . . . will continue at an increasing ratio.'[19]

Captain Clive Boyce experienced a similar situation in a POW camp in Japan where, after an influenza epidemic, he 'was explicitly ordered, "There must be no more influenza".' The men in the camp followed the order 'firstly because they realised my impotence with the Nipponese . . . and all preferred to be outdoors or at their places of work in the event of an air-raid'. Boyce dealt with the problem by diagnosing influenza sufferers with other conditions, thereby technically adhering to his 'order'.[20]

In a remote Railway camp in September 1944, Australian combatant officer Captain Osmar J. Blau recalled a time where a Japanese officer thought there were too many malaria cases and blamed the Allied medical officer. He 'ordered his Korean subordinate to assault this officer about the face and body inflicting grievous bodily harm'.[21] In another example, Captain J. J. Woodward of the Indian Medical Service recalled that one colleague was forced to sign a document stating '"he understood that he was ordered not to let any more men die."—This was during an epidemic of pneumonia in a bad camp with severe dysentery and beri-beri.'[22]

On Ambon Island, there were initially plentiful supplies of food and medicines for the 1,000-plus Australian POWs held there. After a time, all such provisions were withheld, 'despite the oft repeated pleadings of their doctors and other officers'.[23] The Japanese watched most of them slowly starve to death. On Hainan, Australian quartermaster Captain Philip P. Miskin wrote that the Japanese knew a lot about nutrition and food values, but concluded:

> It can be flatly stated, therefore, that the Japanese were coldly and calculatingly pursuing the policy firstly of gradual starvation, and latterly of absolute starvation. On 5 May, 1945, the caloric intake per man was 578—cold blooded murder according to any standard.[24]

Japanese command also interfered in projects that POW doctors initiated to alleviate the lack of food and vitamins. Although vegetable gardens at Changi and other large camps often flourished, they did not always come to fruition. In one camp, Woodward planted many tomatoes to combat neuritis and pellagra, which were causing vision problems in some men due to vitamin deficiencies. When they were almost ripe, a Japanese officer pulled them out. He wrote with despair, 'For those whose vision was failing, the removal of this one of their last hopes was unbearable'.[25] There are many other examples of captors frustrating the efforts of doctors, either directly—such as in withholding supplies—or indirectly, such as destroying hand-built medical equipment.

POW medical officers themselves attracted physical abuse because of their important and unique position. In many camps, they were frequently, sometimes daily, slapped and bashed, while making constant attempts to protect sick men from being forced to work. British doctor Captain R. W. Lennon wrote that after one week on the Burma–Thai railway, Japanese command 'declared that the British Doctors were liars and that they were deliberately keeping men in camp on the pretext of illness, and slowing work on the railway. They then struck each MO [medical officer] several heavy blows on the face with their fists.'[26]

In reports written by POW doctors documenting the conditions in which they lived, there are some remarkably reserved mentions of Japanese brutality. At Nong Pladuk and Ubon camps in Thailand, Lennon and his British colleague Major E. A. Smyth noted that the work was strenuous, but not as bad as some others:

Often men had to work 6–7 weeks without a holiday. Beatings by Japanese guards were almost daily, fortunately at Nong Pladuk and Ubon nothing more serious than depressed fractures of the Malar Bone [upper jaw], fractured mandible [lower jaw], broken noses, loss of teeth, sub-conjunctival haemorrhages, concusions [sic], scalp wounds, contusions, spinous process of cervical vertebrae and one serious case of intestinal contusion following kick in the abdomen.[27]

These were described as relatively good camps. Perhaps when physical abuse became part of daily life, perspective on its severity was somewhat dulled. Tellingly, Dunlop commented that there was little point keeping a record of every beating doled out by their captors: 'There were incessant examples of beatings and sadistic treatment of people, so many that it was a kind of routine and unless someone was actually killed, we did not deal with them.'[28]

Another more sinister kind of physical abuse was medical experimentation conducted by the Japanese on POWs. In an incident recorded by British physician Captain A. J. N. Warrack, doctors were forced to watch a totally unqualified Japanese camp commander, Captain Toheda, attempting to perform medical procedures. Toheda was also the only person who could approve operations or medical discharges of patients. Warrack wrote:

> . . . in the event of the Japanese Commandant being in camp, this officer would insist on performing or at least assisting at the operation itself. As the Commandant's knowledge of surgery was abysmal and his technique conspicuous by its absence, Surg. Cmdr. Cleave's task was made extremely difficult.[29]

Toheda performed procedures such as injecting Allied POWs with soy bean milk, sulphur and castor oil, and intraspinal vitamins. In one instance, in order to determine whether a patient could be discharged, he conducted a rectal examination using a rigid sigmoidoscope. 'The patients were put through a useless, painful and degrading procedure merely to satisfy the sadistic instincts of the Japanese Commandant,' Warrack recorded.[30] It is difficult to imagine the doctors' outrage at having to watch silently as an unqualified man performed appalling and unnecessary procedures on their already suffering patients.

Australian orderly Osmund Vickers-Bush recalled another procedure that many thousands of Australian POWs had to endure—swab testing for dysentery. If the Japanese medical personnel did not have glass rods to insert into the anus to collect specimens, they used bamboo, or even sometimes pieces of wire: 'Many of us had bleeding haemorrhoids and finished up with blood running down our legs.'[31]

The brutality dispensed by the Japanese was in many ways as psychologically cruel as it was physically damaging. A particularly stressful characteristic of the behaviour of the Japanese camp personnel towards the prisoners was its unpredictability. Recriminations and punishments were often meted out for spurious reasons. If a captor wanted to beat someone, an excuse was convenient but not necessary. Maisey commented:

> It should be realised that anyone who interfered with the Japanese in any shape or form was likely to receive at the very least a most severe bashing, and as the years went by, this fear of receiving corporal punishment from the Japanese produced a pathological reaction in the majority of the prisoners of war.[32]

The prisoners knew that no matter what they did they could be beaten, and that there was no strategy they could adopt to avoid punishment. They lived in a perpetual state of uncertainty and fear.

Sometimes whole groups of prisoners would be punished for one man's minor transgression. This could be a failure to salute, not fulfilling one's quota on a work party, or collapsing on a march. A typical example: 'A half blind patient would not see a guard and failed to salute. Any other patients in the vicinity would be made to stand at attention.'[33] Should a prisoner be caught trying to escape, he would be executed in front of the camp, and usually some form of punishment would be applied to the entire camp as a lesson.

The severity of punishment among all the Japanese camps varied, from withholding rations (ultimately as dangerous as any other punishment), to frequent beatings and torture. In a camp near Saigon in 1944, two Australian POWs were caught pilfering Red Cross parcels the Japanese refused to distribute. The men were tied up, beaten repeatedly for days, and given the 'water treatment'—they were force fed water through a hose after which guards would jump on their bloated stomachs.[34]

Individual captors could also display a confusing and contradictory range of emotions and behaviour. When he was with 'A' Force, Captain Rowley Richards wrote, 'Lt Asoto professes sympathy for sick; was unable to watch a boy's hand being sutured but immediately afterwards beat one of his guards insensible.' A month later, after an epidemic of dysentery had broken out, Richards wrote, 'Japs won't allow evacuation of sick. Much trouble with Naito, a drunken and vicious creature.'[35]

Major Hugh Rayson also noted the strange duality of his captors. On one hand, Lieutenant Hoshijima was a constant thorn in his side, yet when he visited the Japanese official at Sandakan, 'I was fed and entertained by Lieutenant Hoshijima as a courteous host to a welcome visitor—a queer mixture are the Japanese.'[36] Maisey also calmly reflected on the bewildering behaviour of a Japanese officer in a hospital in Java: 'it is difficult to understand a man who can severely beat a dentist in the morning, as did Lt Sonne, and then come for dental treatment in the afternoon'.[37] These contradictory natures of their captors were difficult for doctors to cope with, and meant they lived in a perpetual state of uncertainty as to what each hour would bring.

Although premeditated torture was not a routine punishment in POW camps, it occurred often enough—and widely enough—to be a constant fear for the POWs. In Omuta Camp in Japan, Duncan witnessed a range of punishments, 'from mild slapping to physical torture such as putting bamboo splinters into the mouth to keep it open. During the winter the men would be stripped of their clothing and every half hour, cold water would be thrown over them.' He also saw Japanese guards urinating into the mouths of men being tortured.[38]

Maisey wrote that one of the factors contributing to men's low morale in the months following the fall of Singapore was 'the sense of fear of what the Japanese would do as rumour followed rumour regarding various atrocities the Japanese were alleged to have committed'.[39] In Hong Kong, Woodward reflected that the POWs 'had been looked after so long by a system which gave its utmost to avert pain and death that they could not realise that they were now in the hands of savage animals'.[40]

Communication with the outside world was practically impossible, being totally controlled by Japanese camp command. In one example, guards continually told a group of American POWs news they were sure would demoralise them: 'they would come in one day and have a sad look on their face, and they'd say that Clark Gable died today, and of course, that would upset the Americans . . . about a week later, they would say, "Mickey Rooney died".' At the end of the war, when American POW Sam Moody met some countrymen, 'the first thing we asked was: "Is it true that Clark Gable's dead?" They said, "Hell no!"'[41]

Maintaining secret radios was a personal badge of pride for many POWs, allowing some news to filter in. Otherwise, prisoners would only receive mail sporadically, often months or even years apart. British POW John Sharpe was given 38 letters from his mother after liberation, while still in hospital in Changi: 'She had never believed I was dead and written to me every month for more than three years. Reading them I just wept and wept.'[42] The Japanese would also withhold letters as a form of psychological torture. On Ambon, prisoners would receive letters only when they were about to die—letters dating back as far as three years: 'The prisoners did not know whether Ikeuchi [a camp officer] acted to soothe, or tease, the dying.'[43]

## Camp guards

While contact with a camp commander could be daily or sporadic, constant contact with the guards was inescapable. Most acts of physical and psychological abuse against POWs occurred as a result of their daily interaction with these men. The behaviour and attitudes of camp command described above to some degree applied to guards. However, the relationship between POWs and guards had another layer due to the guards' position within the Japanese military hierarchy: many were conscripted Japanese and Korean soldiers, the latter being in the majority.

The way the guards behaved towards POWs is often attributed to the Japanese military code. Discipline in the Japanese military was based on the right of a superior to beat subordinates, a fact not initially understood by many Australian prisoners. Hunt noted that the lower ranks 'were particularly brutal in the presence of their officers'.[44] The high rates of suicide in Japanese military academies due to bullying by upperclassmen were well known in this era. In this system, therefore, Allied prisoners were at the end of a long chain of both command and abuse.

Even among the guards there was a sharp delineation. The cultural backgrounds and behaviour of the Korean and Japanese guards differed, however tempting it may have been for Australian POWs to group them together. When former POWs recall Japanese cruelty, many then add 'the Koreans were nastier than the Japanese'. Much of this can be attributed to the position of Koreans in the Japanese military hierarchy. To the Japanese, they were only slightly higher than Allied prisoners. The Koreans would have felt little loyalty towards Japan, its emperor, or its army, their country having been invaded and brutalised by Japan for centuries. One Korean guard, Yi Hak-Nae, who was tried after the war and convicted as a war criminal, was not able to go home to Korea after serving his sentence 'because of the shame attaching to me as one who had collaborated with Japan to the point of being a war criminal'.[45] Another, Kasayama Yoshikichi, said of his feelings toward the Japanese, 'After the first couple of years, we didn't hide our feelings any longer . . . "Do you think we're going to let you shit on us till we die?" . . . The Japanese apologised and grovelled when they didn't have their rifles.'[46] Towards the end of the war, Dr Stanley Pavillard witnessed three Korean guards attacking a Japanese senior officer in his sleep; one of the guards repeatedly asked Pavillard for poison to kill his Japanese superior.[47]

Most POW doctors explained the Koreans' particularly vicious behaviour towards prisoners as a trickle-down effect: the Koreans were abused and frustrated, so they took out their anger on the only people they could: Allied prisoners. Interestingly, an American POW officer, Captain Clark Taylor, noted that some Korean guards were actually conscientious objectors who had been forced to do POW guard duty because of their refusal to join frontline troops.[48]

In many ways, differences in treatment towards POWs from camp to camp could be attributed solely to the nationality of their guards. At Nakon Patom camp on the Railway, British doctor Lieutenant Colonel J. W. Malcolm noted that the Japanese staff there left the prisoners and doctors alone, whereas several of the Korean guards 'were sadist and took a keen pleasure in kicking patients on ulcers and in the privates'.[49]

## Talking to the enemy

How individual Australian POW doctors dealt with their captors varied significantly. Some, like Dunlop and Hunt, were renowned for being aggressive and confrontational, while others tried to compromise with the Japanese where possible, hoping that when something really important needed to be negotiated the Japanese might be responsive. Some of these doctors are unfairly remembered as being weak, or 'Jap-happy'. British doctor Captain David Christison recalled one British officer whose ability to communicate with the Japanese caused resentment among his peers:

> All he wanted was to get the same ideal as me, to get these men back to Britain alive ... But some dyed-in-the-wool officers thumped the table and they got nowhere. Nowhere. They were suspicious of Janis because he was getting things and they thought he was 'Jap-happy'. He wasn't 'Jap-happy' at all, he was just doing what he could for his men.

Interestingly, Dunlop later acknowledged that his style of communicating with the Japanese was not a useful one: 'In time, I learned that unflinching confrontation was not in the interests of those for whom I cared, and a few Japanese won my respect and even liking.'[50]

While Allied medical officers picked up a few phrases and basic sentences in Japanese, few sought to learn their captors' language, instead relying on interpreters. This cultural unwillingness to engage with the Japanese could be seen in the nicknames given to them. Names such as 'Billy the Pig', 'Liver Lips' or 'Doctor Death' ensured that their captors were not humanised. After the war, these nicknames were often the only way men could identify individuals in their War Crimes Trials statements.

Many doctors wrote letters to their camp commandants in the formal and conciliatory style that they soon learned was often the only effective way of communicating with the Japanese. Always written in English, these letters often requested official interviews on behalf of the doctors and other officers, or forwarded reports detailing the medical conditions of the men with appeals for more food and medication. In one such letter, Captain Ben Wheeler of the Indian Medical Service and another colleague wrote to their Japanese commandant:

> We appreciate only too well the difficulties facing the Commander in these times of war, and we hope the Commander will understand that the points we raise are not complaints but merely an attempt on our part to assist in maintaining some standard of health among the prisoners.[51]

They wrote many follow-up letters, one pleading about individual cases, another listing recent POW causes of death. One letter stated, 'We should like to offer the whole of our bank balances to be used entirely at the Commander's discretion, should they be of any use.'[52]

The formality of these letters disguises the desperation which led the doctors to appeal to their captors for help. Over the few weeks in which these letters were sent by the two doctors, 63 patients died. There was no reply or acknowledgement of any of their correspondence. It is not clear whether in the face of failure, these two doctors persevered in a continuing effort to gain supplies, or just to communicate the basic message that men were dying all around them. Clearly they felt they had to keep trying.

## The Japanese and POW doctors

It is difficult to find an Allied medical officer who believes he was treated better by his captors than other prisoners. The Japanese did not recognise the separate legal status of medical personnel in war as set out by the 1929 Geneva Convention, even unofficially. Japan had not ratified the section of the Convention regarding the treatment of POWs, so Allied prisoners had no legal recourse to protest. Technically, a 1942 Japanese government policy stated that foreign POWs could not be used as labour to benefit the Japanese war effort, but they could be used for the very grey area of 'military labour'.[53] British doctor Lieutenant Colonel S. W. Harris recalled being told by Lieutenant Fukuda, Commander of Shimo Songkurai Camp, that 'International law and the Geneva Convention do not apply if they conflict with the interests of the Japanese army.'[54] The Japanese renounced any of their own soldiers who were captured, so they did not consider themselves to have any reciprocal obligation to care for their enemies.

Their status as doctors did not prevent the Japanese from sending them out on work parties, and as time went on, many doctors did not even bother to keep their Red Cross cards, which designated their protected status in wartime. Rayson dryly noted in his diary that he was told 'more men must go out on working parties irrespective of our medical classification. This may be a source of trouble to Hoshijima at his subsequent trial.'[55] In one Thai camp in March 1944, the Japanese declared medical personnel would be paid upon producing their Red Cross cards. 'A number of blank cards existed in the Camp,' one doctor wrote, 'but they had all been cut in half and were being used for such games as "Monopoly".'[56]

In contrast, in German POW camps, the Red Cross identity card carried by medical personnel automatically distinguished them as non-combatant POWs, with their own rules and permitted duties. Hal Finkelstein, a Jewish-Australian POW who worked during captivity as an orderly in a German POW camp, credits his Red Cross armband as saving his life many times in the face of anti-Semitic guards.

Apart from their unenviable role of often being a buffer between the sick and the Japanese, there was one significant factor that *did* distinguish medical officers from other POWs. They were the only group of prisoners who actually had something to offer their captors—their medical expertise. Japanese officers and guards of all ranks sought treatment from Australian doctors rather than from their own, particularly in the case of venereal disease as they would be punished if they presented with this to their own doctors. In exchange, doctors could ask for supplies of food and medicine. Captain Leslie Poidevin performed circumcisions on some of his captors, as they believed circumcised men went to the front of the queue in brothels.[57] Dr Stanley Pavillard treated a Japanese cook who had tapeworm. Pavillard had a bottle of what he thought was the appropriate medication, though it had no label. He estimated the dose and gave it to the cook. The next day, the man passed the entire 6.5-metre tapeworm. Every morning after that, the cook sent Pavillard a bucket of stew, which he credited with saving many lives as well as improving morale. After the war, Pavillard looked up the correct dosage: 'I was amazed that the Jap had not passed his liver as well.'[58]

This mutual exploitation was a good arrangement, when it was possible. While some doctors confessed to a private reluctance to treat their captors, none recalled an ethical dilemma in doing so. Richards said, 'It's very difficult to withhold your medical knowledge from anybody irrespective of who they are.' It is interesting to note, however, that doctors quickly qualify statements like this by saying that they treated their captors so they could get more supplies, or to curry favour with the Japanese. As Richards said: 'one was sufficiently pragmatic to realise that by doing this for a sergeant or an officer, we might be able to get a little more out of him on behalf of the troops'.[59] Even though they were acting in a professional capacity, the doctors' need to rationalise helping the Japanese in any way was a strong impulse.

Sometimes there was a lighter side to treating their captors, as Captain Lloyd Cahill remembered:

> They used to get a lot of rashes and things like that. Things that weren't terribly serious ... They'd pay you a cigarette for a consultation, so you never let them get really cured, if you got a good one. You'd let him get his rash a bit better, then you'd give him something to stimulate it.

In general, contacts between Australian POW doctors and Japanese command and guards were personal and constant, forming a reluctant symbiotic relationship. The Japanese relied on POW doctors to provide the manpower they needed for various projects, and the doctors needed the Japanese to provide food and medical supplies. That the doctors were occasionally useful to their captors was advantageous, but ultimately it did not protect them from systematic persecution.

## Japanese counterparts

Just as the camp staff were not a homogeneous group, neither were Japanese medical personnel. There were varying degrees of contact between Australian and Japanese medical officers, usually in the form of inspections of camp medical facilities by the latter. Larger camps had a permanent resident Japanese doctor or a small medical attachment. While it is in some way understandable that Japanese camp command and staff would not have had any special feeling for enemy POW doctors, Western notions of a 'professional fraternity' would imply that a sense of mutual respect should 'rise above' the military context and their cultural differences. Certainly, Allied doctors brought this expectation with them into captivity. While this belief was sometimes borne out, examples of collegiality were more the exception than the rule. As Australian combatant officer Colonel Cranston McEachern noted, 'Unfortunately, the brotherhood of medical personnel was not appreciated by the Japanese, and Prisoner of War doctors, though they won grudging respect by their superior ability, were never treated on any plane of equality.'[60]

The expectations and cultural values of Australian doctors were most challenged in their relationship with Japanese medical personnel. The Hippocratic Oath states that doctors must help and respect each other, and treat all sick to the best of their ability. Consequently the Australian doctors were most distressed when a Japanese doctor was cruel—viewing this as a humanitarian *and* professional betrayal.

POW doctors were often forced by Japanese medical personnel to misrepresent causes of death on death certificates, such as writing 'accident' rather than 'malnutrition and dysentery'. In Burma in 1943, Dr Higuchi made Coates record 'diarrhoea' on the death certificates of 30 men who had died from amoebic dysentery.[61] Autopsies—even crude ones in the circumstances—essential to doctors in determining exact causes of death, were rarely permitted. As a result, it was difficult to learn more about the pathologies that were killing prisoners, particularly those tropical diseases of which very little was known at the time, such as the neurological effects of beri-beri. Even when autopsies were allowed, their findings were not always accepted. When Coates, after performing several post-mortems on amoebic dysentery patients, showed his evidence to Higuchi and asked for emetine, he was told that as he did not have a microscope, his 'evidence' was not conclusive. Instead, Higuchi renamed the condition 'Hill diarrhoea'.[62]

Higuchi also ordered more than 1,000 men who were extremely ill to be taken away to other working camps. When Coates protested, Higuchi told him that they could have 'a long rest' when the Railway was completed. Coates bitterly wrote later, 'His words proved literally true for many of these men.'[63] When asked after the war by the Australian War Crimes Board of Inquiry whether he considered that Higuchi had been 'neglectful', Coates answered, 'That would be my view; it may not be the Japanese view. His argument would be that he was under orders; but as a doctor I take it he has certain duties to sick men.'[64] Major Walter Fisher, another Australian doctor working with Coates in Burma, similarly condemned Higuchi more harshly than the other Japanese captors, describing him as 'anti-european, arrogant, ignorant and lacking in the humanity and sympathy which might be expected from a Medical Practitioner to patients and medical colleagues respectively'.[65]

When Japanese medical personnel beat prisoners, they made no distinction between doctors and patients. Some doctors found the abuse harder to bear when it was carried out by 'colleagues'. In Kuching in Borneo, Rayson was beaten by a Japanese doctor. His colleague, Major Howard Eddey, wrote angrily, 'Major Rayson was bashed by Lieut Yamamoto personally. Major Rayson is a man over 50 years old.'[66] This may have been a beating that Rayson recorded in his diary. He was in hospital with a burning fever when he was knocked down several times by Yamamoto, who then fractured his jaw bone, beat him over the head with Rayson's own wooden clogs, and then

> ... attempted to kick my injured leg with his heavy cavalry boots—I was able however to interpose my left leg and take the blow on the shin. I was quite at a loss as to the reason of the assault—it may have been because I had not reported my disability to him.[67]

The refusal of Japanese medical personnel to take heed of their counterparts' professional opinions was also frustrating, especially as the Allied doctors began to question their captors' medical knowledge and expertise. As time went on, the POW doctors increasingly came to regard them as little more than glorified first aid workers, even though some had been trained in the West.

The Western-based Japanese medical profession was established in 1870 when thirteen Japanese medical students studied medicine in Germany. By 1900, Japan had set up its own medical course at the Imperial University, but it was still heavily influenced by the German medical tradition—one that from 1870 to 1914 was considered unequalled. Due to this influence at a key time in worldwide advances in the nature of bacteria and infectious disease, Japan became a pioneer in disease prevention during war.[68] It also established certain military medical structures that were adopted by some Western armies before World War I, such as having a 1:10 ratio of medical personnel to troops.

By World War II, however, this international esteem had been eroded and Lennon's view that Japanese doctors were 'appallingly ignorant of medical knowledge' was a common one.[69] Coates expressed a similarly typical observation: 'Our doctors were even able to show the Japanese doctors appointed to supervise them that Japanese medicine is primitive ... The captors have learned many a lesson from the despised prisoners toiling to ameliorate the awful conditions of their fellows.'[70] Major Arthur Moon noted that the Japanese medical orderly who was ostensibly in charge of the 2,000 Allied POWs at Tamarkan camp on the Railway in 1942 had been a 'rice laborer' before the war.[71]

Major T. M. (Max) Pemberton, a New Zealand doctor in the British Army, served as the senior medical officer at Chungkai and Tamuang POW hospitals in Thailand, and saw many such instances of medical ignorance. In January 1945, when men were still being sent on work parties in Thailand, he recounted an incident in which a Japanese doctor inspected 836 sick men, many with acute malaria. When asked how long a man should remain off duty with malaria, the Japanese doctor suggested two weeks. When it was then pointed out that prisoners were being sent out to work on the second day of a malarial attack, the doctor said that 'he was judging by general appearances and these men that he picked out were fit enough for work'. Five months later Pemberton was still protesting. On 10 June, 300 sick men were made to work for one hour. Pemberton wrote in his diary:

> The IJA [Imperial Japanese Army] medical branch were notified that the working of sick men might prejudice their chances of recovery, to which an IJA sergeant on the spot replied that they were not particularly concerned whether prisoners died or not since there were plenty of padres to bury them.[72]

There are many documented cases of Australian doctors being forced to watch Japanese medical personnel perform rough examinations, prescribe what they considered absurd treatments and, as in the case of some Japanese Camp Commanders, conduct medical experiments on their patients. In Java, Maisey witnessed many distressing incidents including one where a Japanese doctor, Dr Yamani, visited a patient 'with a very distended gall bladder he palpated so violently that the patient vomited'.[73] At Kobe House Camp, Japan, Captain Clive Boyce witnessed a bizarre Japanese treatment for diarrhoea:

> Its principle seemed to be one of counter-irritation applied to the back, where six burn scars were made. The position of these was decided by the width of the feet and of the great toes measured with a loop of string ... Treatment using a smouldering powder was daily for three days, and was unsuccessful.[74]

In a Tokyo camp Private Mick Ryan, who had beri-beri, also received a Japanese treatment that involved burning the skin. Three pieces of cotton wool were placed on his leg and set on fire. 'They would burn away and burn into the flesh causing ulcers—it was dreadful, after 40 years, the scars are still on my legs.'[75]

The Japanese medical officer on Hainan Island, Dr Kakuchi, initially behaved reasonably, even giving Captain William Aitken some badly needed drugs. Over time, however, his visits became less frequent, his behaviour worse, and his responses to requests for help increasingly hostile. Aitken concluded that Kakuchi 'should be brought to task and made to answer for these deaths caused directly by his wilful neglect and disregard of our requests and warnings'.[76]

In a particularly disturbing example of experimentation at Rabaul, New Guinea, Japanese doctor Dr Chikumi gave Australian officer John Gray an injection to make him semi-conscious before removing his heart while Gray was still alive, 'to study his reactions'.[77]

There are numerous examples of clashes between Allied and Japanese medical personnel regarding the correct treatments to give patients. Official medical reports by the Allied POW medical officers thinly veil their disappointment and bitterness towards Japanese medical personnel:

After careful selection and categorisation of sick by POW doctors, frequently they were subsequently reclassified by such Japanese medical officers as Higuchi by making them walk past four at a time while he assessed their condition by his penetrating and all seeing eye.[78]

It may not be fair, however, to apply the Allied doctors' condemnation of the Japanese medical personnel to Japanese military medical professionals as a whole. Allied officers commonly surmised that the best officers were probably deployed with the fighting units. It is likely that this was also true of the Japanese medical personnel.

## The exceptions

'This war, like all wars, will come to an end one day. You're going to run into some good Japanese and some bad Japanese. Treat them on an individual basis. Don't think of every Japanese as being like any particular one.'[79] These were the words of advice given by an unnamed Japanese officer in an address to Allied POWs at Bicycle Camp in Java in May 1942.

Despite numerous instances of cruelty and neglect which came to stereotype the Japanese captor, there were some individuals who actually helped POW doctors, either in attitude or action. In the case of Japanese combatant officers, this usually took the form of ignoring doctors, rather than actively giving assistance. Some camp guards would help to procure supplies for doctors, or turn a blind eye to local black market trading.

Of those guards who were sympathetic to POWs, some were Korean. As one American prisoner saw it, 'once in a while, you'd run into a Korean who hated those Japanese enough that he'd treat the prisoners as well as he could'.[80] Doctors witnessed acts of kindness by Korean guards, such as smuggling food into hospital huts, which they did at great risk to themselves. Pavillard recalled one Korean guard in Kinsayok camp who warned Allied officers when camp searches were to take place.[81] Also on the Railway, a Korean guard called Tatiyama befriended American POW orderly Griff Douglas, giving him cigarettes and engaging in conversation. Tatiyama said 'he wanted to come to the United States when the war was over and go to school, and he was as much a prisoner as I was'.[82]

Lieutenant Colonel Glyn White became friends with a Korean guard known during captivity as Azuarma. White and Lieutenant Colonel Hedley Summons taught him English and in exchange Azuarma smuggled medication to them and protected them from other captors. After the war, in 1969, White happened to pass through Korea. He looked up Azuarma under his Korean name, Kim Yung Duk. They spoke, and within ten minutes Kim was at White's hotel. White wrote that apart from meeting his wife again in 1945, 'I don't think I have ever experienced such an emotional reunion.'[83] After a friendship that lasted many more years, White gave the oration at Kim Yung Duk's funeral.

Some Japanese guards would also help prisoners if it was to their advantage. Dutch combatant officer Colonel Laurens van der Post noted an arrangement in Bandoeng, Java, where a Japanese guard would allow black market trading as long as he received a 'commission'.[84]

Richards recalled an incident where he was saved from a bashing by a guard who professed to be Christian; when ordered to beat him: 'he got me outside and he cursed and swore at me in Japanese and then with his fist hit his hand like that, you know, it just sounded as though he was hitting me . . . And then he told me to go, and boy, I went.'[85]

Boyce found the lower-ranking Japanese medical personnel in one camp (one medical sergeant and two privates) mostly left the Allied personnel to themselves. However, the staff rosters changed frequently, and sometimes their staff replacements would 'endeavour with or without requested permission from the Camp Commandant or H.Q. Osaka, to obtain for us medicine that we badly needed'.[86]

Maisey wrote glowingly about a Japanese doctor who was a great help to him. Dr Mitsufutsi 'devoted every care and attention that he was able to our welfare, but he had no powers of discipline, and was always getting into trouble with his senior officers for trying to do anything for us'.[87] When Maisey saw Red Cross parcels intended for POWs being sold in Batavia by the Japanese, Mitsufutsi intervened and locked up the parcels, giving the key to the Allied medical dispenser.[88] Maisey and Coates also both wrote about Lieutenant Takeo Aonuma, a Japanese doctor on the Railway who was kind to the prisoners. He was 'always courteous, reasonable, honest, sympathetic, and kind' said Maisey, and 'his name will be long remembered amongst all Allied Medical Officers who knew him. On more than one occasion he got into serious trouble with his own people because he tried to help the P.O.W.'[89] At 55 Kilo camp in late 1943, Coates recalled that Aonuma had stated he could not do anything to help the prisoners because it was against Japanese orders, 'but he winked his eye and allowed me to run a black market'.[90] Coates was therefore able to smuggle meat into the camp, which improved prisoners' health.

An American navy doctor, Ferdinand Berley, told of the aid he received in Osaka and Kobe camps from a Japanese doctor, Dr Ohashi, who 'proved to be a very fine person, very much a gentleman, very much a doctor. He was not a military man; he had actually been drafted like many of the people had. And he treated us as fellow physicians. He actually encouraged us to keep our minds busy.'[91] Also in Japan, captured American B-29 flight engineer Fiske Hanley was repeatedly interrogated by the *Kempeitai*, the Japanese secret police. An English-speaking Japanese doctor quietly warned Hanley never to speak about the Emperor or speak his name aloud or he would be executed.[92]

All Japanese personnel were always under the watchful eye of their superiors, so their choice of whether to help or not also had to include considerations of personal recrimination should they be caught. For example, in a camp in Japan, two Japanese doctors who tried to help Duncan paid the price. The first of these men, Dr Murao,

> . . . was accused of being insane by the Commander and relieved from duty in the camp. The next doctor was Cadet Officer Hoshiko. He also went out of his way to help us and was also removed as soon as his activities began to show evidence of bearing fruit.

Duncan concluded that:

> ... any Japanese Army Medical Officer assigned to this camp who attempted to co-operate with the prisoner medical staff by requesting better conditions for the prisoners or forcing the Mitsui Mine Hospital to furnish adequate medical supplies, was usually transferred from this camp in a short period after his efforts were sufficient to receive some response.[93]

While the behaviour of such individuals was sometimes erratic, when they did give aid, it was gratefully accepted. In War Crimes Trials affidavits, Australian doctors and other officers were quick to point out the names and faces of those captors who had been helpful, to aid their case for amnesty. However, in memoirs or interviews the doctors can well remember such incidents of kindness—generally because these happened so infrequently.

There are no discernible patterns as to why these particular individuals took risks to help their enemies. Whether it was a form of rebellion against their own superiors, a sense of personal morality different from their comrades, or in the case of doctors, professional fellowship, may never be known.

## Cultural clashes

The reactions of Allied doctors to the practices of their Japanese counterparts were inextricably bound up with ideas of race, ethnocentricity and ignorance of Japanese culture. In 1942 most Australians knew little about the Japanese or Asia as a whole, and doctors were no exception. Products of a liberal democratic society, medical officers expected that the Japanese army would adhere to the 'laws of war', as defined by Western nations. From their medical training, they were also used to practising medicine that revolved around the concepts of rationality, logic and empiricism. When the behaviour of scientific

Japanese military personnel did not match the doctors' expectations, the disparity created bitter frustration.

During World War I, as allies of the British, the Japanese were known for their excellent care of a large number of German POWs. In doing so, Japan 'sought to secure recognition as a civilised nation by introducing international law, almost in direct translation, and affording it strict enforcement'.[94] Between the wars, however, Japanese culture underwent an intense militarisation, intertwined with ideas of nationalism and race: 'Part of the nationalistic revival included the strong support of old ideals. One of these was *bushido* and the spirit of the samurai.'[95] Education in this period, termed by historian Saburo Ienaga as 'khaki-coloured curriculum', emphasised the glory of military service and the utter dishonour of defeat or capture. During the 1930s a new cult of ultra-nationalism took hold and 'Japanese politics seethed with conspiracies, ideological movements, and secret societies that rejected liberalism, capitalism, and democracy as engines of weakness and decadence'.[96] In addition, aiming to be a world power, Japan needed raw materials in order to continue growing and saw war as a way to gain overseas land and resources. As a result, in 1942 Australian medical officers suddenly faced a Japanese military that did not care about the welfare of its prisoners, and they quickly learned that the rules of 1929 Geneva Convention regarding the treatment of POWs would not be observed.

Although many Japanese doctors had trained overseas, many spoke good English, and some identified as Christian, Allied doctors found it disturbing that a pervasive military indoctrination seemed to override any sense of professional collegiality in their Japanese colleagues. British doctor Captain Bill Hetreed recalled meeting a 'properly qualified Japanese doctor' who had been trained in Germany, who after a long conversation said to him, 'Of course, if I was in your position, I should have to kill myself . . . because I couldn't go back to Japan, having been taken prisoner and made to work.' The Japanese doctors' attitude to surrender and captivity directly echoed the 1941 Japanese field service code which stated: 'You shall not undergo the shame of being taken alive. You shall not bequeath a sullied name.'[97]

When Japanese doctor Lieutenant Yamamoto came across a large group of wounded men from forward companies in New Guinea, he was surprised that they had returned, thinking that 'they could only be a burden to their comrades and soon would realise that if wounded they would be better off dead'. When he then saw an Australian soldier tied to a tree and left to die, he wrote:

> I looked at an 'enemy' face for the first time. He was a young man of about twenty with blonde hair and a pale face . . . He showed none of the solemn realisation that having been captured, he could not return alive. I thought this attitude was very different from us.[98]

Like all Australian POWs who survived the war, former medical personnel have tried to understand their treatment at the hands of the Japanese. Some speculate that many of the Japanese camp personnel were retired or failed officers, to whom command of Allied POWs was akin to imprisonment, or at least a great disgrace. Surgeon-Lieutenant Samuel Stening, the medical officer at Oeyama POW Camp in Japan in 1943, noted that the most brutal captors were those who were medically unfit for the Japanese army, suggesting that this may have produced their feelings of frustration.[99] As well, in most camps, the Japanese themselves were living in a foreign and hostile country—they probably did not want to be there any more than their prisoners.

Recriminations for their treatment of POWs only became a salient consideration for the Japanese towards the end of the war, when the fortunes of their allies soured and defeat became a possibility. From early to mid 1945, the change in behaviour towards the sick and their comrades was plain, particularly after Germany had been defeated in Europe. While there is debate about whether the Japanese were willing to negotiate surrender terms before the Hiroshima and Nagasaki bombs were dropped in August 1945, it is clear that some of those in command of the Allied POWs in 1945 began to hedge their bets, either behaving more humanely or preparing to kill all their prisoners.

While POW doctors' relationships with their Japanese captors remained mostly difficult, abusive, and professionally and personally frustrating, former Australian medical personnel sometimes exhibited a kind of empathy for their captors. Some offered rationalisations such as that their captors were suffering, that they too did not have enough food or supplies, that they were under extreme pressure from their superiors to finish building projects on time, and so on—as if the Japanese could not help how they behaved. This is *not* a common attitude among other POWs.

As part of this rationalising of their captors' behaviour, some doctors downplayed the abuse they personally received. Yet in interviews, when encouraged, they could often describe several incidents in detail, usually changing the subject soon after. This points to the unreliability of memory in oral history, as well as the effect of trauma on memory suppression. British doctor Captain Bill Hetreed, for example, when asked about any personal physical abuse he had received, said that he could only remember being hit once, and that he could not understand why so many people claimed they had been frequently physically beaten by the Japanese. However, his diary, written during captivity, documents several incidents of brutality against him. When asked why there was such a discrepancy he answered, after a long pause: 'By suppressing it, I made it disappear and therefore it didn't exist, therefore I didn't have to worry about it.' Such seemingly offhand explanations for discrepancies surrounding traumatic memory are not unusual among POWs.

Australian doctors found the behaviour of their captors difficult to comprehend and those alive today are still at a loss to explain it. Exploring the motivations of the Japanese camp personnel is problematic: not surprisingly, there has been no comprehensive recording of the experiences of former Japanese POW camp staff such as has occurred among ex-POWs in Australia. The immediate postwar period was, perhaps ironically, the most open time for discussion of Japan's role in the war. There was free discourse in government and academic circles, and a national desire to face the realities of the war and begin the slow physical and psychological reconstruction of the nation. Initially, 'textbooks and other materials issued during the first few years after 1945 clearly stated Japan's responsibility for the conflict'.[100] The author of the first postwar textbook, entitled *Our Nation's Path*, wrote, 'The Japanese people suffered terribly from the long war. Military leaders suppressed the people, launched a stupid war, and caused this disaster.'[101] The 1950s, however, witnessed a complete turnaround in Japan's accepted war history. When Nobusuke Kishi, a former war criminal, became prime minister in the late 1950s, he 'legitimised a great deal of wartime practices and marked the beginning of the distortion of some of the wartime atrocities'.[102] This process continued for decades.

As historian Yoshikuni Iragashi writes, 'postwar Japan's relation to its past is filled with tension'.[103] He argues that in order to rebuild their devastated nation, the Japanese embarked on a collective process of actively forgetting their war experience. Similarly, Ian Buruma writes that in terms of what Japanese schoolchildren are taught about Japan's war, 'Japanese school textbooks are the product of so many compromises that they hardly reflect any opinion at all. As with all controversial matters in Japan, the more painful, the less said.'[104] Despite some outward indications that Japan is making some progress in acknowledging its war actions, little has really changed. An American university professor in Japan noted that 'even among the brightest and best of Japan's younger generation, many know nothing of World War II'.[105]

It is important, however, to keep this period of Australian history within the context of the larger war—everyone suffered in wartime, and atrocities during World War II were not hard to find within any nationality group. As former POW orderly John Higgs reflected, 'I find it much harder to understand the German treatment of Jews than the Japanese treatment of POWs.'[106]

For Australian POW medical personnel, captivity was a time of personal and professional frustration, constant struggle and deep disillusionment, especially with their Japanese medical colleagues. With a few exceptions, a general adherence to intense militarism and contempt for, or at the very least apathy towards, the welfare of Allied POWs was a constant among Japanese captors. They hampered doctors' efforts to work to the best of their professional capacity, and were directly responsible for the doctors' inability to save more men. The doctors' personal records clearly reflect the frustration they felt because of the different value placed on human life by the Japanese, because they did not understand the belief that shame was inherent in surrender, and because they were unable to prevent their captors' cruel and inconsistent behaviour.

Yet POW medical officers seemed to have had the ability to juggle their various roles: one minute they were 'one of the men', commiserating with their patients and trying to keep their spirits buoyed, and the next ministering to a Japanese or Korean man, viewing them as just another patient they were duty-bound to treat. While one would expect this to cause some kind of personal conflict, it was not strong enough to override their sense of professional obligation. It is curious, too, that the Japanese, while relying on the professionalism and unique skills of these foreign doctors, still treated them as badly as they treated other prisoners. Most Japanese camp staff saw medical officers in the same way they saw all their prisoners: as members (albeit non-combatant) of a military that had failed, and as individuals who accepted the shame of being captured.

However, the various captor groups were not the same, and cannot be stereotyped. Each represented to medical officers a distinct challenge and a separate relationship to negotiate. Ignorance of Japanese culture also had an important bearing on how doctors perceived their captors. Over time, Australian medical officers became more sensitive to the differences in the hierarchy and motivation of the various groups, and changed their tactics accordingly for the good of their patients.

# 6

# DOCTOR AND OFFICER

*Much of the story of prisoner of war was a medical one, sometimes about the curing of disease, at other times about the alleviation of its effects, the easing of the dying, and, for much of the time, a broadening of the roles of some medical officers into matters of morale, inspiration to survive, and even leadership.*

BRYAN EGAN[1]

It is often assumed that Australian prisoners shared a common experience of captivity. This does not take into account the many intricate interpersonal relationships that existed between the prisoner groups: medical officers, combatant officers and other ranks. There are also the relationships between different nationalities to consider. Each of these was complex and each posed different challenges for Australian POW doctors.

In Allied POW camps, rank and class generally influenced interpersonal relationships far more than nationality. As former British POW Padre Noel Duckworth stated:

One cheering result comes from this dismal epoch in our lives. The Japanese had always tried to separate and encourage differences in temperament and relationship between the men from the UK and the men of Australia. But mutual suffering, mutual help, and the sharing of a common burden of toil, suffering and degradation, brought them close together in a wonderful union of comradeship and understanding.[2]

To some extent, this was true—there seemed to be little tension between Australian and British POWs of the same ranks. However, due to the unique position held by the medical officers within the POW environment, inter-Allied and internal relationships for Australian doctors were subject to different factors and influences. The special circumstances of captivity produced conflict between some groups, which in many ways reflected the inherent strengths and weaknesses of the British and Australian armies.

## The Australian military in captivity

No Australian serviceman imagined when he joined up that he would spend most of the war as a prisoner. This fact alone made captivity difficult to cope with, but it also meant that all the previously established roles and demarcations in the military structure became less rigid.

For medical officers, however, their professional *raison d'être* remained intact. They too faced unbearable conditions in captivity, but the fact that they could carry out their responsibilities, albeit under duress, set them apart from the ordinary combat soldier or officer. Orderly Bill Flowers commented that a distinction between medical units and fighting units became quickly apparent in captivity: 'We carried on with the work we'd been trained to do, whereas the fighting units suddenly had nothing.' Captain Rowley Richards also observed that 'all the other poor fellows were deprived of their responsibilities and the Japs deliberately removed them from command and responsibility and they just became a bunch of people'. He said that as a prisoner, 'I was one of the lucky ones because I was doing my own job... as a medical officer I had a job to do. I still had my sick to look after.'[3]

Captivity divorced combatant Australian officers from many of their operational duties. Their captors told them what to do and where to go, and forced them to accept a position of subservience. The most senior officers were also often separated from their men and placed in different camps. Even though according to military regulations officers were obliged to attempt escape, this was impractical and dangerous in Japanese captivity and was seldom successful.

The relationship between medical officers and other Australian officers was complicated by the many marked personal differences in their age, rank, education and military experience. Changi was perhaps the only place where the doctors' roles and positions during captivity were similar to what they would have been in an operational context. Here they functioned within a clearly defined chain of command, and followed orders about what they did, with which patients, and at what times. Changi was also the only camp where doctors were generally in plentiful supply. Even in late 1944, British doctor Major R. R. Braganza, who returned to Changi from the Railway, wrote, 'I have no official work as yet... all I do is potter about in the Garden and read.'[4]

In other camps, however, there were instances where the elevated status and vital importance of the medical officers in life or death situations caused conflict between doctors and combatant officers. This was perhaps natural, as everyone in captivity was under extraordinary pressure to perform according to their prescribed roles—roles that were challenged by the realities of imprisonment. Medical and combatant officers alike had to negotiate significant change, both on an individual level and among the larger POW community. Both groups had their own ideas of 'the right thing to do'. Studying these complex relationships between doctors and their fellow officers, who were mostly higher in rank than they were, offers an interesting insight into a little-known area of internal politics in captivity.

To understand how the role of doctors changed in the context of POW camps, it is necessary to explore their pre-captivity place within the hierarchy of the Australian military. Here, although they were considered essential, medical personnel were often relegated to the position of token military personnel, performing an indispensable but essentially civilian service. Captain Robert Pufflett, for example, stated that throughout captivity his identity was that of a medical officer and that rank as such did not interest him.

Unlike other Australian officers who earned their position through training, personal qualities and military expertise, most POW doctors entered the Australian Army once the war started, with little or no military training, and with the expectation that the expertise they would be called upon to use would come from their civilian experience. Although they were officers, they 'were not required to strip themselves of their civilian identity and dignities'.[5] Their motivation was more patriotic and professional than arising from a personal sense of tradition or loyalty to the military.

Captivity produced another evolution in the medical officers' place within the Australian military hierarchy; in the environment of a POW camp, the doctor's role became increasingly crucial. In a situation where critical decisions had to be made about the use of medications and food, doctors increasingly made those decisions. Lieutenant Colonel William Bye was put in charge of this task in Changi throughout captivity. His postwar OBE citation by Major General Cecil A. Callaghan stated:

> To him was entrusted the onerous task of allotting the meagre reserves of drugs, and special foods. This was a task requiring professional skill of a high order and unquestioned integrity as decisions of this nature might have meant life or death to the patients. Lt Col Bye carried out this important duty with distinction.[6]

For Australian prisoners, doctors were also a secure reminder of home and of a relationship that had nothing to do with war. They 'had expectations derived from civil life about doctors in uniform and those expectations contributed to the formation of different roles for different medical officers. The actual medical work they did mattered but the roles they played were often more important.'[7] Captain Lloyd Cahill remembered that 'strangely enough the doctors were in a very powerful position . . . it was almost like you became more than a doctor to them. You became a father confessor and mother and everything else.'

In some camps, doctors had to assume the role of de facto camp commander, accepting responsibility far beyond that generally expected of men of their rank and role. This was sometimes simply a logical progression reflecting the high esteem in which the doctors were held, in a setting where conventional military practices no longer always applied. As with many of his colleagues, British doctor Captain Bill Hetreed took this increased responsibility in his stride:

> It was something that was accepted. If I had been a competent officer, I would have been expecting that as part of my job and I would have been seeking the initiative, whereas at this stage having been landed with it I wouldn't be doing any more than I had to, because the responsibility in the army would be taken over by Warrant Officers or NCOs [non-commissioned officers] or the next rank down. The whole officer distinction of that sort became blurred if you like, or softened, because you had to do things that you wouldn't normally do.

Major Bruce Hunt, known for his forceful personality and leadership skills, often took charge even if senior combatant officers were present. Cahill, who described Hunt as 'a born commander', said he 'just automatically ran the camp . . . it was Bruce Hunt who did everything. Bruce Hunt just did everything, no matter where it was.' Orderly Osmund Vickers-Bush greatly admired Hunt for treating and caring for every man equally, regardless of rank, and he described one instance of this on 'F' Force's march from Ban Pong to their first Railway camp:

> I was weak with malaria and dysentery, and when the S.M.O. [senior medical officer] told me to pick up his bedding roll and carry it, I told him I couldn't. He kept on insisting and when I flatly refused, Bruce Hunt came over and told me not to touch it. He gave the other a dirty look, picked up the roll and threw it

over his own shoulder. This kindly man, who had once been over six feet tall and weighed around fourteen stone, was now down to about nine stone ... I shall never forget the many kindnesses and the help he gave me both during P.O.W. days and afterwards when we got home.[8]

In Java, when British doctor Colonel C. W. Maisey saw combatant officers dejected and ignorant of basic health issues, he also took control: 'the only method to adopt was that of a dictator—to literally try to hammer sense into them, and if that did not succeed then to take matters completely into one's own hands'.[9]

Sometimes leadership was thrust upon the doctors. In a camp in Japan, Surgeon-Lieutenant Samuel Stening found he was not only the sole doctor, but also the sole officer. This situation was not uncommon, as officers and doctors were frequently moved between camps. As Pufflett explained, smaller camps, with their less clear-cut hierarchy, made the division of authority difficult:

> On several occasions I took control of the rations and insisted on using them as I felt, and not as the quartermaster felt. I had a lot of authority because I could say, 'You can go to work, you can't go to work.'

While sustained conflict between Australian medical officers and combatant officers was not common, when it did occur it usually centred on the differences in each group's priorities. In the critically and commercially successful 1957 film *The Bridge on the River Kwai*,[10] the commanding officer, Colonel Nicholson, and the medical officer, Major Clipton, are prisoners in the same POW camp, yet from the beginning they clash. Nicholson demands maximum work output from the men, while Clipton, who is pointedly told, 'you have a lot to learn about the army', struggles to save the men from debilitating work. Although in reality it is doubtful that any commanding officer would have been as unfair and callous as Nicholson's portrayal, the doctor remains a saviour figure, loyal to the men and making no distinctions of rank—'the voice of sanity'.[11]

This cinematic representation reflects a common theme in Allied POW camps: the doctor always had the health of the men as his priority, while other officers attempted to maintain discipline and to lead at all costs. In reality, both groups had the welfare of the men as their first priority—only their methods of accomplishing this differed.

In the camps with the worst conditions, there were arguments between doctors and officers over how best to divide food, finances and duties. The conflict usually occurred because of differing opinions about whether the limited resources should be directed towards the sick or the 'well' men. Sickness itself, however, was not the issue—everybody was sick; it was more a matter of degree. Understandably, the doctors were focused on the very sick patients, while other officers seemed more concerned with preventing the less ill men from becoming sicker—both logical points of view. The doctors were always in charge of distributing the scare food supplies, but as Richards commented:

> If you get any extra food, do you give it to the bloke who you know is going to die, or do you give it to the bloke who's got a chance? So they're the sorts of decisions that were on all the time. Thinking back on it, gosh, it's horrifying.

In Burma in 1943, Lieutenant Colonel Albert Coates felt similar pressure in stretching food supplies:

> Rice was issued in insufficient amounts; meat 20 grammes per man per day in a weak vegetable stew. This was insufficient to keep a healthy man alive and well. How then could it be regarded as a diet for the heavy sick? The meat had to be used to render palatable the soup for the sick. Hence there was none left for the men convalescing.[12]

The responsibility for sharing out scarce supplies was a burden the doctors felt keenly. Lieutenant Colonel Glyn White described deciding how to distribute Red Cross supplies as 'one of the most unenviable tasks

I had to perform during the whole of my POW days'. He was very aware of the difference in priorities between the two groups of officers:

> Naturally, as it always has been, and always will be, the hospital medical officers considered the bulk of the Red Cross supplies should go to the hospital, whereas the Regimental Medical officers who had in the regimental aid posts, many men who, under normal circumstances, would have been in hospital, held strong views also and I had to remember that the supplies had been sent on behalf of all POW.[13]

Maisey often disagreed with other officers over the use of camp funds. He described their attitude as one of 'We will keep the fit men fit. This is a question of survival of the fittest.' He appealed to logic to persuade them:

> I pointed out to them that this was not the correct attitude to adopt, that the survival of the fittest took into consideration that fact that every individual had a fair chance, whether he was sick or not. In other words, the greatest care and attention should be paid to those who were most sick. It must be our policy to save every life we could . . . if we were to be content to watch our men die and give them only a little assistance while at the same time giving as much or even more assistance to healthy men, then we should be guilty of a criminal offence.[14]

As all the prisoners were ill in some way, the responsibility for choosing men for the work parties also fell to the doctors. Captain William Aitken often crossed swords with his commanding officer on Ambon, Lieutenant Colonel William J. R. Scott, as he felt that exhausted men should be rostered rest days to recover their health. Scott, however, believed that such a move would only anger the Japanese. Likewise, Scott frequently refused to protest to their captors over various issues, believing it would invalidate his authority in their eyes. Aitken, however, felt that Scott should have protested to the Japanese vigorously and constantly—as he himself did.[15]

Richards also clashed with his commanding officer, Lieutenant Colonel Charles G. W. Anderson, about forcing sick men to join work parties. One day on the Railway in August 1943, Richards picked only 140 of 350 men as being fit to work. Anderson ordered him to send more out, including officers. Richards reflected that on that day 'group loyalty had taken a beating', and was particularly annoyed that non-medical officers were making medical decisions. He reconciled himself to the fact that 'There was no way that the soldier who demanded the triumph of the spirit over flesh and the soldier–doctor who dealt with the ills of the flesh would ever find a common ground for cooperation.'[16]

At Sandakan, Major Hugh Rayson wrote that one senior combatant officer

> . . . began to show up in a very unfavourable light, being, apparently, definitely in favour with the I. J. A. [Imperial Japanese Army] authority and to keep this position he did not hesitate to sacrifice the interests of the Ps. O.W. He repeatedly challenged my authority over the hospital group notwithstanding the written authorisation I held from Lt. Col. Sheppard.[17]

In all the camps, Japanese command ordered that the prisoners in hospital or on light duties were to receive half the rations of those actually working. However, this order was not carried out by the Australian POWs. If the cookhouse received less food because of the number of non-working prisoners, it was still often shared equally among the men. Although this was a decision made by the commanding officers and doctors, it did cause some resentment, especially when certain items in very short supply such as meat, milk and oil—generally obtained through a black market—were reserved exclusively for seriously ill patients.

Bitterness also occurred among prisoners because of the privileges afforded to officers by the Australian Army. Rank differentiation was often diminished by captivity, but it was still common and a cause of conflict in the camps. Tom Morris and a group of lower ranks, for example, disobeyed an order in Changi to build a separate eating mess for Australian officers, believing that this was unnecessary and unfair.[18]

Australian officers also usually had separate sleeping quarters, a fact not always appreciated by the others. Richards said that while his own commanding officer was an excellent leader who never let officers accept privileges over other men, he was in the minority. There were other camps, he said, 'where some of the senior officers took privileges, got better food. Disgraceful conduct, and the only people willing in those camps to look after not only the sick, but also the well blokes, were the doctors.'

Part of this resentment is explained by the perception of many of the Australian other ranks that they were in captivity *because* of the officers. Though their anger is mostly reserved for British officers, some was also directed at Australian officers for the debacle of the Malaya campaign. Even today, many ex-POWs are at pains to point out that they were *ordered* to surrender. After the capitulation, Lieutenant Colonel Arthur S. Blackburn in Ambon echoed the sentiments of many Australian combatant officers when he ordered them to

> ... take the first opportunity of telling your men that this surrender is not my choice or that of Gen. Sitwell. We were all placed under command of the Commander in Chief N.E.I. [Netherlands East Indies] and he has *ordered* us to surrender. In view of medical reports as to the dangers of living in the mountains, impossibility of obtaining food in the mountains and the fact that no reasonable prospect of escape in ships from the South Coast exists, there was considered by Gen. Sitwell to be no alternative except to obey the order.[19]

Not all studies of the fall of Singapore solely blame the British. Military historian Alan Warren argues that two of the top Australian officers in command, Duncan Maxwell and Gordon Bennett, were both lacking in vision and leadership, describing them as 'unequivocal failures'.[20] Some Australian officers, having failed to perform well during the campaign, in captivity 'attempted to reassert lost authority and dignity. The prisoners met them with resentment, and sometimes contempt.'[21] British doctor Major John Bull commented that he also felt this distrust from Australian officers who, while friendly, 'felt very strongly that the British had let them down'.[22]

Questions of privilege and rank among Australian prisoners have been investigated by historian Joan Beaumont, who says former POWs and Australian historians alike have decided that 'the delicate question of differentiation between prisoners of war on grounds of ranks is best left tacitly ignored'.[23] As Beaumont points out, in reality it is difficult to do so, as this area of interpersonal relationships is crucial in understanding the stresses of captivity. Lower ranks often accused officers of putting their own interests and well-being ahead of their men. Common examples given are of officers eating more food, or complaining about doing duties that they saw as beneath them, such as digging latrines.

Attitudes to officers understandably soured when starvation became widespread and men saw their officers eating better than they were and doing little or no manual work: 'Where chronic malnutrition was the main cause of death even a slight disadvantage was significant, and the officers had a real advantage.'[24] On Ambon, Australian officers grew their own vegetables, and any other ranks found stealing from the vegetable patch were put in the 'cage'—a contraption similar to the one at Kuching (described in Chapter 4). When his friend was caught, Sapper Les Hohl claims he protested to the commanding officer, but his protest fell on deaf ears and the man died.[25] Orderly Vickers-Bush wrote, 'We O. R.'s [other ranks] were not nearly as well off as the officers. At no time did we get an issue of sugar or salt . . . The only eggs we ever got were age-old eggs preserved by sticky, black mud, and these we bought ourselves from the natives.'[26]

When the POWs returned to the base camps from the Burma–Thai Railway in 1943, there were noticeable differences between the officers and the other men. 'The officers might be two stone heavier [and] were likely to be standing in boots and uniform while the other prisoners, after weeks of working in all weathers, were barefoot and dressed in G-strings and tattered shorts.'[27] Captain Victor Brand also commented on the great differences in the prisoners' physiques: 'When men were having a shower, you could easily tell who were the men and who were the officers ... the men were usually shorter, stunted, less muscular and so on, you could see the difference—a very great difference.'

These physical disparities were also reflected to some extent in the mortality rates. In the 2/29th Battalion for example, 361 men died, including only two officers, or 0.6 per cent.[28] Statistics like this, however, do not take into account the fact that there may have been very few officers with any given group of Allied POWs.

It is difficult to judge the actions of individual prisoners given that they all just wanted to survive. Officers had a much higher chance of survival if they did not perform hard physical labour. 'The right not to work could mean, quite literally, the difference between life and death.'[29] This is not to suggest that officers avoided such work wherever possible, but it was most likely a factor in their generally higher rates of survival.

Although Allied officers and non-commissioned officers were technically not required to work for a captor nation under the 1929 Geneva Convention, the decision as to whether or not to honour the Convention was often made at the whim of individual Japanese officers. This in some ways put extra pressure on POW officers, as the lower ranks understandably felt that an officer who did not do any manual labour was not acting fairly. It certainly seems that an Australian officer who joined a work party was either forced to by the Japanese or motivated by individual conscience. In some cases, the Japanese forcibly prevented officers from joining work parties, thus removing the option altogether. As American POW officer Colonel Ilo B. Hard recalled, 'If I were counted in on the party personally, I figured I had to move my share of the dire [sic], if the Jap would let me.'[30] Interestingly, in some camps, Japanese command would allow American officers to have their own batmen—as in the British and Australian system—allowing them to save at least one POW each from working. 'We'd try to pick somebody that was weaker than the others,' recalled Hard.[31]

There is a danger, however, in exaggerating the 'privileges' officers could obtain, or in overstating the shortcomings of some POW officers. There were good officers and less effective officers in the ranks of every nationality, and captivity was bad for all. Even so, Australian POWs did not experience the dissolution of the basic command structure in their military, and even officers who were thought to have failed during the Malaya campaign ultimately retained their rank and authority. However, the environment had changed and was not amenable to a normal army structure in which roles were clearly demarcated and understood.

Despite the many criticisms levelled at combatant officers, and the occasional conflicts between them and doctors, the Australian military as a whole adapted fairly successfully to the changes presented by captivity. Combatant officers are often the scapegoats of POW history, but their contribution and work *with* the doctors was vital. They managed camp discipline, supervised camp hygiene and cooking and division of rations, administered camp finances in order to buy extra food and supplies if there was a black market, and helped to cremate the dead. As historian Jane Flower writes, 'No one who saw the confusion and desolation of the camps of Asian labourers on the railway doubted that there was an advantage in being part of a predetermined military order.'[32]

Captain Roy Mills had high praise for the Commanding Officer of the 2/29th Battalion, Lieutenant Colonel Samuel F. Pond: 'He was on the job every day witnessing what was happening to the men under his control, making appropriate protests at every opportunity, instilling faith in those who served under him.'[33] Several Australian and American officers voluntarily joined work parties to save sick men from working. Some organised the rotation of men on a particular job to ensure a fair distribution of the workload, protested on behalf of sick men when they were on work parties, and often stood between the men and their violent guards. American officer Huddleston W. Wright felt his main role on Railway work parties was to keep the guards entertained and distracted so they would be less likely to mistreat his men. Wright remembered, 'It got tiresome entertaining some little Korean, but as long as we were doing it, we were helping the men.'[34]

In many recommendations written by senior officers, combatant officers and non-commissioned officers are similarly praised. In a 1944 report by Brigadier Arthur L. Varley, of Allied POWs in Burma and

Thailand, he recorded his anxiety that if he died in captivity there would be no record of the exemplary work done by many Australian officers. In recommending OBEs for Lieutenant Colonel C. G. W. Anderson VC MC and Lieutenant Colonel G. E. Ramsay, Varley wrote:

> The conditions under which prisoners lived and worked were such as to break the morale of strong men. The example set by these two officers in their respective camps was responsible for the maintenance of morale, so vitally necessary for the preservation of life itself.[35]

Varley noted the tremendous psychological strain suffered by several combatant officers who had to constantly negotiate with the Japanese, and who were 'subject to the beck and call by day and by night of every Nipponese guard who desired men detailed for the slightest menial task'.[36] Varley himself died in captivity on 13 September 1944, a great loss to all his men.

British doctor Captain Cyril Vardy noted that in his camp in Thailand the Australian officers made an enormous difference to the morale of their men:

> ... there is a totally different, and to me, more pleasant, spirit about their mess—(amongst the officers, among men and between the officers and men). Their C.O. [commanding officer] is friendly—they all chat together laugh play the fool—yet he is undoubtedly their C.O. and if the time calls for it they jump to it (I have seen it time and time again) while in our Mess there is a bloody barrier almost everywhere you turn.—There is hardly any general conversation—just in little groups. (We get secret letters sent round the mess telling us how we should behave towards O.R.s [other ranks]—Ye Gods such piffle at times like these and when after all, we are all P.O.Ws.—No; we are so ... frightfully British don't you know, while they, (the Aussies) are bloody good fellows.[37]

In memoirs and interviews alike, most former Australian POW doctors are quick to praise their fellow officers. Whether this is an accurate reflection of their relationships is difficult to determine. They do not like to criticise the behaviour of men who, as they know only too well themselves, were in a situation of crisis. There are also individual degrees of loyalty depending on how long a doctor was in the military, and what rank he attained. For the young doctors who volunteered for the war and for whom it was their first military experience, rank was comparatively unimportant compared to what they saw as their professional duty, and they tend to be more openly critical than senior doctors of other officers. This difference in loyalty between junior and senior doctors may also be a reflection of personal connections; many senior doctors were close friends with other officers and had long established relationships, undoubtedly affecting their willingness to make critical assessments. White, for instance, counted Lieutenant Colonel F. G. 'Black Jack' Galleghan as one of his closest friends during captivity. He particularly admired Galleghan for his balance between discipline and leadership. In one instance where they disagreed over whether officers should donate most of their pay to camp funds, Galleghan eventually supported White in front of senior officers. At a meeting held to debate the issue, said White, 'I told them just what an officer's responsibility to his troops was and when I had finished [Galleghan] said simply, "Well gentlemen, you have heard what he has to say—and I so order it."'[38]

Naturally, if a doctor had many years of military experience, his loyalties to the army and to his medical colleagues might be divided. Senior medical officers such as White and Lieutenant Colonel Edward Dunlop displayed a clear sense of *military* professional loyalty. This, however, did not always extend to British or Dutch officers. Stationed in Palestine in 1940, Dunlop was heavily critical of British staff officers' attitudes, finding them 'arrogant and patronizing to Australians'.[39]

White had an interesting philosophy about his dual roles of senior officer and doctor: 'If combatant officers and men are ill disciplined, no medical service, no matter how excellent it be, can function efficiently.'[40] In a postwar address, he praised all officers, both medical and combatant:

Many of the officers were quite senior to me in the profession. Many of them are not alive today, but all of them gave me such loyalty, cooperation and help throughout our captivity and so turned what might have been a far more terrible catastrophe, into an experience, which I can look back on, in many respects, as something grand.[41]

In general, whatever conflicts there may have been between Australian doctors and other officers, the Australian military structure functioned well in captivity because it adapted to change. Without the long sense of tradition of the British Army, the Australian Army was perhaps less rigid about structure, and was in many ways better placed to accommodate the new circumstances and rules of captivity. As conditions worsened, the status of Australian doctors increased. In many ways this was not only allowed but encouraged by other combatant officers, who adjusted to the needs of their men, recognising that only by allowing some flexibility in the POW military hierarchy would more men survive. In many ways, this was in stark contract to the British in captivity.

## The British military in captivity—a comparison

Captivity gave POWs a heightened sense of their national identity. Anzac Day dawn services held by Australian soldiers in all camps every year were important and poignant occasions. These offered a chance to reflect on their World War I fathers, and an opportunity to openly acknowledge and grieve for friends who had died in the past years, whether in combat or captivity. On a lighter, but no less nationalistic note, Australian events such as 'Melbourne Cup Day' (with men piggybacking each other as 'horses') and AFL 'grand finals' were staged.

While there were always cultural differences between the Allied nationalities in captivity, rivalry between them was not very deep. British doctor Captain Bill Hetreed observed that when there were any problems between the British and Australian other ranks, it was usually the fault of the former:

We were not accustomed to each other and to be 'thrown into the bag', as this is referred to, did make for difficulties. I think the fault was on our side . . . you know, not being willing to accept differences for the common good.

Yet among most POWs, any rivalry was generally friendly. In one humorous instance, British soldiers in Changi performed the play *Journey's End*. While the British audience appreciated it, Australians heckled, interrupted 'and ended up barracking for the German prisoner'.[42] Real bitterness from Australians only emerged against British officers,[43] and again, much of this hostility can be explained by the failure of the Malaya campaign.

The Australian POWs' great respect for their own medical officers did not necessarily transfer to doctors of other nationalities. This is particularly true of British doctors, which is surprising considering that in practice and training they were most similar to their Australian colleagues. To understand this contradictory attitude, it is important to explore the nature of the British military structure.

Perhaps the clearest difference between the Australian and British militaries in captivity was the latter's almost constant maintenance of distance between the ranks. Given the dire circumstances, many Australians saw such distinctions as irrelevant and grossly inappropriate. Australian Lieutenant Harry Medlin was one who found the British officers' attitudes to formality in Java 'irritating':

> Most of us Australians saw no sense in our troops saluting officers or in officers saluting more senior officers; this did of course lead to friction between Aussies and Poms . . . I found much more interesting and useful activities while being 'in the bag' than going around saluting and being saluted.[44]

Richards thought that the reason British officers were so conscious of their rank was that they all came from the same social class, 'whereas for the Australians you could have, and literally this would happen, you'd have a gunner who was a bank manager and his officer could be one of his tellers'. At the end of the war, when reprimanded by British officers for celebrating with lower ranks, Richards replied, 'I'll drink with them because they are my men. And I might get a little drunk with them.'[45]

While the majority of American POWs were held in the Philippines, several thousand spent time in Changi, Java, Manchuria and Japan, alongside British, Australian and Dutch prisoners. American POWs were quick to note differences between the nationalities in captivity. In many accounts, the Americans firmly identified and immediately bonded with the Australians and Scots. American POW Chaplain Robert Taylor made a typical comment:

> ... we are not as much like the British as the Australians are like we are, you know. The Australian people have this warmth of fellowship, and warmth of attitude, whereas the British is always a Britisher to the last degree. That's not speaking derogatorily against the British. It's just their way.[46]

A remark by American POW Frank H. Bigelow, highlighting the importance of a sense of humour, 'a little guts' and 'taking a chance once in a while', mimics several such statements made by Australian POWs, reflecting a common approach to captivity.[47] A shared colonial background and resulting anti-British sentiment also went some way towards cementing 'sides' against the British. American POW Horace Chumley remarked, 'I've always thought that Australians, the ones I've met, were more like a bunch of wild Texas cowherds than anything else, and they didn't think any more of the Limeys than we did, really.'[48] In a similar vein, Texan POW Luther Prunty commented, 'By that time, the Americans had sort of reverted back to frontier behaviour or something ... the Australians and the Americans there, I know, gave the British nightmares.'[49]

American prisoners were scathing of what they saw as the British attachment to pomp and ceremony, and the inequitable division of work both among Allied forces and between officers and other ranks. Upon meeting British troops in Changi, American officer Colonel Ilo B. Hard commented dryly, 'They still didn't know they were prisoners, in a way.'

When the Americans were given garden detail work, 'we'd come dragging in about sundown that afternoon, and they'd be out playing soccer or having a good time, taking showers and washing. Their clothes were clean, and they were well-fed looking, and our people were dragging in their tracks.'[50] Similarly, American POW seaman Otto Schwartz felt as if 'the British were conducting it as if they were back in London and as if there wasn't even a war going on'.[51]

A notable cause of conflict between the British and American groups was the latter's absolute refusal to salute British officers. Like their Australian counterparts in captivity, American officers allowed a relaxation of military protocol. As American POW Martin Chambers noted, 'Our officers didn't request any of that. That's one thing I'm glad of. The Australians didn't request it; but the British wanted us to salute them, and we wouldn't do it.'[52] Chambers praised the behaviour of his officers saying that they were prisoners too and they 'knew that you had to put up with all that stuff from the Japs all of the time, and they didn't request any additional discipline stuff'.[53]

Naturally, maintaining discipline and some semblance of normality in captivity was important, but generally the British doled out harsher punishments for minor offences than Australians. Australians tended to handle their own disciplinary cases, feeling that conditions were hard enough without adding to Japanese punishments. On the rare occasions when they did not, the ramifications were significant. In early 1942 on Ambon, Australian Lieutenant Colonel William J. R. Scott felt that discipline was eroding rapidly in captivity: 'officers were being openly jeered at [and] NCOs who tried to get men to work were laughed at'. He announced that henceforth he would involve the Japanese in punishments if discipline did not improve. This was met with great indignation, as it went against the 'tradition in the Australian Army of favouring informal rather than formal sanctions'. In attempting to explain Scott's unusual decision, given that he had enjoyed a successful army career during World War I and in the interwar years, Joan Beaumont comments that captivity and the resultant 'bitterness of failure turned him against the men under his command almost from the day they became prisoners'.[54]

Lieutenant Colonel Albert E. Coates (left) and Lieutenant Colonel E. E. 'Weary' Dunlop stand outside their office at the Medical Headquarters, Recovered Allied Prisoner of War and Internees Unit in Bangkok, 15 September 1945. *Norman Bradford Stuckey, AWM Neg No. 117362*

(*Top left*) Surgeon-Lieutenant Samuel E. L. Stening survived the sinking of the *HMAS Perth* and was the only Australian naval medical officer in Japanese captivity. He spent his imprisonment in Japan itself. *AWM Neg No. P04017.061*

(*Top right*) Captain Domenic George Picone was one of the ten Australian doctors who died in Japanese captivity. Picone died at the age of 36 at Sandakan, Borneo—just days before the end of the war. *AWM Neg No. P02467.954*

(*Left*) Lieutenant A. H. MacLean and Major Bruce Attlee Hunt (right) in Melbourne, October 1945. Hunt was one of the most respected and famed Australian POW doctors. *AWM Neg No. 117093*

This photo, taken at Fukuoka Camp 17 in Omuta, Japan, September 1945, shows Australian doctor Captain Ian L. Duncan (second from left) with American medical colleagues including Captain Thomas H. Hewlett (far right). *AWM Neg No. P01662.005*

Thanbyuzayat, Burma, 1942: A Japanese soldier stands guard near the entrance to the POW camp that marks the northern starting point of the Burma–Thai Railway. After the Railway's completion in October 1942, it became a base hospital for seriously ill POWs. *AWM Neg No. 045258*

Nakom Paton, Thailand: An improvised still produced two litres of alcohol from fermented rice every day, which could be used as medical disinfectant. *Norman Bradford Stuckey, AWM Neg No. 118851*

Allied POWs sit in a darkened makeshift eye clinic in Roberts Hospital, Changi. *John Rosson, AWM Neg No. P04485.059*

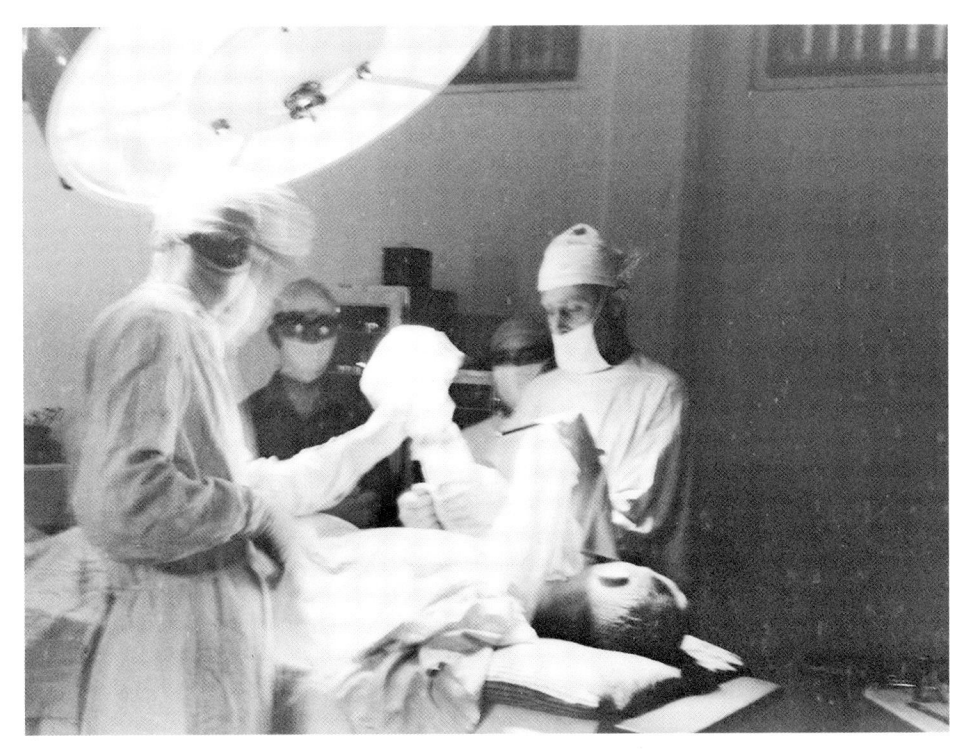

Lieutenant Colonel Charles Harwood Osborn operates on a patient in Roberts Hospital, Changi. This relatively well-supplied surgery was rare in many other POW camps. *John Rosson, AWM Neg No. P04485.051*

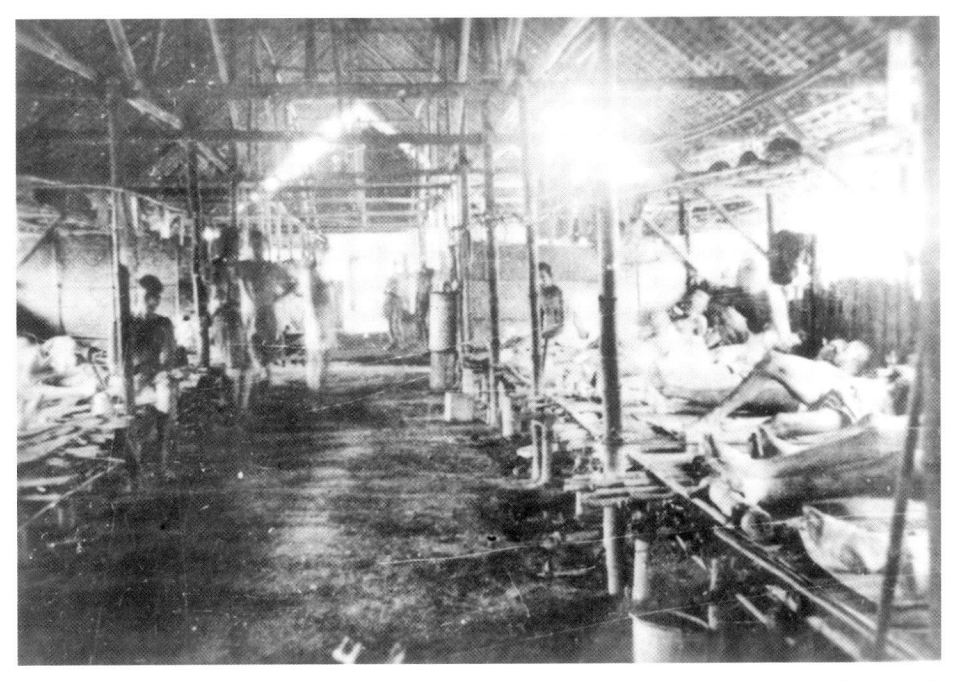

Many Railway camps had to be built from scratch with primitive medical set-ups. This British medical ward at Kanchanaburi, Thailand, is typical—patients are crowded onto sleeping platforms made of split bamboo. *AWM Neg No. P01433.018*

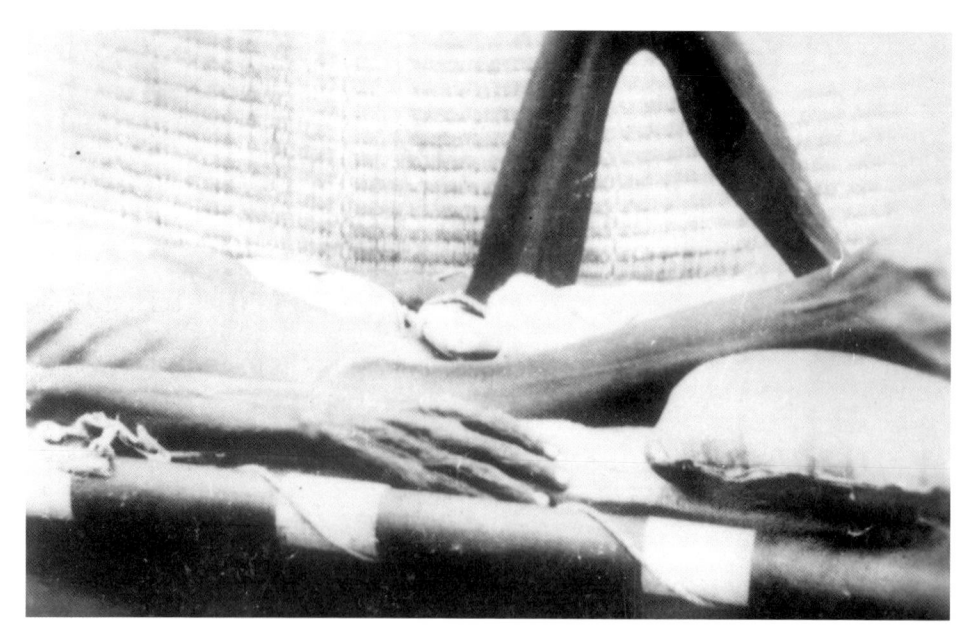

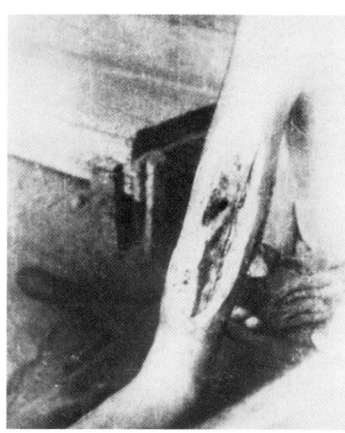

(*Top*) Burma or Thailand, 1945: An emaciated cholera patient. A highly infectious disease, cholera epidemics in the Railway camps were responsible for the deaths of thousands of Allied POWs and many more indentured Asian labourers. *AWM Neg No. P01433.027*

(*Left*) Tarsau, Thailand, 1943: An advanced tropical ulcer on a POW's leg. Tropical ulcers often meant amputation—and sometimes death—for afflicted prisoners. *AWM Neg No. P00761.010*

(*Bottom*) Tarsau, Thailand, c. 1943: Four Allied POWs show the typical effects of beri beri and malnutrition in Japanese captivity. *AWM Neg No. P00761.011*

Allied POWs enjoy their first taste of freedom in Singapore following their release from captivity in Sumatra. *Courtesy Imperial War Museum, London: HU 69972*

Examples of artificial limbs constructed in captivity for the many amputees. *AWM Neg No. 100946*

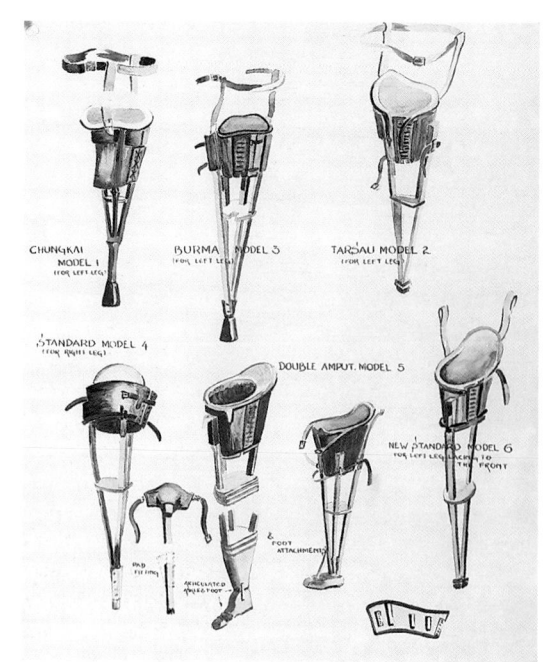

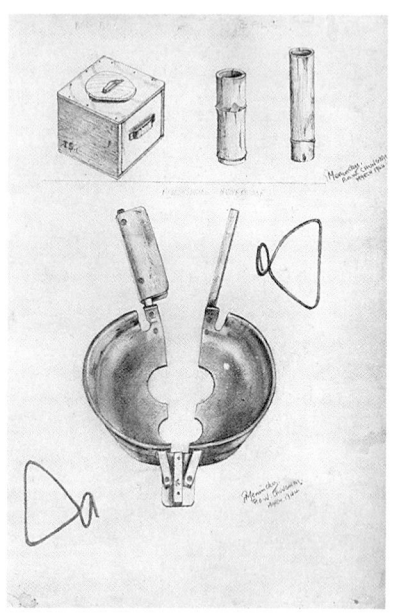

Medical instruments were improvised in many POW camps where supplies were scarce. Shown here are a bed box, bottles made from bamboo and an amputation retractor. *P. Meninsky, AWM Neg No. 101044*

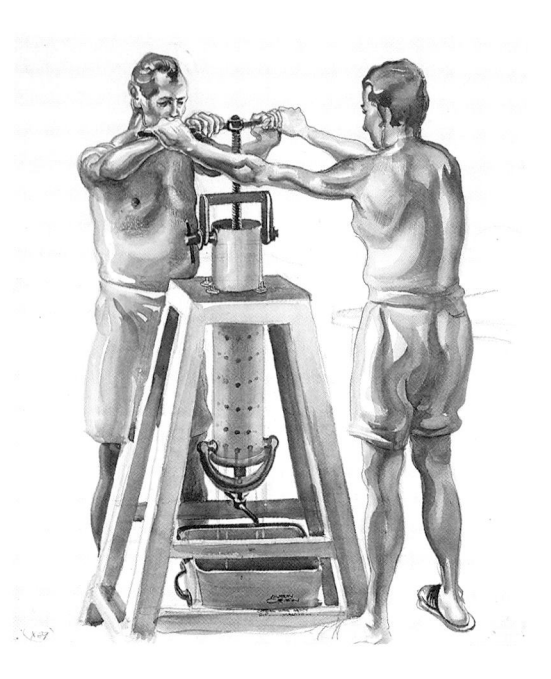

An ingenious press for extracting much-needed vitamins from rice polishings. *Murray Griffin, AWM Neg No. ART26454*

Scott's authority effectively ended in October 1944 on Hainan, in an incident that directly reflected the lower ranks' resentment of officer privilege in captivity. When a lower-ranking Australian was caught showering in the time allotted for officers, Scott made good on his threat and turned him over to the Japanese. The man was strung up by his thumbs and beaten severely by a group of Japanese with pick handles. His men, including other officers, were disgusted with Scott, who himself was devastated by the unexpected brutality of the punishment. Not surprisingly, two Australian medical personnel, furious that Scott's actions had so seriously endangered the health of one of their men, spearheaded a confrontation with Scott, along with other officers.[55]

Maintaining camp discipline was challenging for all Australian officers, as the men resented being disciplined on top of having to endure the appalling conditions of the Japanese camps. This was particularly understandable when their 'crimes' often involved measures to simply stay alive, such as sneaking out of camp at night to scrounge for food—in itself a dangerous exercise. In Omuta camp, Japan, Captain Ian Duncan witnessed the executions of five POWs who had stolen food for their own survival.[56]

Colonel James H. Thyer, an Australian combatant officer, believed strong discipline was crucial during captivity for maintaining a sense of cohesion and soldierly pride. At a lecture on leadership to officers in Changi in June 1942, he considered the postwar ramifications of losing control of discipline:

> We must remember that the circumstances of Singapore are being widely discussed in Australia. If we go back a disorganised rabble, the people will be inclined to say it was no wonder. On the other hand, if we go back a disciplined body the people of Australia will feel that the loss of Singapore was due to circumstances beyond our control . . . We must think of our future in civil life.[57]

Colonel 'Black Jack' Galleghan, the 'well respected tyrant', voiced similar sentiments when he famously said to Australian POWs, 'You are not going home as prisoners of war, you will march down Collins St as soldiers.'[58]

One might assume that Australian POWs would make a distinction between British medical and combatant officers, as in the Australian situation, but in general this was not the case. The main difference was that while Australian doctors successfully negotiated their dual positions as officers and doctors, British doctors identified more as *military* officers. As a result, for Australian prisoners, British medical officers became tarred with the same brush as other British combatant officers.

Australian medical officers for the most part did not enforce rank and were sometimes addressed by their first names by staff and patients, or by the generic 'Doc'. British doctors were rarely so informal, and usually ate and slept with fellow officers. When he was in Adam Park camp in Singapore in 1942, Rayson found himself in conflict with a British officer who felt that Rayson should stay in the officers' quarters, even though Rayson 'preferred to remain with the hospital and the men'.[59] Australian orderly Dick Armstrong commented on the differences between the two groups of doctors:

> Every one of our doctors—captains, majors and colonels, they always insisted on a doctor–patient relationship. I never heard a single doctor say, 'You'll address me as "Sir"' . . . It's informal and not got that class distinction that the Poms have . . . You know that even in Australia today, if you don't have the personality to command respect, you won't get respect.

Australians also resented what they saw as an attitude of racial superiority displayed by British doctors. A doctor popular among Australian POWs was Pat Wolf, with the Indian Medical Service, who had saved the lives of many Australians suffering from cholera. Armstrong expressed disgust at how British doctors treated Wolf:

> He was practising medicine on what the British in those years called an 'East of Suez' Medical Licence. He could only practise

medicine on people whose racial origins came from east of the Suez Canal: India, China, Afghanistan, or whatever, 'But don't dare touch a white man'.

This attitude is interesting considering many Australians at that time were equally xenophobic towards Asian cultures. Perhaps the difference is that through his actions and behaviour, Wolf had proved himself a doctor first and therefore gained the loyalty and respect of Australian POWs.

Corporal Doug Skippen, a British POW orderly, commented on the familiarity between Australians and their doctors:

We weren't as familiar with our doctors as the Aussies were. Our doctors were *respected*. The Aussies, I suppose they were respectful and they got on and they were easier with their doctors. Bruce Hunt always called me by my Christian name [while] our officers always called me 'Corporal'. But now I was 'Doug'.

Here again is shown the difference between earned respect and a respect enforced by rank. Skippen and Hunt became very close, and Skippen still thinks of Hunt as one of the greatest men he has ever known. After the war, Hunt even asked Skippen to move to Australia to work with him.

The Australian Army was a relatively young one and prided itself on being an egalitarian meritocracy. In its self-perception, the upper ranks generally rose from the lower, not from a tradition of bought commissions, as was historically common in the British military. In truth, this perception was by now inaccurate and outdated, but Australians continued to see themselves as an army that believed authority came from earned respect and from having proven oneself to be a competent leader. One particularly graphic example of this attitude occurred on the Railway in 1943, when Armstrong almost hit a British officer. When later asked why, he explained that the officer had called him 'A damned Colonial'. He continued: 'I threw the bloody shovel down and walked over and I said, "Don't ever call me a Colonial or I'll punch your face in. I'm an Australian".'

Another perspective provides perhaps the most interesting comment on the differences in behaviour between Australian and British medical officers. Dr Frans V. B. Du Moulin, a Dutch POW medical officer, noted:

> As a result of the common sharing of hardship and suffering, the usual military distinctions between the different ranks amongst the allied POWs gradually faded into feelings of solidarity, bordering on fraternisation. This disappearance of stratification in military rank did not apply to the British, who in line with their conservative spirit, preferred to maintain, even in prisonership, a strict distinction in status and ranks of field officers, regular officers, non-commissioned officers (NCOs), and the soldiers with their corporals ... The British Officers for example, kept displaying their badges, even when clad in a 'twajat' (loincloth) only.[60]

Dr Moulin wrote scathingly about the British officers' maintenance of batmen to perform duties such as 'laundering his uniforms (if any were left)'. As a doctor, he objected to their insistence on parading their squads at the end of long work days: 'The men, exhausted and barefoot, were called to attention ... vigorously accepting their sergeant's habitual shouting.'[61] Du Moulin saw it as a case of poetic justice when British officers, who had insisted on having a private cubicle latrine built for their use, suffered a scabies and ringworm outbreak, the communal seat providing a perfect spreading ground for infection.

In a telling statement, one British officer wrote, 'This treatment of officer prisoners of war is without precedent in the whole history of modern war, besides being a direct breach of the Hague Convention. It will not be forgotten or forgiven for a hundred years.'[62] Yet he only mentions the mistreatment of officers, not the mistreatment of the more numerous other ranks, who arguably suffered a great deal more. It would be unusual for an Australian officer to have made this kind of distinction in a report.

Accurately or not, the Australians also saw British officers as lacking ingenuity or initiative. Captain Lloyd Cahill observed that when their troops moved into an area, British officers were 'absolutely hopeless' at making camp, and had no idea of jungle conditions:

> They had no latrines and they had the cookhouse anywhere at all, probably near the latrines, and they got cholera and they were just unable to cope with the whole situation. They were ill-equipped in every way and of course they died.

Richards described what he felt made the Australians stand apart:

> Necessity, ingenuity, and the talent for improvisation that had furnished many a bush hut in the pioneering days of Australia had devised the Burma-Railway cot: a simple frame of bamboo supporting two bamboo poles run through either side of large rice sacks.[63]

Australian orderly Gordon Nichols believed that the British were less able to adjust to their new surroundings than the Australians, particularly because they had been used to doing things a certain way in Singapore. He remembered such British pre-captivity practices as resting during the hottest hours of the day, wearing shirts with a padded spine intended to protect the cerebrospinal fluid becoming too hot, and malaria cases being isolated and treated with great care. But with captivity came a different way of doing things:

> We worked without shirts at all, no period of rest in the afternoon and not the proper drugs. So, we soon found out that things were altogether different. Now the Australian soldiers somehow were able to cope with it, but the British were not so good at coping with it.

Australian personnel also noticed that some British officers were less generous than their own officers with their money. Most Allied doctors (and, indeed, lower ranks as well) argued that on those infrequent occasions when POWs received pay, officers should hand from half to three-quarters of theirs to a camp fund for the sick to procure black market supplies of food and medicine where possible. Maisey wrote about the refusal of fellow British officers in his camp in Java to do this:

This was vetoed by the senior officers in command at the time on the grounds that an officer must have money to keep up appearances, to pay for a batman, etc. I held the view that an officer is an officer by virtue of his moral character and his leadership rather than by what he has in his pocket.[64]

This was a common source of quarrel between Australian and British officers. Maisey also recorded his disgust with the way in which the officers in his camp distributed money. They would only allow money to go to men in their own units; 'for all they were concerned, men from units which had no money—such as sailors and merchant seamen who had been cast ashore penniless—could starve to death'.[65]

Like the Australian medical officers British doctors often praised their medical colleagues, but they bemoaned the behaviour of their combatant officers. Maisey wrote of the outstanding selflessness of one officer, Flight Lieutenant J. Lillie RAFVR (Royal Air Force Volunteer Reserve), who always gave half of any money he received to the camp fund: 'In comparison with the extreme selfishness of 99% of all other officers, I thought his conduct was outstanding.'[66] British doctor Major N. Courtney Lendon similarly condemned many of his comrades:

The psychological attitude towards labour of both Officers and Other Ranks at this time was one of demoralised and stuporose indifference... rumours of more dreadful happenings elsewhere were readily believed, while news of brighter days ahead were treated with the casualness of past experience.[67]

British doctor Captain David Christison also described what he saw as the failings of some of his fellow officers: 'Some of them were just lying down and didn't seem to do anything much. If you were in a camp where there were extra officers, they didn't bestir themselves and see anything to do, they just tended to lie up.' His colleague Captain R. B. C. Welsh wrote bitterly in his diary about two brigadiers in his camp who seemed to contribute nothing and actually put *on* weight: 'Football is the only relief from the constant bickering and backbiting in the officers' part of the camp—especially those sick in hospital.' He was also frustrated at the attitude of his commanding officer, Major Read, for two reasons—overworking Welsh's orderlies, and favouring the men from Read's own unit: 'a heinous offence for the C.O. of a mixed unit'. Welsh wrote angrily, 'We just muddle along and pretend we are better Britishers for doing so. Futile and maddening.'[68]

Major D. W. Gillies wrote of an interesting predicament his British colleagues faced when balancing military and medical obligations. He alleged that senior British officers in his camp were forcing doctors to classify them as sicker than they actually were, to avoid responsibilities: 'It isn't easy of course for a young Captain, say, to tell some old burbler of a Lt. Col. that there is damn all wrong with him except lack of guts, and of course if the said M.O. [medical officer] is a Regular, he has to think of his future.'[69]

Overall, Australian doctors did admire the most senior combatant British officers. Captain Roy Mills' comment that 'the top British officers were magnificent' is typical. But distinctions were often drawn between the behaviour of particular groups of British officers. For example, one Australian doctor voiced his complaint that there was a party of British officers who were malingering in hospital, receiving full rations. He was moved to another camp, and believes this was the reason. Captain Victor Brand summarised it thus: 'Australian officers on the whole were better than the British officers. There were some British officers who seemed to think that the war was for their benefit and the men were for their benefit.'

## Allied doctors in captivity

Although POW doctors usually treated their own countrymen, this was not always the case. Sometimes the doctors were too ill to perform their duties. Doctors allocated to work parties on the Railway could also be moved arbitrarily as numbers of sick prisoners necessitated. In any given camp, Australian doctors often found themselves working with one or more medical colleagues of different nationalities, as well as treating their patients.

There is little evidence of conflict between the Allied doctors. They were loyal to their own militaries, but they were also loyal to each other as colleagues. Many Australian doctors had trained, if not in the same institutions in the United Kingdom, then according to similar syllabuses. That they were also in camps with Dutch, American and Indian doctors also increased their feeling of professional solidarity.

Australian and British doctors for the most part got along very well, united by a professional duty of care and enthusiasm. One typical comment was provided by British doctor Major John Bull at Kranji in 1943:

> The Australians were pretty much a hotchpot [sic]. Some of them were quite elderly and had been in the first war, others of them seemed to have been unemployed before being scooped up by the army. These seemed a poor lot. But the Australian medical officers were good chaps, nice and able chaps.[70]

Gillies showed a similar attitude, demarcating Australian medical officers from the rest: 'we find them quite decent fellows individually. It is the Australians in the mass who become frightful.'[71]

Doctors shared information, new medical techniques and ways to substitute for their usual tools and equipment. When an Australian doctor joined a Railway camp, Welsh wrote that he 'told us about his improvisation of bamboo cannulas for intravenous work; and that he injects intravenously filtered river-water and rock-salt saline solution—rather heroic'.[72] Any conflict between doctors was more often due to a personality clash rather than to any intrinsic national or cultural divide. For Australian medical officers, working with doctors of different nationalities served to reinforce their self-identity. The practice of consultation and sharing of medical techniques with colleagues was one they were used to, and that familiarity continued to breed professional and personal affirmation.

A British report on Roberts Hospital, Changi, praised all the medical personnel there, and commented that the biggest cause of stress in medical officers was in fact British patients:

> At the best of times, where food is concerned the British soldier is none too free with his appreciation. When it is not to his liking he is never slow at coming forward . . . I had my time fully occupied in meeting these complaints and trying to teach the grumblers that the Jap ration was unsatisfactory and what extra food we possessed was to be preserved for a 'rainy day'.[73]

Flight Lieutenant A. N. H. Peach recorded that a Dutch Dr Heysteck had cheerfully informed his British colleagues that British patients allegedly preferred Dutch doctors to their own.[74]

When there was conflict between doctors of diverse nationalities, there is no doubt that it was most often between the Dutch and the British. In a mixed camp in Java in 1944, Maisey wrote:

> The jealousy and suspicion between British and Dutch was during this period pathological in its intensity. Mistakes and unfortunate incidents were bound to occur on account of the language difficulty, but such was the mental attitude of the majority of people that this would never be looked at in a reasonable way.[75]

Maisey attributed the conflict between the two groups of doctors to many factors such as language difficulty and professional jealousy, stress caused by lack of privacy, and ignorance of cross-cultural variance in behaviour and medical ethics. He did not expand on this last point, merely acknowledging that they were at odds. However, he did consider some extenuating circumstances that may have influenced the behaviour of the Dutch. They were particularly persecuted by the Japanese because of their historical connections with local communities who were hostile to the Japanese, and this contributed significantly to their stress.[76] The Dutch were also the occupying colonial power of the East Indies, a resource-rich area that Japan planned to 'liberate' for their own interests.

The majority of Dutch and Australian doctors worked harmoniously together. Skippen believed this was because Australian doctors were more willing than the British to learn from their Dutch colleagues. He maintained that the British officers' reluctance to consult with the East Indies-born Dutch was responsible for the British troops not faring as well as they could have in the camps: 'Well you see, being British, we don't follow these natives: "He's a black native and you don't pay any attention to what he's talking about." If we had I think we'd have done better.' The Dutch tended to be looked down upon by the British for allegedly being less 'civilised' and less hygienic. Yet despite this misconception, the Dutch survived better than everyone in tropical conditions.

When doctors did not make such unnecessary distinctions, it was appreciated. After the war Lieutenant Colonel Thomas Hamilton received a grateful letter from a Dutch senior medical officer, Dr Bloemsma, who wrote to thank two Australian medical officers 'who both have done so much for the Dutch patients'. The first was Major Alan Hobbs, of whom he wrote, 'Always and at any time ready for anyone, his name with the Dutch patients was a by-word for medical skill, humanity and kindness.' The second was Australian dentist Captain Stuart T. Simpson, who worked tirelessly in captivity:

> Captain Simpson had still more Dutch patients to treat as we had no dental service of our own in the P.O.W. camps . . . Speaking of Captain Simpson in our circles means remembering an extremely good, kindhearted and efficient dentist to who we all have many reasons to be grateful.[77]

There are no simple answers to explain why nationalities experienced varying mortality rates on different Railway forces and in different camps. While many theories have been put forward, many Australian POWs contend that they almost always survived in better numbers than the British. In some cases, this is patently true, such as on 'H' and 'F' forces on the Railway. While statistics vary wildly between sources, mortality rates among British, Australian, Canadian and American troops were generally similar—between 25 and 36 per cent. Predictably the lowest mortality rate was among the Dutch at 23 per cent.[78]

Why did British personnel die in higher numbers than other Allied groups in the same camps? Some POWs have suggested they started off with a worse state of health, having grown up in the Depression in Britain, that officers were less competent at enforcing hygiene standards, that poor morale translated into poor health and lack of organised facilities for men to look after each other, and that they failed to heed the advice of other nationalities' doctors, particularly the Dutch. All of these are true to some extent. When orderly John Higgs passed two British camps on the Railway at Songkurai camp 2 and Kami Songkurai, he was shocked at the difference in conditions from Australian camps. They 'were depressing and foul almost beyond belief. There was a universal air of hopelessness, almost all seemed ill and despondent, the camp grounds were filthy and slimy with human excrement, there were bodies lying both inside and outside the huts.'[79]

After persistent entreaties to the Japanese, Coates was allowed to set up a POW hospital in Tanbaya, Burma, to receive those men who were too sick to work. Before long, British camp patients started to arrive. Higgs remembered:

> Even now, more than fifty years later, it is hard to recall or write about the horror of those late-night trains without feeling sick ... When the truck doors were opened the stench that emerged was overwhelming. Scarcely a man was not covered in his own filth or that of his companions, and it required pretty stern resolve to lift men out ... One of the two occasions when I wept in frustration was when, on the arrival of one train, we laid out the bodies of several men who had died—this on a train trip of scarcely 50 kilometres.[80]

One of the main differences between British and Australian soldiers in captivity was their relationship with their respective officers, including medical officers. Many British officers (including doctors) tended to adhere to rank and formality to try to maintain discipline. Unfortunately for morale and group cohesion, enforcing distinctions between the ranks served to widen the gaps between officers and other ranks. Australian prisoners respected their doctors because they gave priority to their medical role over their military role. British doctors did not command the same respect because the men saw them as being more like their fellow British officers in both action and attitude than their Australian medical colleagues.

On the whole, Australian medical and combatant officers adapted well to the constraints of captivity, realising that only a willingness to change as circumstances dictated would ensure the maintenance of discipline and morale. This was perhaps an intrinsic strength of the Australian military—the more flexible and accommodating a military structure under the intense pressures of captivity, the better it survived. While a blurring of authority between medical officers and their fellow combatant officers may have occurred regardless of the circumstances, the doctors—whatever their rank in the army hierarchy—cemented their position of leadership through their actions, attitudes and skills.

# 7

# BEYOND THE CALL: COPING IN CAPTIVITY

*Dr Ehlhart did the best he could. He often said: 'I am horrified at the way men are dying, without God, with no comfort or hope. How can one minister to so many? I'm between the living and the dead. I do not know what to do'.*[1]

Captivity under the Japanese was a terrible ordeal, but it was both harder and easier for doctors compared to other POWs. This had a significant effect on how they coped—and ultimately *why* they coped. In a postwar report, Captain Ian Duncan wrote:

> All [Allied POWs] were subject to severe and unremitting stress for the term of their captivity. They had to deal with a barbaric enemy who did not recognise the Geneva Convention and who were sadistic and unpredictable. They had to endure starvation and malnutrition. They were exposed to many illnesses and diseases as well as injuries when in a weakened condition both mentally and physically. They had to labour under extremely harsh conditions for an indefinite term. They were denied news from home. They were subject to Allied bombing. Some were close to the atomic

bomb, especially those in the Nagasaki area . . . the average weight of prisoners at the end of the war was 84lb [38 kg].[2]

Thirty years later, Thomas Hewlett, a former American POW doctor in Omuta camp with Duncan, wrote: 'we survivors still face disabling physical and emotional problems which can be traced to our experience'. He described in detail some of the scenes he witnessed, such as a nineteen-year-old Australian soldier being forced to kneel for 36 hours in snow in a camp in Japan; the soldier's feet later had to be amputated. Another POW was caught trying to learn Japanese, and was used as a target for the Japanese guards' bayonet drill, stabbed 75 times.[3]

The memories of POW doctors are vivid, even more than 60 years after the war. They can clearly recall events they witnessed or decisions they were forced to make which sometimes spelled the death of men. None could ever have envisaged the environment they would find themselves in or the decisions they would have to make. Unlike other prisoners, Australian doctors experienced specific professional and personal pressures with which they alone had to cope. However, certain factors enabled them to find a particular kind of resilience during captivity, and the strength to survive the experience.

## Professional frustrations

In a postwar report, British doctor Lieutenant Colonel C. W. Maisey described the most direct and immediate psychological problem that faced every POW doctor: the professional frustration caused by the day-to day-struggle of having to practise medicine without the appropriate equipment.

> During the first six months, all doctors developed a frustration complex. It is an experience that one has to suffer to realise fully—that of seeing around one hundreds of sick men, many of them dying, and being unable to give a single drug of any value to them in their disease.[4]

Captain Colin Juttner too recalled it was 'terribly frustrating because you knew what you could do if you had the wherewithal to do it. It was very tragic in a way. It's hard for me to talk about it now.' Captain Rowley Richards put it this way: 'When you knew that with the blokes who had malaria all you had to do to help them was to give them some quinine, that was heartbreaking, absolutely.'[5]

Fantasising about clean, well-equipped medical environments was common among medical officers as they watched men die from causes that could easily have been prevented by better medical supplies. In late 1942 at Tarsau camp in Thailand, British doctor Captain Cyril Vardy performed an emergency appendicectomy on a patient lying on two packing cases pushed together. Vardy 'thought of all the beautifully tiled [operating] theatres we have known—chromium plate, tiles—lights—water—we had bamboo, old petrol tins and a dixie.'[6]

On the Railway, Australian orderly Bevan Warland-Browne assisted Lieutenant Colonel Albert Coates in operations:

> I used to assist him by sterilising all the instruments and on one occasion we had some artery forceps and he said, 'They're no good' and he threw them on the ground and of course he was thinking he was in the Royal Melbourne Hospital. There wasn't another pair. It was the only pair there was so I had to rush and grab them, re-boil them and sterilise them again and give them back to him.[7]

Doctors went to great lengths to find substitute treatments or even just ways to relieve pain. A feeling of helplessness developed over having to practise what Duncan termed 'makeshift medicine'.[8] In Manchuria, surrounded by tuberculosis sufferers, Captain Des Brennan struggled with the limitations of his environment:

> The thing that haunts me most, to this day, is the fact that these guys in Mukden were dying and I could do bugger-all about it—I couldn't do a thing as a doctor. If ever I have learnt anything about consolation of the sick and dying or some sort of compassion I had to try and practise it then. I had to say to these guys, 'look

you are doing better, you'll get better.' That was the hardest thing for me—that I could do nothing for these people.[9]

When Dr Stanley Pavillard was nursing a diphtheria patient on the Railway for whom he had no treatment, he simply sat with him and held his hand until the man died. Pavillard reflected sadly:

> Episodes of this kind left one completely washed out, and unable to control one's emotions ... the repeated experience of such suffering ceased to affect one so violently, leaving only a vast tolerance of other people's shortcomings and a feeling of weariness and old age.[10]

## Pushing the limits

As the physical and mental health of POWs deteriorated, their dependence on the doctors greatly increased. The resulting psychological toll on the doctors was significant, particularly since most of them were young and most had little or no training in tropical medicine. As Hewlett later remarked: '[O]ur education had not prepared us for years in prison camps; thus we had no way of predicting the medical sequelae that might hound the survivors to their graves.'[11] Captain Lloyd Cahill was only 28 when he was captured in Singapore, yet at one point he found himself the sole medical officer with a work party of 1,000 men: 'If anybody had told me of the responsibility I'd be taking subsequently, it would have given me the horrors.'

As Geoffrey Gill has written, 'the spectrum, extent and exotic nature of disease seen on the Burma–Thai project had not been experienced before (or since) in British medical military history,'[12] and doctors' medical training often proved irrelevant in Japanese captivity. They quickly found that they had to rely on their wits and personal strength to take calculated risks and hope that their attempts would succeed.

Major Bruce Hunt carried with him one book on tropical medicine—*Medico-Tropical Practice: A handbook for medical practitioners and students*, written in 1920. Although Hunt treasured this book, its practical benefits were limited. For bacillary dysentery, a condition about 90 per cent of POWs had throughout captivity, it prescribed 'absolute rest in bed', three pints of milk daily, alcohol if needed, saline, enemata of olive oil, hot fomentations to abdomen and perineum, and antidysenteric serum—all measures that were completely impossible to carry out in captivity. For cholera it advised a diet of nothing but 'iced whey, iced champagne or iced brandy and water'. For the vitamin B1 deficiency disease beri-beri, the suggested treatment is bitterly comical in the context of Japanese captivity: 'Care must be taken to cut off white rice from the patient's diet.'[13]

Orderlies experienced similar pressures to the doctors. In some cases, there was no doctor in a camp so the whole burden of medical care fell to men who had very little medical training, and in some cases none at all. When orderly Ray Connolly was the sole medical carer in one camp for more than 1,000 men, he tried treatments that he says he would be too frightened to try today. An Australian driver with the 105 Transport Company, Walter McEwan Cobden, found himself in the same position as Connolly, but with even fewer qualifications. In July 1945 at Niki camp on the Railway there was no doctor and Cobden 'was acting as a Medical Orderly looking after any sick, who were not in a hospital, but were put in a hut in the camp'.[14] Cobden remembered caring for an Australian POW who had been beaten so badly by the Japanese that he died two days later.

Orderly Bevan Warland-Browne had with him a copy of *Martindale's Pharmacopeia*, which he bought in Kuala Lumpur before the surrender: 'I managed to keep it all through the war and when I . . . had a bit of spare time, I'd read it all through and I got formulae out of there and a bit of guidance of what to do with this and that.'[15]

Of all the medical challenges the medical staff faced, the most frightening was cholera, due to the speed with which it spread and the large scale of the outbreaks. Pavillard wrote, 'I had never seen a case, but I was almost obsessed by the fear of it: the section of my textbook on tropical diseases which dealt with cholera was the only part of that book which escaped being used as cigarette paper.'[16] Watching men die swiftly and painfully of cholera was harrowing for the medical officers. Juttner recalled a patient who died within hours of becoming ill:

> I can remember him—he was a big bloke too, quite a nice fellow, laughing and joking with his [mates]—not that they had much to joke about, but you know what I mean, they were mucking about, fooling about at breakfast. At 4 o'clock in the afternoon he was dead of cholera.

Australian 2/29th Lieutenant Frank Nankervis remembered a similar case on the Railway: 'We had a bugler who played Retreat, Lights Out, one night—and they played Last Post over him the next morning. As quick as that.'[17]

Cholera was difficult to diagnose if a patient was suffering from a variety of medical problems; anyone who was suspected of having cholera was quarantined. A particularly cruel consequence of this was that a prisoner who did not have the disease would then face contracting it. This made the task of diagnosis all the more difficult.

One lucky survivor of cholera was orderly Private Dick Armstrong. He was isolated on 'Cholera Hill' at Shimo Songkurai camp on the Railway, and credits his survival to an early dose of epsom salts which 'flushed him out' at an early stage of the infection. After his recovery, he volunteered to stay and nurse his comrades, a sad and difficult task: 'to merely keep the place clean and cremate the remains of your Mates is a bugger of a job and working with those who are dying by inches as they vomit their lives away is a heartbreaking task for the toughest of men'.[18]

As discussed previously, in trying to protect their patients, medical officers were bashed and even tortured, for example being forced to kneel for days, or being beaten until they were unconscious. Often these incidents were for no discernible cause. In St Vincentius Hospital, Java, Australian officer Captain James Goding witnessed the beating of a Dutch medical officer:

> [Japanese Lieutenant] SONE would ask GONLAG a question in broken English and while GONLAG was endeavouring to reply SONE would strike him and then speak again. This went on for at least 45 minutes and by the end of that time Dr. GONLAG became very weak and exhausted and had sustained a very large haematoma [collection of blood] over the left jaw ... I saw Dr. GONLAG repeatedly over the next seventeen months and I consider he had not completely recovered from the effects of this beating.[19]

When arguing with the Japanese over work quotas, Hunt received such a severe beating that he was 'virtually insensible and had a metacarpal [hand] bone fractured by three guards wielding bamboo canes'.[20] Dealing with the abuse directed at them, having their efforts consistently obstructed, and never knowing how their captors would react to certain situations added a significant burden of severe and unremitting stress. Captain Leslie Poidevin recalled:

> You were living under fear all the time, and pretty severe fear because they were using their bayonets a lot. I mean we'd seen heads cut off by this time, and we knew that if we didn't obey we were going to get either locked up and tortured or even worse, annihilated.

Some doctors were able to cope with some of this abuse by learning the system. According to Pavillard:

> By standing up to the Japs, even at the cost of a beating, one could often get one's way ... Sometimes it was possible to choose one's posture carefully and then by a well-timed yell lead the Jap to suppose he had scored a direct hit when in fact he had not. You had to be quick to get away with this.[21]

## Ethical dilemmas

For many doctors, the worst task was the daily selection of work parties. Duncan said, 'Being a doctor in the camps was a terrible responsibility.

You played God.'[22] As Hank Nelson writes, POWs' feelings of helplessness were constant, and they relied on doctors to make decisions for them:

> Prisoners could not make rational decisions in their own self-interest: they could not know whether it was better to join a work party or not, whether it was better to feign an illness or conceal one. Ignorance was a central part of the frustrating impotence of being a prisoner.[23]

Richards described a typical scenario where the doctors and the Japanese would negotiate over each man:

> Occasionally we would get to the stage of having what we called a blitz sick parade where the Jap would come along and he'd say 'What's the matter with him?' and I'd say, 'He's got malaria. Four days no duty.'
>
> 'No, two days.'
>
> 'Alright, three days.'
>
> 'Right.'
>
> And so we'd come to the next one and so it would go on... finally if I was getting nowhere I would pull the final joker out of the pack which was, 'Ah, you send this man to work and this man dies' and this is all done in Pidgin Jap of course, 'and this man dies when I get back to Australia', again no hesitation in our minds that we were going to get back to Australia, 'when I get back to Australia my ichiban'—that's number one—'will say to me, "Why did this man die?" and I will say, "Ah, Yamamoto sent him to work", and my number one will talk to your number one and you'll be punished.' And with one exception it worked, it always worked... I pulled it a little bit too effectively with one bloke on Jeep Island and he gave me the thrashing of my life. But you know, but this day-to-day thing was on, you know, it was a battle.[24]

The level of despair such responsibility caused the doctors was beyond measure. After meeting a returning work party, British doctor Captain

H. Churchill wrote in his diary at Hindati Camp, Thailand, about one of the Japanese guards:

> I saw the outline of his round head and promised myself that if I ever got the chance to hit that hard skull I would smash it. 'These men are all ill', I said angrily; 'They cannot work.' 'Be quiet', the gunso shouted, 'or I will send you into the forest to take their place.' 'Send me', I said; 'I want to go'.[25]

Major Kevin Fagan once had to select a group of prisoners to go to a Thai camp where the conditions were so bad that they were sure to die. He expected them to be angry with him, but instead they all came and shook his hand and thanked him for everything he had done. He remembered this as one of the hardest experiences of his captivity. Dick Armstrong recalled that it 'nearly broke Major Fagan's heart'. When Armstrong spoke to Fagan in 1990, he was still haunted by what he had to do and by the fact that 'not one man had rebuked him'.

Choosing work parties on the island of Pulau Bukkum off Singapore in 1942, Captain Robert Pufflett, the sole medical officer, struggled with weighing the good of individuals against the well-being of the whole group:

> Those suffering from nervous problems, depression, could be given a help in not working for one, two or possibly three occasions, but after that I thought that they were running my sick parade and I was being placed in a vulnerable position. I was of the opinion that giving way to nervous and depressed soldiers could only be done in a limited way in such circumstances, but I was not achieving anything for them and I could be jeopardising the rest of us.

This was a common problem. In 1945 the doctors in Changi faced the same hard decision when they received a transfer of men from Kranji camp who had pulmonary tuberculosis:

> It is realised that under present conditions where the greatest good must be done for the greatest number that it may not be able to

maintain the present standard of treatment on the other hand [sic] one is very loathe [sic] to see these patients fade away and die after much (relatively) has already been done for them.[26]

On the Railway, Pavillard discovered a malingering 'trade' among prisoners, where the same specimen of abnormal stools would be presented by a number of individuals so they could avoid work. When Pavillard changed his sick parade in a way that made this practice impossible, he was accused by some men of being a Japanese collaborator. But he felt that 'I had succeeded in protecting the interests of the genuinely sick.'[27]

On the Railway, Vardy examined seven young POW patients but he had only enough drugs to treat one of them. Unable to choose which patient should receive the injections, the medical staff found another way to make the impossible decision. Vardy wrote in his diary: 'it upset me—seven fellows—all under 25—all I think knew what was going on—we eventually put their names in a hat and Coney an Australian won.—dreadful.'[28]

Pavillard worked out his own way of selecting which patients would receive medication when there was not enough for all: he gave married men first preference, especially those with children. He also would give men placebo injections of water when he had no drugs, hoping that it would give them some psychological comfort.[29]

Medical personnel were sometimes forced to resort to euthanasia. There are few documented cases, but the constant movements between camps means it probably occurred more often than has been recorded. Orderly Osmund Vickers-Bush was in a camp on the Railway when the Japanese told the prisoners they would be going back to Singapore but that they could not take the cholera and smallpox patients with them. Vickers-Bush wrote of the terrible decision that had to be made:

> What was going to happen to them? We could not leave them alone to die. I was soon to find out. The Maj. gave me a bottle of morphine and a syringe and told me to go through the hut to see if any of them were alive. If so, I was to give them an injection and be sure they were gone before I left them. When they saw me, they begged

me to put them to sleep. I had no choice, and this is how they went to their last, long rest. I cried and cried like a baby, but I am sure God will forgive me for what I did.[30]

## Personal Tolls

On top of the many daily pressures faced by POW doctors, they also experienced the same personal stresses as any other prisoner. They grieved at the loss of friends and colleagues, and all of them were sick at various times during captivity.

A close friend and fellow officer of Pavillard contracted cholera. As he died, 'he took my hands in a tight grip and whispered, "Pav, write to my wife, tell her I love her."' Pavillard wrote, 'I had not the heart to throw his body into the common pit, since we had lived as brothers, sharing what little we had.'[31] Although Pavillard was busy and exhausted, he buried his friend himself. Likewise, Pufflett remembered he broke down 'when the fellow alongside of me died of cerebral malaria—a great friend whom I liked'.

Such situations also exacted a great personal toll on orderlies. Many of the most distressing and poignant stories of medicine in captivity are provided by these men. Once on night duty in a Thai jungle camp, a patient in the ward called to Vickers-Bush:

> I turned over to where the voice came from. I looked and said, 'Who called?' This man said, 'I did, Vic.' I looked at him. His hair was grey, and of course like the rest of us, he was very emaciated . . .
> 'Yes, what would you like to talk about?'
> 'Don't you know me?'
> 'No, I don't.'
> 'It's Ralph.'
> 'Ralph who?'
> 'Ralph Jones.'
> I looked at him again and I said . . . 'I'm afraid you're not the Ralph Jones I know.'

'Don't you remember Dulcie?' he asked.

With that, it clicked. It was Ralph Jones. I turned my head away and cried.[32]

When asked about their own health in captivity, most doctors responded that they 'didn't think about it' or that 'there were others worse off than me'. Yet, when probed, it emerged that they were often as sick as their patients, and completely incapacitated for periods of time. Cahill gave a typically modest answer: 'I had one bad bout of dysentery and quite severe. I was lucky. I had repeated malaria and beri-beri, fortunately not terribly badly. Eventually I got cardiac beri-beri but that cleared up.'

Pavillard was so sick with avitaminosis on the Railway that he suffered from severe night blindness. When performing an emergency appendicectomy one night, he had to hand over to someone else because he could not see what he was doing.[33]

In a medical report written on the Railway Lieutenant Colonel Thomas Hamilton talked about doctors who 'fought sickness in themselves as well as their patients'. He noted that the doctor sent to relieve Richards 'who, in spite of Chronic diarrhoea had been working from June '42 without spell' himself contracted bacillary dysentery. He also feared that the eyesight of an Australian doctor working at Nakon Patom on the Railway, Captain Thomas Le Gay Brereton, would be 'permanently impaired', presumably from avitaminosis.[34] Maisey wrote that of the six doctors in a Javanese camp, 'there were always two who were too sick to work, and on one occasion we were all sick and Lieutenant Colonel King and myself were the only ones who could get up and walk about at all'.[35] When a British doctor contracted cholera in a Thai camp where there were many cholera patients, orderly Ray Connolly made a significant treatment decision: 'a doctor who was urgently needed as far as I'm concerned, took priority'.[36]

While all the Australian doctors were ill at some time, very few died in captivity (9.5 per cent) compared with the general Australian POW population (36 per cent). This is interesting given that many orderlies died from frequent contact with disease, especially cholera. Why was the mortality rate of POW doctors so much lower than that of the men? There were some practical considerations—doctors were rarely members of work parties, they were obsessed with hygiene, and they had access to medication, when it was available. On the other hand, they worked long hours, were constantly in contact with contagious diseases and often suffered prolonged periods of great stress. Arguably, what kept them alive had less to do with physical factors than with the psychological value of knowing the importance of their work and the satisfaction of saving many lives.

Doctors often felt guilty when they became ill, as if they were showing weakness and letting their patients down. 'Never let a patient see you can't cope,' maintained Richards.[37] Sickness was a reminder of their mortality at a time when they knew that they above all others had to stay alive. Richards, for example, 'stubbornly refused to admit weakness and exhaustion in himself although he watched his own men with the anxiety of a hen with chicks'.[38]

With all the above examples of how captivity was a very difficult experience for doctors, evidence shows that they coped relatively well with their years as POWs. The question is, how?

A determination not to get dragged under by their circumstances goes a long way to explaining the resilience the POWs doctors displayed. As Richards reflected:

> We were basically optimists, stick our heads in the sands ... Two things that I talk about: one is 'reality rejected', you know, we became very very competent at rejecting reality. Then the other thing was 'disappointment deferred'. You know, we'd say, 'All right we'll be home by Easter'. Come Easter, 'Oh no no, I bet we'll be home by Christmas' and so it went on.

Doctors were able to 'switch off' to some extent, and focus on a particular situation's demands without giving too much thought to their role in it. When choosing work parties, Juttner said:

This was the great tragedy of the whole thing and I think it made you a bit hard and a bit tough too . . . you had to lose a lot of your sympathetic side I think, to be positive about things. It was just a matter of making a decision and you had to make the decision, which was often difficult.

Pavillard explained his own philosophy for coping:

We had to re-shape and re-direct our whole outlook: life became a game of make-believe and we acquired the knack of turning our attention entirely away from personal comfort and deprivation . . . all too often I saw men failing to adapt themselves to this make-believe game, this mental camouflage of reality, and then in consequence becoming morose and gloomy and in the end invariably dying.[39]

This was also a common strategy for facing their own illnesses. If doctors were sick, they would rarely admit it. At one stage on the Railway, Duncan suffered from a range of medical problems including malaria, dysentery, beri-beri, pellagra and tropical ulcers. But he believed it was a fatal mistake to acknowledge disease: 'If you let yourself get depressed, you were liable to die.'[40]

They were also often inspired by the attitudes of their patients. In a typical example on Hainan, Captain William Aitken noticed that those men who became very depressed 'often gave up the battle for life and allowed themselves to drift away'. Others who, despite being extremely ill, kept up a 'most cheerful outlook on life', stayed alive.[41] In Manchuria, Captain Des Brennan wrote in his diary that the men who had seemed to give up had told him that they had consciously chosen death over continuing to live in captivity.[42] Similarly, Richards noted that with those men who exhibited periods of 'intense fear, anxiety and deep depression' it was very difficult, if not impossible, to turn their attitudes around. Quite understandably, some men 'seemed to take stock of their situation, then decide that the ugly round of illness, convalescence, exhausting toil, mistreatment, semi-starvation and illness again was not worthwhile. They lay back on their sleeping platforms and died.'⁴³ That a positive mental attitude could in many ways sustain one through periods of physical weakness seems to have been a strong belief among the doctors. Cultural attitudes to showing emotion also played a part for some. Richards commented, 'I was brought up in the mid Victorian era where you had a stiff upper lip and all that and you didn't show any sign of weakness... There's no way I would have let people know.'⁴⁴

Living in the present was another important coping mechanism. British doctor Major D. W. Gillies found that in the worst times, such as when he was on the Railway in 1943, his prewar life seemed to fade into the distance as the physical and mental effort of the constant work consumed all. In his diary he wrote to his wife, 'everything else, including you I'm afraid, faded rather into a remote sort of background... you were like a lovely country once visited that one longed to return to.'⁴⁵ Like many other doctors, Captain Victor Brand did not allow himself to reflect too closely on his position, nor his future. 'We didn't intellectualise it,' he explained simply.

Decades later, Richards reflected on the brain's fascinating capacity to continue to shield particular memories: 'most of us have a selective recall of memory. We remember things that we want to remember and we forget the things we don't want to remember and then there's the question of just straight out subconscious denial: it didn't happen.'⁴⁶

In any case, doctors were all so occupied with the day-to-day task of keeping others alive that they simply did not have time to meditate on their situation. Some doctors describe rising in the morning, doing sick parades for a few hours, attending their patients, then tending to the returning work party at night until falling asleep, exhausted. This pattern could be repeated daily for weeks, allowing little time for contemplation. In many camps, especially on the Railway, doctors worked up to 20 hours a day. Any spare time was spent sleeping. Richards said, 'we were too busy surviving to be indulging in psychological problems... too busy trying to stay alive'. Duncan reflected, 'I was lucky because I had a job to do. I was busy. I think that saved my life.'⁴⁷ Similarly, Poidevin stated, 'I lived for my work and naturally all my thoughts were on medicine.'

This was true for some British doctors too. When faced with a diphtheria outbreak in Changi, Gillies wrote that he was 'fed up with the sight and smell of it'. However, the constant work 'kept us sane and prevented the frightful soul-rot which is rather too evident in some of the non-medical community'.[48]

When doctors were not busy caring for patients, they occupied themselves with a variety of other activities, all designed to make time pass. For example, in the doctors' diaries, one can see lists of books read, countless recipes swapped, letters to loved ones that would never be sent, designs for future houses and, in the case of Captain Peter Hendry's diary, meticulously detailed star and constellation maps. To escape the pressure of his work, at night Richards planned his future, 'where he would be free and going on with his civilian life in private practice'.[49]

Despite captivity's difficulties and frustrations, doctors knew that the responsibilities they faced were ones that only they could assume. Medical officers coped, because as Pufflett explained,

> They had to. They had a job which was different. Psychologically I can see why the medical officers came out better than the rest ... the rest had no purpose other than to keep up the spirits of the men, and they couldn't do that, being sandwiched between the Japanese and the ranker.

Taking responsibility for maintaining morale was part and parcel of how doctors saw their role—and indeed their mere presence often helped patients maintain the will to live. Pavillard outlined the lengths they went to:

> ... once a man lost the will to live drugs and treatment were useless. We used every possible subterfuge to keep the men cheerful, even sometimes inventing false news of the progress of the war, and sometimes we succeeded. If a man was past caring about such things it was now and again possible to make use of the deeply ingrained habit of military discipline: one could order a man to

recover and even threaten him with court martial if he died. This may seem a little far-fetched, but I have known it to work.[50]

When medicine failed, doctors used their personalities to will dying men to hang on—sometimes in remarkable ways. Orderly Dick Armstrong recalled a time when they received some boxes of rotten meat. Hunt 'gave us a pep talk in which he told us to eat it. As it had been boiled it was sterilised, and would do us more good than harm and the maggots were actually protein which we sorely lacked in our diet . . . Bruce Hunt ate his share with the rest of us.'[51]

Once, when Brennan was unable to do much for his patients, he resorted to more novel means of encouragement:

> So we came out and we said, 'You there, where do you come from?'
> 'My parents came from Hungary.'
> 'Well I've never seen a bloody Hungarian croak as easily as that. Don't give up. You've got to keep going.'

Others used different tactics to raise spirits, which could be just as effective. Cahill remembered one day in Songkurai camp on the Railway:

> They were really down in the dumps, miserable the lot of them. So I started an argument which would be the heavier . . . the steel in the Harbour Bridge or the *Queen Mary*? . . . it went on for weeks, all these experts coming up with so many pounds.

His men also made a deal that the first child born to a POW after liberation would win the 'Songkurai Cup' (which was duly presented to the first child born, on her 21st birthday). In a similarly humorous vein, Hendry remembered another spirited role he played—the lead in the musical 'Hawaiian Hedi and the Harlot'.

In other words, survival in the POW context did not only mean returning home alive. In such desperate and depressing circumstances, for POWs psychological survival was just as important. Doctors represented saviours, father figures, confidantes—roles that were all the more important as often there was no chaplain in a camp. British doctor Captain P. G. Seed noted that without the presence of female nurses, his medical care became much more personal: 'men died in my arms metaphorically speaking. I was the last human being they would have contact with in this squalid death at the other end of the world from their homeland.'[52]

## Raison d'être

Upon being taken prisoner in Singapore, the vast majority of Australian soldiers found the first few days confusing and disorienting. They had to negotiate the transition from fighting their enemies to being their prisoners. They had little knowledge of their captors or what imprisonment would hold:

> Seeing the vast army assembled in defeat, many men could not understand why they had done so little to impede the Japanese. And defeat was followed by insult. By ignoring them, the Japanese had shown their contempt: thousands of Allied soldiers were no danger to them. The surrendered men had no secure signs of who they were, what they should do, or what was going to happen to them.[53]

Doctors, however, had no such crisis of identity and role. Despite the difficulties of the situations that faced them, they considered themselves fortunate. They needed less time for the radical readjustment to being taken captive, unlike combatant soldiers and especially officers. Many doctors attribute their psychological survival to the fact that before, during, and most importantly *after* the war, they remained doctors.

This sense of overriding purpose was also shared by another civilian group in the military: chaplains. As American POW chaplain Robert Taylor explained:

> My profession provided me with an opportunity to be busy ministering to others and serving with others all the way through. We were very fortunate as chaplains, you know. The field was always ripe.

There were always people to whom you could minister and serve. I think this was a great contributing factor to my survival.[54]

In spite of the terrible circumstances, doctors were able to take some satisfaction from their work. An example of this can be seen in a letter written to the *Medical Journal of Australia* by former POW medical officer Alan Hazelton in 1992. He begins by discussing the 'regular meetings of a group of general practitioners in the late 18th century, at a pub called *The Fleece*' and draws a parallel with meetings of POW doctors sharing ideas and techniques during captivity. Hazelton ascribed great importance to this 'meeting of minds', regardless of the context of captivity:

> I felt that in common with the doctors gathering at The Fleece, it was possible for doctors of the mid 20th Century to make meaningful observations and devise therapy despite the lack of resources. Perhaps the doctors of fading years of the 20th Century can recapture the use of commonsense and apply the resources which are at hand to the benefit of the majority of their patients.[55]

The importance Hazelton gave to POW doctors' accomplishments showed not only that he felt their medical experience was historically interesting and important, but that the ways in which they combated their adversity stood as a lesson future doctors would be wise to learn.

Captivity represented a professional hiatus for doctors rather than a waste of time. This is evinced by many comments written in their medical reports during imprisonment and immediately after liberation. From the beginning of captivity, doctors formed medical societies and lecture groups in many camps. With such a cross-section of doctors in age, experience, nationality and medical specialty, there was a keenness to learn from each other while they had the chance, particularly for junior doctors—as illustrated in the following encounter. Hendry, a young doctor as a POW, intended to become a surgeon after the war. One day in captivity while reading an anatomy book, an old man walked up to him and asked what he was doing. Hendry announced he was studying to be a surgeon. The man replied, 'Well, that's the easy part. The second part's the difficult part.' Hendry retorted, 'How would *you* know?' The man replied dryly, 'I'm the Chief Examiner for the College of Surgeons in England.'

Even in remote camps in which there were often only a handful of doctors, this practice of forming groups to share their professional knowledge and experience was common. Quite apart from their practical benefits, these sessions provided a link between the doctors, reinforcing their sense of belonging to a professional elite whose traditions and *esprit de corps* would not be destroyed by circumstances beyond their control. Major Howard Eddey even wrote a complete book on anatomy during his captivity, begun on two rolls of toilet paper.

Dedicated to the pursuit of knowledge, the doctors continued to have faith in empiricism and believed that if they experimented enough with what they had at their disposal, eventually they *would* find solutions to the problems they faced. As Richards explained,

> You're faced with a situation, it becomes a challenge to fix it, and then you analyse it and do all the usual procedures: come up with a hypothesis, test it, and if it doesn't work, then you go back and do it all over again.

Various experiments were conducted in many camps to assess different treatment or diet regimes. Though often rudimentary, some met with great success. For example, Captain Jacob Markowitz, the renowned Canadian doctor with the British Army, pioneered a technique for using defibrinated blood in blood transfusions. (The fibrin removed from defibrinated blood is the major component of blood clots. It is removed so blood does not clot before it is transfused.) Markowitz supervised 300 transfusions, and the technique was successfully used by other medical officers as well. In 1944 he presented a paper on the technique to the 'Nakom Paton Medical Society'. Written in a consummately scientific manner—one would never suspect the primitive conditions in which his study was conducted—it quoted, from memory, research going back many years. This exciting breakthrough kept the doctors interested in their work and gave a sense of pride in their profession.

In another example, Dunlop noted that when Coates arrived at Nakon Patom, he 'stimulated great interest in the hospital clinical society by showing a case in splendid condition following this operation [ileostomy] many months previously'.[56] Coates even described his years as a POW doctor as the best work of his life, despite having been 'for nearly three years in a backwater as remote from medical culture as if we had been at the North Pole'.[57]

When doctors were alone in camps, this group identity and mutual professional and personal support was sorely missed. As the sole medical officer in a camp in Japan, Surgeon-Lieutenant Samuel Stening 'felt keenly his professional isolation, having no opportunity to discuss problems with others'.[58]

Captivity did not dull their zest for new knowledge and intellectual exercise. A 1944 Red Cross report on Formosa POW Camp 3 recorded a plea from Australian doctor Captain Patrick O'Donnell for some up-to-date medical textbooks: 'As malaria is main disease at Camp, inquires whether further supplies of atebrin could be sent. As medical doctor, should welcome up-to-date medical textbooks, especially on tropical diseases. Feels that 2½ years of imprisonment have brought him behind in his profession.'[59] There was also a sense that what doctors were doing eventually may be useful to the outside world. They could publish their findings and experiments in medical journals—they knew only too well how little was known about tropical disease at the time.

This sense of being men of science able to add to the body of medical knowledge for the greater public good even led doctors to appeal to Japanese doctors for supplies and better equipment. While discussing the many cases of tropical ulcers, Coates wrote:

> These ulcers, so prevalent a year ago, and now fortunately only represented here by old scars, deformities, and amputated legs, provided a most fruitful field of investigation. Being deprived of

bacteriological and biochemical equipment at the same time those ulcers were prevalent, we were unable to do more than carry out the gross clinical observations. Much valuable information was lost. We have the medical talent here and we are confronted by medical problems which could be solved in many cases if the appropriate equipment were available . . . Research of value to future generations of mankind could have been undertaken if such ordinary facilities were present . . . Medicine knows no national or racial limits, and a discovery which may yield local results in aiding cure [could have] far-reaching effects.[60]

Unfortunately for Allied prisoners, his Japanese colleague did not accede to Coates' request.

One meaningful aspect of their imprisonment was that doctors learned about conditions and treatments they otherwise might not have experienced in their civilian careers. While the reintegration of other POWs back into civilian life was 'as challenging as the battle for survival in the prisoner-of-war camp',[61] the doctors could look back on their years as prisoners with pride in their research, as well as their humanitarian achievements. In a postwar article in the *Medical Journal of Australia*, Duncan marvelled over a range of surgeries and procedures that had been done on 'these emaciated, exhausted men' in the environment of captivity. These included the removal of gall bladders, kidneys and spleens, draining liver abscesses, draining fluid from the pericardium (the sac around the heart), cranial decompression, and the surgical resection of rib segments.[62]

After the war, some doctors published medical articles, gave talks, and shared the knowledge they had gained, although admittedly this process took decades for some. Clearly, the doctors felt no shame in having been prisoners of the Japanese.

In that era in Australia, doctors were highly respected intellectual and community leaders, and their decisions were rarely if ever questioned or criticised. During captivity, doctors such as Coates and Dunlop performed hundreds of amputations on tropical ulcers. Those patients did not question their decisions to amputate, then or now, because they trusted them. The knowledge that their decisions would be trusted and upheld was one factor that helped the doctors shoulder the burdens of POW medicine.

Part of this confidence also made doctors take risks with their own health. Many tried out substitute medical treatments or unfamiliar foods on themselves. On Hainan for example, Roy Harris recalled that Aitken insisted on 'testing' all food first. This was also for a practical reason: 'Captain Bill Aitken always said to us, "Now boys don't eat anything until I've tried it. If it makes me sick I've got enough medicine to cure myself. But I haven't got medicine to cure a hundred men."'[63]

Just their presence in the camps provided a familiar and sane moral centre, a place for prisoners to take comfort. In many ways, the men viewed them as almost infallible—so when doctors paid the ultimate price for their efforts, the shock felt by the POWs was profound. In early 1942, Major Alan Hobbs noted in his diary that the death in Changi of Australian medical officer Major Gilbert Jose from malaria caused a panic among the men, and made them more conscious of their health and hygiene.[64] When popular doctor Major Kevin Fagan became seriously ill:

> For days everyone went around with concerned faces and many brought gifts from their meagre possessions and their rations in the hope that they would help his recovery... I doubt that the illness of any other man in Singapore would have produced such a reaction.[65]

What enabled doctors to cope in captivity was the psychological advantage of continuing to serve in a useful role they knew and understood. Not only did they keep their professional identity intact, but to a large extent they were also able to adapt and broaden their role.

However, for most doctors, their incarceration by the Japanese was by no means easy. In his memoir, Pavillard illustrated the heartbreaking and grim realities of the experience:

In describing these days, I may have given an impression of callousness, as though I and the other doctors were past feeling and suffering the situation. In a sense our emotions were anaesthetized: we could not have remained sane otherwise. But then and for a long time afterwards we were liable to find memory reasserting itself at night-time, and to wake up screaming from the black depths of nightmare: this still happens to me from time to time, and once again I see the jungle, the rain, and my friends turning liquid in a pit of flies and maggots.[66]

# 8

# THE LONG SHADOW: AFTER THE WAR

*... the spectacle of the emaciated skeletons of men on the one hand, and the oedematous, water-logged wrecks on the other, many with rotting, gangrenous ulcers of the legs, emitting a nauseating stench, lying in their pain and misery, was such as I never wish to witness again. The daily procession to the graveyard was a reminder to those still alive that death would soon end their suffering. The memory of it is not easily obliterated.*

LIEUTENANT COLONEL ALBERT E. COATES,
JAPANESE WAR CRIMES TRIAL STATEMENT, 1946[1]

Harry 'Happy' Smith, formerly an entertainer at the Hoyts Centre in Sydney, was the leader of the 'Changi Concert Party'. When he was a POW he played the 'Changi piano', which was carried into the camp after the fall of Singapore and was treasured by many POWs as a meeting point for concerts and singing. It was carefully transported back to Australia after the war, and is still in the Smith family's possession. The importance of such historical items was evident at a 1998 reunion held in Newcastle, New South Wales, where hundreds of ex-POWs, their wives and families sat in an auditorium and sang those songs that had been sung in captivity. Tears were shed and memories shared.

Most accounts of Australian imprisonment by the Japanese usually end in 1945. Yet for those POWs who survived, the years that followed were equally hard. The caring role of the medical staff who had looked after them in captivity continued for many years after the war ended. In several ways, the POW doctors remained key figures in their lives.

Just as doctors had a unique experience of captivity, their experience of postwar life cannot be equated with that of the general ex-POW population. In later years, they were forced to confront their own issues of reintegration into civilian life, both personally and professionally. In some ways this was an easier process for doctors because of the continuity between their prewar and postwar careers. In other ways, however, their adjustment was uniquely difficult. Although keen to put the experience behind them, whether they liked it or not, they would figure prominently in various postwar issues that were to arise.

## Going home

> Someone asked 'What do you think of Frank Sinatra?' I piped up in a cheeky voice, 'Who in hell is Frank Sinatra?' and with a surprised look on her face this person said, 'D'you mean to tell us you have never heard of Frank Sinatra?' I retorted, 'Have you ever been locked up for three and a half years? How the hell d'you think we would know Frank Sinatra?'[2]

On 6 and 9 August 1945, atomic bombs fell on Hiroshima and Nagasaki. A few days later the Pacific War ended. Many Allied POWs held in Japan witnessed the mushroom clouds on the horizon and knew something significant had occurred, but liberation still came as a surprise. The knowledge that the war was over filtered through to the camps throughout Asia at different times. In many, the Japanese commander called the senior Allied officers to his office and announced the news, reading

Japan's formal statement of surrender. Others took their time, fearing reprisals from prisoners. For many Australians, however, retribution against their former captors would have required much more physical and emotional energy than they had remaining, and few reprisals are recorded. Australian POW Tom Morris, who was still in a Thailand camp when told of the war's end, said, 'There was no feeling of euphoria, just an overwhelming tiredness.'[3] POWs could now walk around their camps without fear of abuse from their captors, hoping that repatriation was not too long away. Several camps conducted memorial services—a chance to grieve for those who had died over the past three and a half years. At Omuta Camp, Japan, a service held on 16 August commemorated 'our deceased comrades: young men, the sons of loving parents who shall miss them and wait in vain for their return'.[4]

Repatriation of Allied POWs depended on how isolated the camps were and levels of sickness among the men. Those on Ambon, for example, had to await repatriation by Navy ships. The sickest were taken first, and as previously mentioned there were national differences here: overall, Dutch prisoners were in better health than Australians, while the worst in health were the British troops.[5] The medical officers remained in the camps, refusing to be repatriated until everyone else had gone. As Allied food and medicine drops began arriving in camps throughout Asia, stuffed with rich and long-unfamiliar foods, men were still dying. The foods and drugs were an immediate help, yet doctors and officers had to regulate the distribution of the food as men became violently ill from the radical change in diet. Butter, bread, meat and other rich and almost forgotten foods were not well tolerated by men who had subsisted mainly on rice and watery vegetable soup for three and a half years. Private Harry Leslie recalled that the first time he and his comrades ate meat they were all terribly sick.[6] POW doctors advised repatriation medical teams that due to the recent change in diet, 'Anorexia, fever, vomiting, distension, colic and Diarrhoea have been common, and are likely to continue intermittently for some weeks.'[7]

The realisation that medicine had progressed in the outside world also was brought home to the doctors as they discovered a new drug called penicillin that was revolutionising medicine. For the last two years of the war it had been mass produced and distributed among Allied medical teams. Yet none of these POW doctors had ever heard of it and did not know of its powerful antibiotic properties. The discovery was bittersweet: penicillin, had it been available to them, would no doubt have saved many prisoners' lives.

Similarly, when Atebrin was distributed by repatriation medical teams among Australian POWs, there was almost total suppression of malaria within a month.[8]

Australian Army Rescue teams began to arrive in camps, initiating the process of evacuation, interview and repatriation. Instructions given to interviewing officers stressed the period before captivity: the Malaya campaign, Singapore and related matters, 'to ensure that a worthy and an accurate record of the experiences of their unit is included in the official history'.[9] While they were also instructed to ask about the men's experiences during captivity, these recollections were considered less important: 'Although the first aim should be to obtain recollections of the battle leading up to a man's capture, experiences in captivity, particularly if they were specially picturesque or illuminating, are also of great value.'[10]

Yet the interviewing officers seemed highly interested in the captivity experiences of the POW doctors. Such reports praised uncritically the work of the medical personnel, fostering a perception that these men were the 'heroes' of captivity. This was also based on the testimonies of other prisoners who were, according to one report, 'universally laudatory of the work of AAMC [Australian Army Medical Corps] in the camps'.[11] A similar report stated, 'The story of CHANGI is the triumph of Medical Services over obstruction frustration and oppression. I hope that full credit goes to all ranks of the AAMC for their epic efforts.'[12] The author of these reports, Lieutenant Colonel George T. Gibson, of the 2nd Australian POW Reception Group, described what he had heard of the doctors' work in captivity as a 'medical epic' and urged Official Medical Historian Allan Walker to obtain 'The full story of Thailand.'[13]

Recognising that POWs would have ongoing medical complications arising from captivity, the professional opinion of their doctors was immediately sought. They briefed the medical teams on what to expect when they received ex-POWs for assessment and on the intricacies of their multiple health and dietary problems. As many men were suffering from a number of conditions—acute and chronic tropical diseases and infections, on top of malnutrition and vitamin deficiencies—the POW doctors' expertise was needed to establish priorities and decide on treatment regimes.

Repatriation took months for some Australians. Many former POWs released in Asia while awaiting transport home indulged in leisure activities they had only dreamed about during captivity, illustrating the old POW joke that upon release the second thing they would do is take off their packs. Cases of venereal disease increased for the first time in years among newly liberated soldiers.[14] It may have been a response by POWs to reassure themselves that they could still perform sexually. Prolonged malnutrition had robbed men of their libidos early in captivity, and anxiety about postwar sexual dysfunction was common.

For some, this period proved a difficult transition in terms of preparing to return to 'normal' life. One former POW who was being assessed by the 102 Australian Convalescent Depot in Burleigh Heads, Queensland, requested to stay there another two months 'as he feels he will be more "balanced" after that period'.[15] The relief of liberation was also tempered by grief, as men found out what had happened to other prisoners. Dr Roy Mills wrote that he felt a 'terrible numbness, as we learned the fate of members of our unit and of friends in other units'.[16]

While doctors continued to perform their duties, incidents of other ex-POWs going AWOL (absent without leave) were common. Where ex-POWs were awaiting demobilisation in Australia, breaches of discipline became a widespread problem. They were reported as 'insubordinate and difficult to control'.[17] One report noted that while recovered POWs 'should be treated with every sympathy and consideration it is essential that such treatment should not be allowed to result in lack of discipline'. Although they should be treated with 'tolerance and tactful handling, these personnel are still soldiers and will conform to AMF [Australian Military Forces] standards of discipline'.[18] The harshness of the strict enforcement of such measures shows how little Australian authorities knew about or were prepared for the psychological impact of captivity.

In anticipation of receiving ex-POWs at 102 Australian Convalescent Depot, activities such as weekly movies and access to a piano were requested 'to keep these personnel occupied at night'.[19] Another report noted the 'discontent which still seems to exist among these Repatriated Prisoners' and requested various automobile parts so that 'in addition to manual workshops, interesting mechanical activities should be available to hold the interests of such personnel during treatment'.[20]

Assessments of ex-POWs' behaviour during repatriation was judged according to their prewar position as soldiers and hence did not apply to doctors. Disciplinary problems arose among a group of seventeen ex-POWs at the 102 Depot, due to their drinking, and 'truculent and discontented' behaviour: 'They talked loudly about having been promised they would be discharged and their spokesman (possibly self-appointed) was definite in his statement that they didn't regard themselves as soldiers any longer.' The particular bond between ex-POWs was also evident: 'These men are very loyal to each other and herd together and though they may at times disagree with the tactics of the others, they do not mention it outside their own circle.'[21]

A comparison with ex-POWs from the European theatre of war (EPOWs) showed that the EPOW remained well-behaved and, unlike his counterpart from Asia, had 'not forgotten that he is still in the army and accordingly adjusts himself to his environment'. It was doubted that their Asian camp counterparts would 'ever make satisfactory Army adjustment'.[22] Even at this early stage, the greater readjustment problems among the latter group was ascribed solely to their poor physical condition.[23]

The long-term ill health of these prisoners received comparatively little public attention. The media wanted to hear tales of torture, and stories that consolidated every backyard rumour of Japanese savagery. POWs 'found it difficult to counter with a list of diseases ... a history of illness could be evidence of ill-fortune, and survival then equally became a matter of good luck.'[24] Unfortunately, the media were not interested in their ongoing health issues and 'began what seemed to amount to a campaign to convince readers that these men were alright'.[25]

As the military medical authorities were preparing to receive the ex-POWs, many families still did not know whether their men were even alive. The initial reunions between the former POWs and their loved ones caused a great deal of anxiety and apprehension. Some men had been captured while single; others were married with children—but the images of their lives that they had carried and nurtured during captivity were rarely what they returned to. Although most POWs had put on a lot of weight by the time they were reunited, and for the first time in three years had been receiving adequate medical care, the shock of their altered, aged appearances was a memory many of their families still carry. Having joined up at fifteen, Bob Rolls was nineteen when he returned home from the camps. He was looking for his father at his battalion's release at the Melbourne Showgrounds. A 'fellow walked along, and I said to him "G'day, mate". He said, "Hello, Digger. Welcome home. I'm looking for Bob Rolls. Do you know him at all?" I said, "Yes, Dad. I know him".'[26]

Families of returning POWs were advised by the Repatriation Commission not to ask them about their experience, fearing that it would only keep reminding them, and that not discussing it would help ex-POWs put it all behind them.[27] Returned Australian POW Roy Whitecross commented that in any case many people simply did not believe the ex-POWs' horrifying stories of captivity.[28]

While there was an understanding that ex-POWs would have suffered through their ordeal, Repatriation Commission authorities believed a former prisoner 'should not be encouraged to regard himself as a palpably abnormal person, with a spirit scarred, a mind warped or a body weakened by his experiences. That such changes will occur in some individuals is no doubt true, but we must not brand these men as necessarily so affected.'[29] They suggested that POWs should not be made to feel different from non-POW returned servicemen and women, as a sense of shared experience would be of more comfort to them. Of course many ex-POWs were not eager to share their stories. Former POW orderly John Higgs recalled his first meeting with his parents: 'What I remember most about the reunion was that we could find so little to talk about; Mum just sat beside me with her hand on my knee, and Dad did his best to conceal his tears.'[30] As historian Michael McKernan writes, 'many men simply could not speak; no one, they reasoned, except a fellow prisoner could ever understand'.[31]

The continuing physical and psychological problems of former POWs took a significant toll on their families. Among Gull Force survivors, families members attested that 'Depression, restlessness and moodiness demanded sometimes more tolerance and patience.'[32] Ill health forced some men to be frequent hospital visitors, and particular 'behavioural quirks' required a lot of emotional support and understanding—such as panicking at the sound of overhead aircraft, a continuing obsession with food, and tensions with children that may not have had father figures for four years of their childhood.[33] On the other hand, just to be with their loved ones again was a constant blessing. Dr Peter Hendry, for example, met his four-year-old daughter for the first time when he returned to Australia: 'When I arrived home, she came rushing up and jumped into my arms and said, "You're my Daddy". It was wonderful.'

## War Crimes

Immediately after the war, doctors played a crucial role in testifying at Japanese War Crimes trials. Their authority and expertise in empirically assessing captors' treatment and cruelty were heavily relied upon. Japanese War Crimes trials were largely based on medical information:

> . . . they were cases in which one or more of the following behaviours was alleged: withholding medical and related supplies, forcing ill men to work; maltreating medical personnel, maltreating patients, preventing the ill from obtaining medical care; conducting illegal

or unethical experimentation; withholding food; functioning in a medically incompetent manner; wilfully neglecting the welfare of the sick and injured; interfering with International Red Cross supplies; and finally, performing euthanasia.[34]

Doctors' testimony provided crucial facts about Japanese neglect through medical records, specific information about lack of medicines, and precise knowledge of nutrition and calorie amounts. They could quote from valuable records and diaries that had remained hidden in the camps. These were now open for inspection, and records that had been buried at various stages of captivity (often in gravesites to ensure the Japanese would not search there) were recovered.

From the beginning, therefore, doctors were important spokesmen for the POW experience. That their statements were regarded as essential and authoritative also served to indicate their accepted status within the ex-POW community.

## Postwar physical health

At the end of the war Dr Ian Duncan interviewed every Australian and English soldier in his camp. He was the only medical officer in the camp and felt it was his duty to record their disabilities. Their responses surprised him:

> And you'd say to them, what diseases have you had as a prisoner of war. Oh nothing much Doc, nothing much at all. Did you have malaria? Oh yes, I had malaria. Did you have dysentery? Oh yes, I had dysentery. Did you have beriberi? Oh yes, I had beriberi. Did you have pellagra? Yes, I had pellagra; but nothing much. All these are lethal diseases. But that was the norm, you see, everyone had them. Therefore they accepted them as normal.[35]

The Repatriation Commission was in no doubt that the medical legacy of captivity would be a complex one, and immediately after the war ended drafted reports on how to cope with the problem. The Commission realised that:

> There is a general consensus of opinion that the physical sequelae of serious illness are more likely to affect Ps.O.W. (J) than any other class of repatriates or ex-servicemen. These sequelae are likely to affect their rehabilitation adversely, unless they can be looked for, diagnosed and cured.[36]

The Commission took full account of the expertise of ex Japanese-held POW (JPOW) doctors. It set up a Repatriation Committee composed entirely of doctors, including four Australian ex-JPOW doctors. A further seventeen advisers provided information to the Committee, nine of whom were ex-JPOW doctors. As Lieutenant Colonel Edward Dunlop advised in a report to the Commission, 'whilst the number of ex Ps.O.W. medical officers is small, and many are preoccupied with their own rehabilitation . . . their special knowledge and the confidence they engender in ex Ps.O.W., born of shared experience, renders their co-operation most valuable.'[37]

Many studies have been undertaken both in Australia and overseas on the long-term impact of captivity on the health of POWs, but these have often been slow to reach the attention of the public and the civilian medical profession.[38] In Australia over the postwar decades, various studies of ex-POWs found that their mortality rate was higher than that of the non-POW population for up to fourteen years after the war, before flattening out.[39] Many former prisoners continued to be plagued by the tropical diseases and other medical conditions they had contracted in the camps. New medical problems also developed which the men believed were the direct result of their POW experience. However, the important findings of these and other studies were little publicised.

For decades after the war, the Liverpool School of Tropical Medicine continued to see many British ex-POWs who had strongyloides worm infestations that civilian doctors misdiagnosed, attributing the strange skin patterns produced by the worm to stress. In a 1980 study of 602

British ex-POWs by Dr Geoffrey Gill and Dr Dion Bell, 128 men still had a tropical disease and 20 per cent of them still had strongyloidiasis. Gill and Bell's study also revealed that four men still suffered from tropical ulcers—one of whom had ulcers that had never healed—and that other persistent health problems from captivity were liver disease, duodenal ulcers and post traumatic stress disorder.[40] Another study by Gill and Bell two years later showed that of 898 former POWs, 5.5 per cent still endured long-term effects of malnutrition, resulting in nutritional neuropathy conditions such as burning feet, optic atrophy and sensori-neural deafness.[41]

It was not only illness that caused the POWs' ongoing medical problems. The physical abuse by their captors also had a lasting effect. One of Gill's subjects still had ten rib fractures 36 years after a beating he received in captivity. Nine per cent had persistent ear disease, mostly the result of 'general beatings, blows to the head with the flat of a sword and, in one case, a pencil thrust through the ear'. Three suffered permanent hearing loss from the dropping of either the Hiroshima or the Nagasaki bombs.[42] Many more medically significant results could have been found, but as the research took place so long after the war, many former POWs had already died.

A comprehensive study of the health of 600 Australian ex-JPOWs was conducted in 1984 by a group of former POW doctors and their colleagues. It found that more than a quarter of the men still had hookworm and chronic digestive problems, hundreds still had amoebic dysentery, one-third had tinea, 22 per cent suffered from impotence (judged not to be due to psychological factors), 15 per cent had permanent visual damage from malnutrition, 25 per cent had bronchitis, and half had chronic back problems from injuries sustained in captivity.[43] Suffering from hookworm, Osmund Vickers-Bush wrote:

> For many years after we came home we were treated with chenapodium and tetra-chloride followed by 2 oz. mag. sulph. (Epsom Salts). Our motions were hot fluid and we couldn't move far from

the toilet. The mixture had a vile taste something like diesel oil and petrol. This treatment left us very weak for days.[44]

Other common problems were premature senility and particularly recurrent malaria. Even back in 1945, Major Burnett Clarke wrote, 'Large numbers of patients who have returned to Australia can tell of 30, 40 or 50 recurrences.'[45] In the early 1960s, former POW Lieutenant F. Stuart Peach was one of many who still experienced frequent malarial attacks.

As with other POWs, poor health would stay with the doctors for the rest of their lives. Being medical professionals had not made them immune to the ravages that three and a half years of captivity had wrought on all those imprisoned. British doctor F. E. Cayley wrote that after many years:

> I gradually found my attacks of malaria were getting less frequent. But the strongyloides didn't clear up till a new treatment came out ten years later. If I went to a party, they would creep about under my skin. I am still liable to get upset tummies. My terrible dreams and the fear took a long time to go.[46]

Of the original 106 Australian doctors who were prisoners of the Japanese, ten died in captivity and seven were given a medical discharge status of 'D', which meant they were granted an immediate, 100 per cent disability pension. One of these men had begun the war as the youngest of the POW doctors: Roy Mills. After the war he spent two years in hospital recovering from severe tuberculosis.

Many POWs praised the Repatriation Commission (now called the Department of Veterans' Affairs) for its care of returned prisoners. Mills, for one, said he was 'eternally grateful' for the care he received. Dunlop, however, was more critical, especially of some of its early mistakes. He felt ex-POWs were assessed too soon after liberation, when they 'had enjoyed a few months of idleness and the luxury of good food in quantity', which caused a feeling of 'well-being and confidence'. This feeling, in Dunlop's opinion, was soon to prove 'illusory and transient'.[47] He also cited problems with medical assessments made by doctors inexperienced in tropical and starvation diseases, and by POW medical records being disregarded due to their 'unorthodox nature'. Former POW orderly John Higgs, by now an unacknowledged expert in tropical disease, recalled his farcical medical examination:

> One of the doctors who examined me appeared almost too young to have qualified and was quite bemused as I rattled off the range of diseases that I had racked up. He stared at his notes for some time, then advised me to 'take things carefully' and expressed the view that 'your life has probably been shortened by ten years or more'.[48]

In the United States, American ex-POW Granville Summerlin met the same lack of medical expertise. Suffering from unhealed tropical ulcers, and in hospital for a year after liberation, Summerlin felt his doctors 'were very unfamiliar with all the tropical diseases and stuff. They didn't know anything about it in the States.'[49]

Dunlop claimed many men had been discharged without adequate examination, citing the case of one man who been discharged with amoebic dysentery without receiving any treatment. Duncan felt the Commission should have granted all ex-POWs a provisional 'temporary disability' status for twelve months. Dr Bruce Hunt concurred, stating that many liberated POWs had gone straight back into the workforce once they returned home, with no adequate period of rest and recuperation.[50] He added that all ex-POWs exhibited a form of 'asthenia'—an 'unnatural fatigue and feeling of inadequacy'. Dunlop said no POW was immune to this asthenia, regardless of their status or previous profession, himself included: since his return, family members had noticed in him a lack of interest in recreational activities and 'some personality changes'.[51]

Once a decade or so had passed, men were finding that medical conditions from captivity, such as bowel and digestive problems, were still with them, and that some injuries had never healed. Because of the lack of comprehensive medical records in the camps—despite all the best efforts of the doctors—there was often little hard evidence that injuries or chronic conditions were a direct result of captivity, making claims for compensation difficult. Also, many former prisoners did not seek medical help in the early postwar period, wishing to put the experience behind them, and not wanting to be a 'parasite' on the government. As Dunlop suggested, many newly liberated POWs also played down the state of their health when they were being medically assessed, knowing that the faster they were deemed medically fit, the sooner they could be reunited with their families: 'it is known that some examinations were rushed through'.[52] Many also assumed 'with the confidence of youth, that they would soon shake off their disabilities' and so they 'failed to put on the official record the detail of their problems that would have made their later claims for compensation unassailable'.[53] This bureaucratic difficulty was also experienced by British POWs. John Sharpe, a former POW with the Leicestershire Regiment, received only a 40 per cent pension when the Ministry of Pensions determined that his rheumatism could not be proven to be connected with 'my lying on a damp floor for three years or vitamin deficiency . . . That decision hurt and still does.'[54]

However, in Australia, this lack of disclosure by the liberated POWs when they were being initially medically assessed was taken into account as early as 1947, when the Repatriation Commission foresaw that this might count against men's interests in the future: 'It is quite conceivable that the information on the proceedings of Final Medical Boards is incomplete, which could be prejudicial to the applicant.'[55]

Another problem was that POWs were complaining of medical complications that did not fit neatly into a disability category recognised by Repatriation guidelines. One doctor who was finding it difficult to classify the men's problems reported that 'they complain of tiredness, and fatigue, morning nausea and dry retching, vague abdominal discomfort and distension after meals, a feeling of restlessness and lack of concentration, and are obviously worried in themselves that they don't feel well'.[56]

It was in this respect that the ex-POW doctors became crucial to the ongoing welfare of many ex-prisoners, being in the unique position of having been their carers during captivity, but also being respected practising medical professionals. Ex-POW doctors such as Mills, Duncan and Dunlop spearheaded many campaigns to gain official recognition of the connection between illnesses suffered by the POWs in captivity and their continuing complaints. For decades several sat on panels set up by ex-POW associations to help them receive compensation for long-term physical and psychological problems. Duncan recalled that in 1992 his panel reviewed more than 500 POW veterans, many suffering from stress-related problems.[57]

The Repatriation Commission in 1947 recommended that for ex-POWs 'there should be created a close patient-doctor relationship akin to that encountered in the practice of "family physicians"'. It added that 'towards that end medical practitioners who shared their experiences in the hands of the Japanese, and therefore are known to them, should be available for consultation and advice'.[58] Over the following decades, it was common for ex-POWs to seek treatment and medical advice from their former POW doctors. Many expressed discomfort in seeing other doctors, as they felt they were misunderstood or classed as malingerers. In this way, their former doctors continued to remain a source of comfort and support in civilian life.

In hindsight, where the Repatriation Commission failed in its long-term planning was in not doing more to make civilian doctors aware of the medical problems that ex-POWs would face, for many of these doctors 'were not alive during the war' and could not 'understand what veterans were going through'.[59] In 1990 a pamphlet entitled *Lifelong Captives* was prepared by the Department of Veterans' Affairs, aiming to educate civilian doctors about 'the hardships these men and women experienced and the physical and mental legacies which they carried'.[60] That this was not produced until 45 years after the war shows how long this process of recognition took.

In terms of compensation for ex-POWs, payments of £32 were distributed to POWs from the sales of Japanese assets in Australia; some later received equally small payments from the sale of other overseas assets. In 1974 the Whitlam government granted free medical treatment to all ex-POWs, ending the stipulation that health problems had to be connected to their experiences in captivity. Various other campaigns for compensation from the Japanese government were conducted, the main one by a multinational group of 25,000 former Far East POWs who petitioned that $34,500 be given to each survivor. This appeal was overturned by the Japanese courts in 1998 after a three-year battle. Many POWs were not surprised. Tom Uren, a former Labor minister and ex-POW, commented that the campaign was directed towards the wrong government: 'I always argued it was the responsibility of our government because they were the ones who sent us to war.'[61] Uren felt it was more important that Japan ensure that its postwar generations learned the truth of their soldiers' actions during the war.

In 2001 the Australian Government granted all surviving ex-POWs (or their widows) a one-off payment of $25,000 in recognition of the unique hardships they experienced.[62] The Japanese government did eventually pay war reparations to many Asian countries, although these payments were for economic reconstruction, not to compensate individual victims. Other ex-prisoners still argue that financial compensation by the Japanese is of secondary importance compared to a sincere acknowledgement of regret.

Doctors themselves were rarely involved in such high-profile compensation actions. Some, such as Dunlop—who during captivity sustained 'a burning hatred of them with only a few exceptions'—advocated forgiveness of the Japanese after the war, and 'the importance of international cooperation and understanding'.[63] While he described the Japanese as an 'insect society, with a pattern of blind, unswerving acceptance of leadership whether towards good or evil', Japan's successful rebuilding of itself after the war gave him a different perspective: 'There was much to admire in Japanese courage and deadly earnestness of purpose.'[64] Understandably, many ex-POWs did not share Dunlop's pioneering attitude. As Bill Flowers said, 'They want us to forget and forgive. Well you can't forget . . . I don't forgive those who caused the death of fellows who were good friends of mine. Why should I?'

## Postwar psychological problems

As well as the long-term physical repercussions of captivity, psychiatric illness is also comparatively common among former POWs. Decades after the war, Dr Ian Duncan noted that 'Many ex-prisoners have not gone through one day with an incident, word or smell evoking memories of prison.'[65] The incidence of psychiatric illness in POWs has been difficult to quantify accurately as many men chose not to seek help for the psychological problems they faced after the war. Despite this, however, enough studies have been done to show that the psychological impact of captivity on postwar life was complex and widespread. Indeed, only two years after the end of the war, the Repatriation Committee acknowledged that 'some men and women are finding difficulty in re-establishing themselves in civilian life'.[66]

Unusually for this time, the Repatriation Commission recognised among ex-POWs a psychological problem it called 'neurosis', which it said was of 'prime importance'. However this was followed by the assertion that all veterans would suffer psychologically, and singling out POWs for special treatment would only make them feel worse. Men who had been prisoners of the Japanese were not to be made to feel 'that they are a class apart from the general run of discharged members of the Forces'.[67] A 'leading Sydney psychiatrist' who had experience with European and Japanese POWs was also quoted as stating, 'At present neurosis among prisoners of war is minimal and what has occurred is mild in character and easily cured. Proper rehabilitation would successfully prevent any unusual degree of nervous illness amongst this group of men.'[68]

Various studies worldwide would prove this assertion wrong and demonstrate that the incidence of psychiatric illness was much higher among former prisoners of the Japanese. A 1970 study by Dr M. D. Nefzger showed that in the first ten years after release, ex-POWs had a higher mortality rate than the normal population, and that this was only partly due to suicide and accidents.[69] Gill reported in his 1980 UK study that 209, or 34.8 per cent, of his subjects were diagnosed with 'significant psychiatric illness'. Only in seven of the men was this due to non-captivity experiences: 'All the usual symptoms of anxiety and depression were present, but weepiness (many cried at interview), retardation, poor memory and obsessive traits and nightmares of their POW experiences were specially common.'[70] He described one particularly sad case:

> Since being a POW in the Far East, this patient had suffered bouts of depression, feelings of inadequacy, poor memory, night sweats, indecisiveness, reluctance to mix, weeping, retardation and headaches. He had never seen a doctor about this and said 'I haven't even told my wife'. He cried openly while recounting his lonely mental suffering since repatriation and said how much better he felt at having 'got it off his chest'.[71]

In Australia, a study by Duncan and colleagues similarly showed that 46 per cent of POWs surveyed experienced constant anxiety, and 20 per cent felt an 'inability to cope'.[72] Unspoken psychological effects of their ordeal included recurring nightmares and flashbacks of particular events or brutalities they witnessed. Many also 'exhibit symptoms of stress; some have minor obsessive behaviour characteristics (they wash excessively, they abhor waste, or they do not like to be alone); some suffer periodic depression, intensified by "survivor guilt".'[73] In the 1960s, when former Australian orderly Bevan Warland-Browne visited Japan for an international Rotary conference, his first unconscious instinct on getting out of the plane at the airport and seeing Japanese guards was to bow to them.[74] Former POW orderly John Higgs found his memories of Railway camps also came back to him in unanticipated ways:

> The pervading smells of the camp—of incontinence, of decay, of gangrene, of death, of burning—were impossible to evade, nor have they since been fully erased from memory. Even now, an occasional odour from, say, a Hong Kong back street or some such is enough to remind me of one of the worst features of that miserable place in Burma.[75]

Former American POW orderly Griff Douglas worked with dysentery patients on the Railway. Part of his duties involved washing their soiled and bloody blankets every morning in the river. Years after the war, he found he could not change his new daughter's nappy without vomiting.[76]

A 1986 study compared the rate of psychiatric illness, including anxiety and depression, in POWs and other veterans of the Pacific and South-East Asian campaigns. Despite the fact that the ex-POWs had fewer hospital admissions, the rates were higher in this group. Significantly, the authors concluded that although the experience of both groups was extremely traumatic, that of ex-POWs of the Japanese 'was almost incomprehensible'.[77]

Many ex-prisoners would only discuss their feelings when in each other's company, making the reunions and group activities of Australian ex-POW associations crucial. Dick Armstrong said that it was while nursing cholera patients on the Railway that 'most of us began building around ourselves brick walls of self preservation through which we allowed no one except our fellow prisoners to enter. In many cases we still maintain those "walls of privacy"; even today.'[78]

Wives of ex-POWs also found support at POW reunions from other women who were having similar problems coping with the erratic and often distressing behaviour of their husbands. Duncan's study found that 'men had accepted their often apparent disabilities as a way of life and had lived with them uncomplainingly for years', and that only by talking to their wives was 'the true story' revealed.[79] His study also noted that most of its 600 subjects showed signs of depression, and that the rate of broken or unsatisfactory marriages was extremely high.

Much has been written about post traumatic stress disorder (PTSD, also known as 'K-Z syndrome', 'shell-shock', 'war neurosis' and 'combat fatigue'), and that Australian ex-POWs were experiencing it long before the term passed into common language. A study of 108 former World War II POWs at Melbourne's Heidelberg Repatriation Hospital found 45 per cent were suffering from PTSD,[80] with many other studies also showing higher rates of chronic depression and anxiety.[81] 'Debriefing' and ongoing counselling after the war may have alleviated years of mental distress, but the science of psychiatry was still in early development, and the long-term effects of trauma had not been widely investigated. After the war, men suffering from stress were labelled 'troppo' and 'psycho'. Mills noted that, perhaps as compensation for these feelings, in the men from his unit there was a common attitude of pushing to achieve beyond their abilities, a 'continual need to strive'.[82]

## Psychological impacts on doctors

While no comparable studies were conducted of doctors as a group, anecdotally, these psychological problems seem to have been less prominent for doctors in postwar life. The continuity of their careers from captivity to civilian life was certainly one important factor in this, alongside several other important features that set the doctors apart.

Over the postwar years, many Australian POWs found themselves trying to rationalise their experience or find something positive in it:

> They believed it had made them more tolerant and understanding of others, while strengthening their own characters. They treasured the mateship that their shared suffering had nurtured. For all its horrors their captivity remained the most intense experience of their lives.[83]

While this was also true for the doctors, they had less need to find reasons to come to terms with their captivity—they knew they had done their best and that they had saved lives. Some continued to receive letters from people all over the world thanking them for saving their lives. Sometimes these men spent years tracking down doctors through ex-POW associations. Dr Phil Millard received two letters from former British POWs, one of whom wrote in June 1986: 'I have long felt the wish to write to you to thank you for all the dedication and skill with which you saved my right leg 44 years ago in Tarsa[u] POW camp.' In the very primitive surgical conditions in that camp, Millard saved Russell Ong's leg from amputation by applying a skin graft. Ong felt that 'with the start you gave me, I threw off my self-pity, and mentally began the process of living again, *because I wanted to*' (Ong's emphasis). In 1980

Ong was diagnosed with carcinoma of the nose and sinus, and he said his wartime connection with Millard helped him through this experience as well. He ended his moving letter with 'you and a few others from your profession, are rarely out of my thoughts'.[84]

From the beginning of liberation, doctors returned to civilian life congratulated for their work as POWs—work that was easy for people to understand. Doctors were seen as heroes who had kept men alive against heavy odds. On the other hand, the public had little comprehension of what other POWs had actually done and how they had worked, particularly in camps that were not well known. Bill Hammon worked in Manchurian mines for two years as a POW. When he retired to the mining town of Cessnock in New South Wales, he met a local miner who remarked, 'But you wouldn't know anything about coal mining would you?' Hammon replied, 'I've got news for you!'[85]

There is an implicit undercurrent that what was being praised was the doctors' *action* versus the perception of *inaction* of the other POWs in captivity. Returning to a culture that could not reconcile an Allied victory with the horrific POW experience, some POWs felt others saw them as having been shamed by being taken prisoner, robbed of their role in war and at the whim of cruel foreign captors. Former Australian POW officer Lieutenant Harry Medlin recalled that, when being repatriated on a ship, he heard

> . . . a broadcast to ex-JPOWs telling them they should not feel guilty, that their country was proud of them, and all this crap. It would have been better not to have said anything. Because all of a sudden you think, hell, am I supposed to be guilty about something?[86]

This is not to suggest that the doctors' transition to postwar life was easy or uniform. Their experiences too were severely traumatic.

During his first year after liberation, Dr Robert Pufflett just stayed at home with his parents, reading and trying to catch up on what he had missed. He described it as 'probably the worst year of my life . . . I'd lost four years . . . I'd missed everything. Missed all my friends, everything.' Unlike most POW doctors, he refused to continue contact with any of his former fellow prisoners except for a few officer friends, and he never joined an ex-POW association or took part in reunions. After many decades, he reflected, 'I think the whole thing isolated me, and I've been isolated ever since.' He never discussed his experiences, even with his family. When asked if his wife had ever questioned him about his experiences as a POW, he replied:

> No. No. Her brother was a prisoner of war but I never knew him. No I've never talked to anybody. I've never talked to anybody like I have to you on this occasion. I suppose it's because I'm reaching the end of the road, and it doesn't matter now as far as I'm concerned.

Commenting on the apparent rise of PTSD in the later decades of the twentieth century, Dr Rowley Richards said that every POW, including himself, would have suffered from it. He added, 'Every now and again when I give talks to various groups, they say, "What counselling did you have?" My reaction is, "Hang on, what's counselling?" There was no such thing. It was a case of "get on with it".'

As with many POWs, difficult memories caught up with doctors eventually, and for some became harder to suppress. As the daughter of Dr Colin Juttner recalled, 'In his last years, Dad suffered from quite severe depression. War memories flooded back and plagued him and he became more moody . . . he seemed obsessed with his POW years and talked about them with me a great deal.'[87]

Some doctors remained haunted by the pressures their roles brought and the horrors they witnessed. Dr Gordon Marshall, the Australian dentist on Ambon who was forced by circumstance to provide medical care for his men, died in 1972 saying he 'never really recovered from his war time experiences'.[88] It was noted in his obituary that during his postwar career, he constructed dental instruments by hand—possibly a legacy of his war years. The memories of captivity were similarly long and powerful for Dr Ian Duncan. When interviewed in 1993 as a 77-year-old, he still could not watch a baseball game because it reminded him too much of seeing prisoners beaten to death with baseball bats.[89]

Dr Roy Mills, an extremely kind and sensitive man, initially refused my first invitation to be interviewed. Two years later, after I had interviewed many of his friends and had 'checked out', he contacted me and said he was ready. While Mills had been interviewed many times before about his POW experiences, he wrote to me after my first visit about the anxiety the memories still produced: 'We look forward to your next visit. I was exhausted for two days after the last, but the biggest factor was the mental preparation and lack of sleep on the night preceding—it is silly, but it happens.'[90]

Such examples show that doctors were by no means immune to the psychological impact of captivity. While they may have blocked out or rationalised most of their experiences at the time, they too endured a painful legacy.

## Careers after captivity

> The doctor is still a champion of the individual; he stands at the springs of life and death in peace as in war, and as a citizen he must accept this challenge.[91]

While ex-POWs had certain bonds that would always unite them, postwar life saw everyone go their separate ways and try to establish normality again. In a follow-up study of Gull Force survivors, Joan Beaumont found that in the decades after the war, many men changed careers a number of times, some through soldier settlement schemes, while others found their chosen career soon after the war and stayed with it until retirement. However, she argued, 'many (though not all) felt they had suffered professionally', such as by being less able to cope with work-related stress and responsibility, having poor concentration, or simply finding working indoors too claustrophobic.[92] Former Australian POW Reg Nossiter found that his nerves were so bad after returning home that he couldn't be around large groups of people. He felt his previous employers demoted him in order to keep him 'out of the way'.[93]

Dr F. E. Cayley's attitude on returning home to England after the war was typical of many POW doctors:

> I found my wife, my father and my sister. My mother had died. I was thirty, weighed about seven stone, wanted children, and had to find a job, get rid of my diseases, get my psyche settled down, and bring my medical knowledge up to date.[94]

Some doctors experienced anxiety about returning to their medical career—one in which they had also missed opportunities for advancement. Mills recalled, 'You were conscious there was a lot you didn't know but the thing that worried you most was that you might be blissfully ignorant of something that everybody else presumed you did know.' At St Vincent's Hospital in Sydney after the war, Richards was anxious to 'catch up':

> I remember one of the things that I was keen on doing was as many plasters as possible. I remember one of the other residents—'Oh, I've done two or three, I don't need any practice, you can do them if you want to.' You know, that sort of attitude. We were flat out trying to catch up for what we'd missed out on.

Like many other prisoners who had lived for years where all thoughts surrounded food and survival, Hendry found his POW experience had given him a new outlook on what was important in life. He said of his return to civilian life, 'They were talking about things I didn't understand. The local theatres and social gossip. It drove me mad, the yak yak yak and the noise . . . suddenly we came back to a world which was frivolous.' This reshaped sense of values accompanied many doctors back to Australia. Richards stated that his years as a POW taught him that 'possessions were only things and I would never let them possess me. Of infinitely greater value were our relationships and mateship.'[95]

The POW experience influenced many of the doctors in choosing or changing their medical specialties after the war. For example, some switched to obstetrics and gynaecology, a branch of medicine far removed from men and death. Others who had never been interested in surgery, but after years of being forced to do it found they enjoyed it and became surgeons after the war. Having learned so much about tropical medicine, British doctor Bill Hetreed decided to spend his career in Africa specialising in it. Mills, although he had originally wanted to be a surgeon, became a chest specialist after the war. During captivity he received a chest injury during the Malaya campaign, and he also contracted tuberculosis, naturally giving him a very personal interest in that area of medicine.

A former American POW, Dr Murray Glusman, specialised in neuropsychiatry after the war, focusing in particular on aggression, fear and anxiety. His son commented, 'It wasn't until quite recently that I realized that perhaps his war experiences had something to do with that, having been so traumatized . . . his attempts to come to terms with that in some ways was instrumental in the direction of his future career.'[96]

There were other, less tangible influences. Dr Des Brennan said that his years as a POW doctor reduced his tolerance for unnecessary suffering and made him 'learn to accept death'. Richards, on the other hand, did not share Brennan's feeling: 'I don't think I've ever come to terms with patients who die. I didn't then and I still don't.' What he *did* learn as a POW doctor were unique assessment skills. At one point during captivity when he was ill and feeling disheartened, he said to Albert Coates, 'When we get back we'll never see any malaria, we'll never see any dysentery. We're just wasting our time.' Coates replied, 'Well you've learned something that only a few doctors ever learn, most never learn, and the ones who do learn it take a lifetime to do it.' When Richards responded somewhat sceptically, Coates explained, 'You know when a man is sick.' At the time Richards thought, 'What a trite, stupid statement to make.' But after the war he realised Coates was right:

> We could tell at a distance if anybody was a bit sicker than he was yesterday or whatever . . . There would be occasions when somebody would come with a minor complaint and you'd realise that there was something really behind it. You develop that something, being able to recognise when somebody was sick.

On a lighter note, Hendry recalled going to a party when he first got back to Australia where he was reunited with an old medical friend, who after fifteen minutes told him, 'You know, I think it did you the world of good being a POW—you were an awful bastard before.'

The careers of other medical personnel were similarly affected. After working as a POW orderly for three and a half years, Gordon Nichols found a desk job too boring, and spent the next 40 years with the NSW Ambulance Service because he had found the medical work of captivity so stimulating. Redmond Sheedy, a sergeant with the 2/3rd Machine Gun Battalion who also spent captivity as an orderly, pursued a career in medicine after the war because he had developed such a keen interest in it.

Gunner Jim Dixon and Lieutenant Bob Goodwin, soldiers with the 2/10th Field Regiment, both became doctors after the war. They wrote that through watching the work of their POW doctors, 'we have been driven by the role model provided by such people as Kevin Fagan, Albert Coates and those many doctors and medical professionals who had such an influence'.[97]

Many doctors who served in captivity went on to have prestigious careers. Professor (later Sir) Michael Woodruff became a world leader in organ transplantation, performing the first kidney transplant in 1960 at the University of Edinburgh. He may never have taken this direction in his career had it not been for a chance reading of a medical textbook in Changi which discussed skin grafts in abdominal surgery.[98] Another was Dr John Cade, who revolutionised psychiatry by discovering the uses of lithium in patients with bipolar affective disorder (formerly known as manic depression) in 1948.[99] During his 25 years as a lecturer at the University of Melbourne he taught thousands of medical students about the intricacies of mental disease. The Royal Melbourne Hospital dedicated a wing to his memory in January 2000, and Neil Cole wrote a play about his life called *Dr Cade* which was performed in Sydney in 2003.

Several doctors had medical fellowships and university bursaries named after them to commemorate their legacy. Some who were so honoured include Dr Glyn White, who became a renowned specialist in neonatal paediatrics, Sir Albert Coates, who was a pioneer in neurosurgery, and Dr Hedley Summons, a leader in otolaryngology (ear, nose and throat surgery). Dr Burnett Clarke continued his prewar specialisation in radiology, becoming a renowned authority in the field but ultimately paying the price for his career-long exposure to radiation.

Over recent years, I have met dozens of former students and colleagues of these doctors. Many remembered being in awe of these men and knew of their POW experience. Interestingly, most commented that they rarely if ever openly referred to their POW years or work.

Museum exhibits in Australia, England and Thailand, established to commemorate the Japanese POW experience, all acknowledge the important role played by doctors in captivity. Many doctors also received honours and awards after the war. Dr Bruce Hunt, hoewer, was angered that many medical officers did not receive the official recognition he believed they deserved. In a 1948 letter to politician William Kent Hughes (a former POW of the Japanese himself), Hunt wrote scathingly that senior officers often had no real 'first hand knowledge' of what the lower ranks, non-commissioned officers and medical personnel had suffered or achieved in captivity:

> Had you this knowledge not only would you have heartily endorsed the recommended promotions, but you would have refrained from making such a silly mess of the list of all recommendations for decorations sent in by Lt. General (now Brigadier) Galleghan. The omission of such gallant and distinguished medical officers as Kevin Fagan and Roy Mills from that list and the inclusion in their stead of a number of regimental officers who did routine work in relative comfort in Singapore Island throughout the captivity makes the list farcical and valueless in the eyes of all who really know who did what from 1942 to 1945.[100]

Fagan in fact received a personal letter apologising for his non-inclusion in a list of 8th Division Honours, particularly for his work with 'H' Force on the Railway. He had been recommended for an OBE but was only listed as having been Mentioned in Dispatches. The letter thanked him for his service 'nobly done but rewarded in a very minor way'.[101]

Several doctors made pilgrimages to POW sites decades after the war. Many of these were conducted between 1991 and 1995 to coincide with the 50-year anniversaries of significant dates. The 'Hellfire Pass' Museum in Kanchanaburi, Thailand, opened in 1998, commemorating the work and lives of Allied POWs lost in its construction, after a Herculean effort led by an Australian living in Thailand, Rod Beattie, to uncover sections of the track that had been overgrown.

## Why 'Weary' Dunlop?

One of the most common questions I encountered while researching this book was 'Why is Sir Edward "Weary" Dunlop the famous one?' How did a POW doctor become the most recognisable war figure in Australia? Why was he singled out among the 106 Australian doctors who all did much the same work in captivity, endured the same hardships and personal pressures, and many of whom also went on to prestigious postwar medical careers? How did he come to be so venerated, as seen in the quote below:

> Significantly, the towering Australian figure thrown up by the war was a POW doctor, the extravagantly lionised 'Weary' Dunlop, who never fired a shot in anger ... it is a wonderful thing indeed that Australia's pre-eminent hero of World War II should be a healer, a nurturer and preserver of life rather than a destroyer of it.[102]

Dunlop became the public face of all the POW doctors, and of all Australian POWs. Prominent statues of him stand in Canberra, Melbourne and his birthplace, Benalla in Victoria, and his image is often used in any media stories about the war. He was knighted in 1969, named Australian of the Year in 1977, awarded an AC (Companion of the Order of Australia, the highest Australian honour) in 1987, and his state funeral in 1993 was a televised event. Documentaries have been made about him, and countless articles and books written. He was commemorated on a souvenir 50-cent coin and is even the subject of a school textbook.[103] Yet it was probably the year-long 'Australia Remembers' campaign of 1995, which marked the 50-year anniversary of the end of World War II, that largely elevated his profile to POW 'hero' to the exclusion of all others. When he died he was probably the best-known veteran in Australia, and he arguably still is today.

There are many factors that help explain Dunlop's popularity. The status accorded to medical personnel in war had already been established during World War I by John 'Simpson' Kirkpatrick—another medical 'hero' who, with his donkey, became better known than the combat personnel.[104] To some extent, Dunlop was already Australian 'hero' material before he joined the war: he was a country boy who had worked hard to put himself though medicine, he was a rugby star who played for Australia, and he was a forceful and charismatic personality who happened to have great faith in his own abilities. Reluctant to delegate responsibility, he was described as being 'more like the hero-surgeons of the 19th century when the surgeon really was a one-man band'.[105]

After the war, through his marriage and his professional position, he became part of the 'Victorian establishment'. He outlived many of his POW colleagues, and published his war diaries in the 1980s, a time when interest in the POW experience was increasing. Following the publication in 1997 of his bestselling biography by Sue Ebury—*Weary: The Life of Sir Edward Dunlop*—he became a household name. It was a name that came to symbolise a larger spirit of human generosity. In a 1998 speech to the Gladesville RSL Club, former Australian Prime Minister John Howard declared: 'And it will be a reminder of the exultation [sic] of men like "Weary" Dunlop who said that always remembering the past tragedies, we should look to the future and we should build links between Australia and the nations of Asia.'[106]

There are some who think Dunlop was not an appropriate choice to be the public face of the Australian POW experience. For example, he was not a member of the 8th Division, whose group identity and bonds are very strong. He also became a POW on Java, not at the fall of Singapore, a key event that contributed to the group identity of Australians in captivity. As well, while Dunlop was on the Railway at various times, he spent most of his time in captivity at base hospitals, so some feel he did not 'have it as hard' as other doctors.

During the war, Dunlop was admired by many for his leadership qualities, but among ex-POWs his reputation did not extend past those who knew him personally. He was liked by colleagues, and was regularly praised in reports written by British doctors he worked with—as were many other Australian medical personnel. In the first few months of captivity in Bandoeng with British, Australian and Dutch prisoners, Dunlop was chosen camp commander. Dutch Colonel Laurens van der Post recalled it was a logical decision, based on Dunlop's leadership qualities and that 'it was to be a war for sanity of mind and body, and who, we asked Weary, could be more fitted to conduct such a war than a doctor and healer?'[107] Later, on the Railway, he was appointed commanding officer of 'Dunlop Force'; in a letter signed by eleven other officers, Lieutenant Colonel Galleghan stated, 'all combatant officers of the party agree to come under Comd of Lt-Col Dunlop for purposes of discipline'.[108] Dunlop was also an excellent administrator, as demonstrated by the reams of medical, financial and other reports he wrote: 'For someone whose ambition was to spend as much time as possible in an operating theatre, Weary always found it ironic that so much of his prison camp existence was devoted to financial matters.'[109] While administration was a vital job in captivity, in the postwar years this was overshadowed by the more dramatic aspects of the surgeries he performed in captivity, and his celebrated conflicts with captors.

In Melbourne stands a large statue dedicated to Dunlop in the grounds of Kings Domain, a short walk from the Shrine of Remembrance.[110] On the steps leading up to it are the names of other POW doctors. This is also a feature of his statue in Benalla. Unfortunately, there are several errors: even though there were only 106 POW doctors, 122 names are listed, and in a serious omission, only recently corrected, Surgeon-Lieutenant Samuel Stening was not originally included.

In the larger POW community, attitudes towards Dunlop vary. Some ex-POWs, both medical and non-medical, have felt angered by the 'token' inclusion of other medical personnel and the lack of consultation with them about the memorial. One ex-POW wrote of his annoyance about other doctors not receiving equal attention:

> Most POWs said that to select one of them for special mention was an insult to the remainder and that a monument to them all instead of a statue to one, would have been a better option. I personally think a 'War Veterans Home' would have been the best option instead of wasting all that money on a statue.[111]

As another example, an Australian documentary made in 1989 featured Dunlop making a return trip to Hellfire Pass in Thailand, along with a group of other ex-POWs. Except for one passing reference to Albert Coates, no mention was made of any other doctor.[112] One could be forgiven for thinking that Dunlop had been the only doctor in Japanese captivity and that he alone had saved all those who returned. I have met hundred of ex-POWs who never met Dunlop and were eager to tell me stories of 'their' doctors.

Part of the reason for this book was to highlight the incredible work other Australian doctors and orderlies did and to put Dunlop's contribution in perspective. He was a good leader and a capable doctor, but to suggest he was the 'best' or somehow more important than the other 105 Australian medical officers is absurd. In the preface to the 2001 edition of her biography, Sue Ebury describes him as an Australian icon 'alongside Don Bradman, Ned Kelly and Phar Lap'.[113] Such fatuous comparisons are both misleading and meaningless.

Consider this citation: this officer was 'repeatedly beaten and knocked about because of the strong stand he took regarding sick and ailing men, he never weakened, and a great deal of credit goes to him for the few deaths recorded in this particular camp'.[114] It sounds like something you would read about Dunlop, but it is actually about Captain John Akeroyd's work while caring for prisoners in Japan. There are literally hundreds of such descriptions of other doctors' bravery and suffering. It is quite possible that any of the other 105 doctors could have been as famous as Dunlop. Certainly, in speaking to hundreds of ex-POWs, Dunlop's name is not mentioned more than that of any other doctor, except in the context of his postwar fame.

Many other doctors were remembered with great affection. Cahill said of Kevin Fagan:

> He was probably the most loved man in the whole of the camp . . . when he got sick at one stage, he had a gastric ulcer . . . he would be in hospital, and you'd find the men queued up to see him, and they'd go up with their last cigarette to give to him.

With Fagan on the Railway, Lieutenant Frank Nankervis remembered witnessing both his surgical skill and personal values:

> I actually saw him performing a skin graft, experimenting taking skin, peeling skin, and putting it over a wound, and I saw him take the covering—which was only a leaf with a bit of rag wrapped around it—and when he took the leaf off there was the leg healed. When I later met Kevin Fagan I reminded him of that operation, and he remembered that was the first skin graft he ever attempted. I said, 'What you don't know is that that man was one of the greatest scoundrels that was on the Line.' And he said, 'He was a *patient*.' That's the kind of man he was.[115]

Bruce Hunt was another doctor POWs often mention with admiration. Former POW Norman Derrington said he doubted Dunlop could have done a better job than Bruce Hunt: 'I've seen Hunt stand there and cop an awful bashing from the Jap, then say "I still cannot send these men out today".'[116] John Higgs remembered Hunt's work on 'F' Force's 300-kilometre march to start building the Railway. He 'must have marched twice as far as the rest of us. He was sometimes at the front, at others down along the line, counselling, comforting, bullying, handing out drugs from the meagre supply to the most desperate, and generally helping by sheer example to lift flagging spirits.'[117]

Medical historian Bryan Egan points to Captain William Aitken on Hainan Island as an outstanding example of a medical officer working in difficult circumstances: 'by his energy, brilliant medical extemporisations and sheer fearlessness [he] was as important and successful on Hainan as was Dunlop in Thailand and Burma'.[118] These men are only a few of the 105 doctors of whom the same things could be said that are constantly repeated about Dunlop.

What is not generally well understood is that Dunlop's fame arose more out of what he did *after* the war, not during it. Much of his postwar energy went into building bridges of communication between Australia and Asia, setting up foundations and scholarships at a time when many Australians were still very anti-Asian, the scars of war too recent. As one example, he set up a medical exchange program between Australia and Thailand, including the establishment of the 'Weary' Dunlop Boon Pong Exchange Fellowship. He was also the kind of person who enjoyed public speaking and using the media to raise the profile of Australian POWs and their continuing suffering.

Everyone would agree that Dunlop did extraordinary work and with great compassion and dedication, both during and after the war. Even though the attention he received after the war has caused some controversy, Australian ex-POWs were lucky to have had someone such as Dunlop to constantly bring attention to their experience, ensuring it was not forgotten, and to advocate that those who survived needed ongoing care. In the United Kingdom, by contrast, there has been no single ex-prisoner of the Japanese who has held a similar place. In the United States, a continuing obsession with Prisoners of War/Missing in Action from the Vietnam War has completely eclipsed the experience of the 25,000 Americans who were incarcerated by the Japanese during World War II. POWs of the Pacific have to all intents and purposes been obliterated from American public memory: the term 'POW' in the States today almost always refers to those who fought in Vietnam.

Yet there is a larger issue to explore connected with Dunlop's role in Australian memory. As with any war, with its attendant human losses, a nation naturally looks for heroes to help remember the more positive aspects of such armed conflicts, and Australia after World War II was no exception. At first the focus was on the highly decorated men and women, especially the Victoria Cross winners. It was not until Dunlop became publicly known that there was an acceptable 'POW hero'. His fame signified a great shift in Australian attitudes to war post-Vietnam in the 1960s and 1970s where the focus changed from lauding combatants' achievements while fighting to celebrating a *non-combatant* for work he had done in a *non-operational* war context.

In the abnormal situation of a Japanese POW camp during World War II, doctors clearly became of greater significance than in traditional military command structures. In this way, it makes sense that a doctor would be a 'hero' figure in subsequent histories of the POW experience. Certainly, Dunlop is almost exclusively represented with positive attributes—his strength, charm, tenacity and compassion are always stressed.

There is a self-conscious unease among Australian military historians in finding a place for POWs in the Australian war experience. POW history has few 'heroes' in the traditional sense: in captivity, there were no battles, no advances and few situations where the usual military parlance can be used. As the perfect mixture of military officer and civilian doctor, Dunlop provided the solution. It is noteworthy, however, that his civilian characteristics are always stressed. Most Australians remember him far less as a commanding officer with years of military experience than as a compassionate and caring doctor—the very antithesis of war.

For the 106 Australian medical officers who were prisoners of the Japanese, the challenge of keeping their men alive was a cause that went to the heart of being a doctor. Whatever the differences in their backgrounds, age, motivation for enlisting, experience or expectations, they were joined by the bonds of their profession. It gave them a reason for not giving in to the feelings of despair and powerlessness they all periodically felt.

That one in three Australian prisoners died in Japanese captivity sometimes overshadows the fact that two out of three survived. While many suffered ill health and psychological trauma for the rest of their lives, there is little doubt that the outcome would have been much worse had it not been for their doctors' efforts.

Many aspects of postwar life were uniform for all those who experienced captivity. It is rare to see a former POW waste food, and for the rest of their lives, they all shared an intense appreciation of the most basic values.[119] Dr Kevin Fagan said that he never stopped feeling grateful for the ordinary things of life: 'bread and butter, a bit of jam on your toast in the mornings, a glass of beer when you're thirsty... when it comes to the end, the only thing that matters are the people whom you love and who love you.'[120] The doctors also never ceased appreciating having tools and medicine in ready supply and being able to practise in proper hospitals with supportive colleagues.

All ex-prisoners experienced varying forms of postwar trauma, from nightmares to depression and severe anxiety. All grieved for friends and comrades they had lost in often horrific circumstances. But some of the trials of postwar life were different for doctors. They had to contend with losing four years of their careers during a period of great advancement in medical knowledge. They needed to relearn their skills and in some cases change the direction of their career. They still felt guilt, frustration and despair over losing many patients and for having to undertake work for which they had not been trained. They continued to question decisions they made that sometimes resulted in the death of their men.

However, there were crucial differences from other POWs in the circumstances in which doctors re-entered civilian life. They had the psychological advantage of having served in captivity in a role they knew and understood, and one that was in critical demand. Another crucial difference was the respect and admiration they received. Captivity provided few positive memories for other Australian prisoners, apart perhaps from sharing an experience that forged the strongest possible bonds between men.

To many Australian ex-POWs, medical officers *are* the heroes of their war years. This small group of doctors successfully negotiated the complexities of their varied roles within a bleak environment, and through their work, brought thousands of men home to their families. While captivity was in many ways a heartbreaking experience for medical personnel, it was also a triumphant one.

Looking back in 1999 on his life and on his career, Dr Des Brennan remarked, 'How lucky we have been. There can be no other life as fascinating and as rewarding as ours... "Thank God I became a Doctor".'[121]

# GLOSSARY OF MEDICAL TERMS

**Amblyopia**: a condition in which the vision in one eye is weaker than in the other, causing differences in the visual information being received by the brain. Among other causes, it can be due to a poor diet—'nutritional amblyopia'—most commonly due to lack of riboflavin.

**Ascariasis**: an infection caused by a parasitic worm called ascaris that lives in the small intestine and can grow up to 30 centimetres in length. Ascariasis is a common human worm infection and is most prevalent in tropical and subtropical areas where sanitation and hygiene are poor. Most people have no symptoms.

**Ataxia**: an inability to coordinate voluntary muscle movements, and a loss of motor control. It can have several causes including deficiencies in vitamins E and B12.

**Avitaminosis**: any of several diseases, such as scurvy, beri-beri or pellagra, caused by a deficiency in one or more essential vitamins.

**Beri-beri**: a vitamin deficiency disease caused by a lack of or inability to absorb thiamine (vitamin B1). It is characterised by the inflammation of multiple nerves (polyneuritis), heart disease (cardiopathy) and oedema (swelling).

**Cholera**: a form of infectious gastroenteritis (intestinal infection) that results in intense vomiting and profuse watery diarrhoea. This can lead to rapid dehydration which, unless immediately treated, may be fatal.

**Dengue fever**: an acute mosquito-borne viral illness with sudden onset and symptoms that include headache, fever, severe joint and muscle pain, swollen glands and a rash. Endemic throughout tropical regions, it is also known as 'break bone' or 'dandy' fever. Victims of dengue often suffer from contortions due to intense joint and muscle contractions.

**Dermatitis**: inflammation of the skin, due to direct contact with an irritating substance or vitamin deficiency or to a reaction from an allergy or stress. Symptoms of dermatitis include redness, itching and, in some cases, blistering.

**Diphtheria**: an acute bacterial disease that usually affects the tonsils, throat, nose and/or skin. It is usually transmitted from person to person by breathing in diphtheria bacteria after an infected person has coughed or sneezed. Diphtheria can lead to breathing problems, heart failure, paralysis and sometimes death.

**Dysentery**: inflammation of the intestine, often with pain, diarrhoea and/or bloody stools. Dysentery can be fatal, usually because of the severe dehydration it causes. There are two main types: bacillary dysentery, an acute infection of the intestine by shigella or salmonella bacteria, characterised by diarrhoea, fever and abdominal pains; and the more serious amoebic dysentery, which produces ulcers in the colon due to infection with an amoeba. This single-celled parasite is transmitted to humans via contaminated water and food. Amoebic dysentery can be accompanied by amoebic infection of the liver and other organs.

**Hookworm infection**: an intestinal infection caused by the hookworm parasite, which measures between 8 and 13 millimetres. It is estimated to infect over 900 million people worldwide. The most significant risk of hookworm infection is anaemia due to loss of iron (and protein) into the gut. The hookworm enters the body through the skin; walking barefoot in soil contaminated with faeces—the source of hookworm larvae—is the most common form of exposure.

**Malaria**: an acute or chronic disease caused by the presence of protozoan parasites of the Plasmodium family in the red blood cells, transmitted by the bite of anopheline mosquitoes. It is characterised by periodic cycles of chills, fevers, sweats, muscle aches and headaches that can recur every few days or weeks. There can also be vomiting, diarrhoea, coughing, and yellowing (jaundice) of the skin and eyes. There are two general types of malaria. Benign malaria is not as serious as malignant malaria and there is a decreased chance of complication of the organs. Malignant malaria has a rapid course and after infection patients have a poor prognosis. They can develop bleeding problems, shock, kidney and liver failure and complications of the central nervous system.

**Malnutrition**: a condition in which the body does not receive enough of the nutrients it needs. This is due to inadequate or unbalanced intake of nutrients or their impaired assimilation or utilisation.

**Oedema**: the presence of abnormally large amounts of fluid in spaces and/or organs of the body, such as lungs or legs.

**Pellagra**: a vitamin deficiency disease marked by dermatitis, gastrointestinal disorders, mental disturbance and memory loss, associated with a diet deficient in niacin and protein.

**Pneumonia**: an infection of one or both lungs, usually caused by a bacteria, virus, or fungus. Prior to the discovery of antibiotics, one-third of all people who developed pneumonia subsequently died from the infection. It is usually contracted by breathing in small droplets that contain the bacteria or virus that cause it. People who are in a weakened state or have low immunity are particularly vulnerable to infection.

**Post traumatic stress disorder (PTSD)**: a disorder that appears after a physically or psychologically traumatic event, considered outside the range of usual human experience, such as conditions of warfare, assault or torture. It can be characterised by symptoms such as experiencing the event, numbing of responsiveness to the environment, exaggerated startle response, feelings of guilt, impairment of memory, and difficulty concentrating and sleeping.

**Ringworm**: any of several contagious diseases of the skin, hair or nails caused by fungi and characterised by ring-shaped discoloured patches on the skin that are covered with vesicles and scales. Also known as tinea.

**Scabies**: an infestation by the itch mite *Sarcoptes scabiei*. Mites have eight legs and are approximately ⅓ millimetre long. They burrow into the skin, producing intense itching that tends to be worse at night.

**Stomatitis**: a painful infection with ulceration, swelling and sloughing off of dead tissue from the mouth and throat due to the spread of infection from the gums. Mechanical trauma, irritants, allergy, vitamin deficiency or infection can cause it.

**Strongyloidiasis**: a parasitic disease caused by the roundworm *Strongyloides stercoralis*, which is an unusual 'parasite' in that it has both free-living and parasitic life cycles. The female worms produce larvae parthenogenically (without fertilisation), which are passed in the host's faeces. Some of the larvae then develop into 'free-living' larvae, while others develop into 'parasitic' larvae. The latter infect the human host by penetrating the skin where some remain. Other larvae migrate to the lungs via the circulatory system, penetrate the alveoli into the small bronchioles, and are 'coughed up' and swallowed. Once they return to the small intestine, the larvae mature into parasitic females.

**Tapeworm infestation**: an intestinal infection caused by the parasitic tapeworm, which can grow very large in the human gut. The eggs usually enter the body via raw or undercooked meat. Symptoms can include abdominal pain, fatigue, weight loss and diarrhoea.

**Tropical ulcer**: a chronic sloughing sore of unknown cause, usually occurring on the legs and prevalent in wet tropical regions. Deformities of the knee and foot, gangrene and tetanus may occur.

**Tuberculosis (TB)**: an infectious disease caused by the bacteria *Mycobacterium tuberculosis*. It most commonly affects the lungs, but can also involve almost any organ of the body. A person can become infected with tuberculosis bacteria by inhaling minute particles of infected sputum in the air. The bacteria are released into the air when someone who has a tuberculosis lung infection coughs, sneezes, shouts or spits.

# Appendix A

# AUSTRALIAN POW DOCTORS

This list includes the 106 Australian medical officers who were prisoners of the Japanese military during World War II.
* *indicates the 44 doctors who worked on the Burma–Thai Railway.*

| Surname | Other names | Rank | Serial number | Unit |
|---|---|---|---|---|
| Aitken | William | Captain | VX31470 | 2/21st Battalion (BN) |
| Akeroyd | John Finch | Captain | VX18194 | PSL Australian Army Medical Corps |
| Anderson* | Bruce Hunter | Major | VX47449 | HQ 8th Div. |
| Anderson* | Claude Leonard | Captain | W17 | 2/4th MG BN |
| Andrews* | Howard Lyell | Major | VX39316 | 10th Australian General Hospital (AGH) |
| Barrett | Alex Keith | Captain | NX35102 | 2/18th BN |
| Boyce | Clive Rodney | Captain | QX23518 | 2nd Aust. Con. Dept |
| Brand* | Victor | Captain | VX39085 | 2/29th BN |

219

| Surname | Other names | Rank | Serial number | Unit |
|---|---|---|---|---|
| Brennan | Desmond James | Captain | NX71022 | 2/3rd Motor Convoy |
| Bristow | Vincent George | Captain | VX39436 | 1st Ind. Coy |
| Brown | Maxwell Mansfield | Captain | TX2109 | 2/40th BN |
| Burnside | Kennedy Byron | Major | VX45320 | 2nd Aust. Mob. Bact. Lab |
| Bye | William Alick | Lt. Colonel | NX70581 | 13th AGH |
| Cade | John Frederick Joseph | Major | VX45001 | 2/9th Field Ambulance (FA) |
| Cahill* | Francis Joseph | Captain | VX39702 | 2/9th FA |
| Cahill* | Richard Lloyd | Captain | NX35149 | 2/19th BN |
| Cameron | Ian Thomas | Major | VX47129 | 2/9th FA |
| Catchlove | John Pelham | Captain | VX39223 | 10th AGH |
| Chalmers* | John Sneddon | Major | TX2150 | 2/4th Casualty Clearing Station (CCS) |
| Claffy | Francis Patrick Christopher | Major | NX70579 | 10th AGH |
| Clarke | Burnett Leslie Woodburn | Major | QX22806 | 13th AGH |
| Coates* | Albert Ernest | Lt. Colonel | VX39198 | 10th AGH |
| Conlon | Victor Alexander | Captain | VX39972 | 13th AGH |
| Corlette* | Ewan Lawrie | Major | NX350 | 2/2nd CCS |
| Crabbe | Gavin Murray | Captain | TX6071 | 2/10th FA |
| Crankshaw* | Thomas Pilkington | Major | VX62081 | 13th AGH |
| Cumming* | Gordon David | Captain | NX70385 | 2/10th FA |
| Davidson | Peter McLean | Captain | QX6476 | 2/21st BN |
| Davies* | Geoffrey Francis Seymour | Major | NX76351 | 13th AGH |

| Surname | Other names | Rank | Serial number | Unit |
|---|---|---|---|---|
| Derham | Alfred Plumley | Colonel | VX13486 | Assistant Director Medical Services, HQ Malaya |
| Dick | Robert | Major | NX70970 | 2/3rd Motor Convoy |
| Drevermann* | Ernest Barclay | Captain | VX61260 | 13th AGH |
| Duncan* | Ian Lovell | Captain | NX35135 | HQ 8th Div. |
| Dunlop* | Edward | Lt. Colonel | VX259 | 2/2nd CCS |
| Eadie* | Norman Basil Menzies | Lt. Colonel | VX14845 | HQ Java |
| Eddey | Howard Hadfield | Major | VX61356 | 13th AGH |
| Fagan* | Kevin James | Major | NX70643 | 10th AGH |
| Farmer | Adrian Ward | Major | WX11015 | 10th AGH |
| Fisher* | Walter Edward | Major | NX70506 | 2/4th CCS |
| Frew* | John Lewtas | Captain | VX39181 | 13th AGH |
| Furner | Carl Russell | Major | NX70516 | 10th AGH |
| Gillies | Douglas Neil | Captain | NX76360 | 2/1st Hvy Bty |
| Goding | James Russell | Captain | VX14906 | 2/2nd Pioneer BN |
| Godlee* | Theodore | Captain | WX11067 | 2/13th FA |
| Greville | Ronald Wellesley | Captain | VX39059 | 2/5th Field Hygiene Section |
| Gunther | Carl Ernest Mitchelmore | Major | NX76596 | HQ Malaya |
| Hamilton* | Thomas | Lt. Colonel | NX70505 | 2/4th CCS |
| Harvey | William Cotter Burnell | Lt. Colonel | NX70668 | 10th AGH |
| Hazelton* | Alan Richard | Major | NX35134 | 2/10th FA |
| Heinz | Ian Conrad | Captain | VX39258 | 10th AGH |

| Surname | Other names | Rank | Serial number | Unit |
| --- | --- | --- | --- | --- |
| Hendry* | Peter Ian Alexander | Captain | NX35147 | 2/10th FA |
| Higgin* | John Perceval | Captain | NX34949 | 2/4th CCS |
| Hinder* | David Clive Critchley | Captain | NX76302 | 13th AGH, later 2/19th BN |
| Hobbs* | Alan | Major | SX10761 | 2/4th CCS |
| Hogg* | Tulloch Graham Heuze | Captain | TX2185 | 13th AGH |
| Home | Arthur Robinson | Major | WX11151 | 13th AGH |
| Hunt* | Bruce Attlee | Major | WX11177 | 13th AGH |
| Huxtable | Charles Reginald Ralston | Captain | QX22801 | 13th AGH |
| Jeffrey | Roderick Lionel | Captain | NX34761 | 10th AGH |
| Jose | Gilbert Edgar | Major | SX11028 | 10th AGH |
| Juttner* | Colin Percival | Captain | SX14044 | 2/9th FA |
| Krantz* | Sydney | Major | SX13978 | 2/4th CCS |
| Le Gay Brereton* | Thomas | Captain | NX76180 | 2/4th CCS |
| Maffey | Reginald Errol | Major | NX70158 | 2/10th FA |
| Marsden* | Ernest Ambrose | Major | NX70674 | 10th AGH |
| Maynard | Roy Bryant | Major | VX46174 | 10th AGH |
| McNamara | William Joseph | Major | NX71018 | 5th AGH |
| Millard* | Philip Thornton | Captain | NX76511 | 2/11th FA |
| Mills | Frank Harland | Major | NX70671 | 10th AGH |
| Mills* | Roy Markham | Captain | NX35139 | 2/10th FA |
| Moon* | Arthur Alexander | Major | NX455 | 2/2nd CCS |
| Murphy* | Patrick Francis | Major | NX70489 | 2/10th FA |
| Nairn | Bertram William | Major | WX11168 | 13th AGH |
| Oakeshott | John Bernard | Captain | NX76223 | 10th AGH |
| O'Donnell | Patrick Neil | Captain | VX39183 | 10th AGH |

| Surname | Other names | Rank | Serial number | Unit |
|---|---|---|---|---|
| Orr | Robert Graeme | Major | VX60748 | 13th AGH |
| Osborn | Charles Harwood | Lt. Colonel | VX42966 | 13th AGH |
| Parker* | Richard Grey Vernon | Captain | NX71143 | 2/10th FA |
| Phillips | Henry Anthony | Major | VX39055 | 10th AGH |
| Picone | Domenic George | Captain | QX6380 | 2/10th FA |
| Pigdon | Douglas Clelland | Colonel | VX39275 | 13th AGH |
| Poidevin | Leslie Oswyn Sheridan | Captain | NX71114 | 2/12th FA |
| Pufflett | Robert Delmont | Captain | NX70378 | 10th AGH |
| Rayson | Hugh | Major | NX34706 | 2/10th FA |
| Richards* | Charles Rowland Bromley | Captain | NX70273 | 2/15th FA |
| Robertson | Sandy Edwin John | Captain | NX35101 | 2/10th FA |
| Rogers* | Eugene Augustine | Major | TX2199 | 13th AGH |
| Searby | Julian Johnstone | Major | VX45273 | 2/9th FA |
| Sheppard | Edmund MacArthur | Lt. Colonel | NX34665 | 2/10th FA |
| Smith | Alan Frederick | Captain | NX77245 | 3rd AGH |
| Speirs | Robert Bradley | Captain | NX34905 | 2/18th BN |
| Stening* | Samuel Edward Lees | Surgeon-Lieutenant | N/A | *HMAS PERTH* |
| Stevens* | Roy Halford | Major | VX39043 | 2/12th FA |
| Summons | Hedley Francis | Lt. Colonel | VX40219 | 2/9th FA |
| Taylor* | John Lindsay | Captain | NX79453 | 2/30th BN |
| Tucker | Horace Finn | Captain | VX39095 | 4th Anti-tank Regiment |
| Uhr | Clive Wentworth | Major | QX19079 | 10th AGH |
| Vincent | Frank Robertson | Captain | VX57546 | 10th AGH |

| Surname | Other names | Rank | Serial number | Unit |
|---|---|---|---|---|
| Watson | Heyworth Alexander Wigglesworth | Major | VX66657 | 13th AGH |
| Webster | Robert Marriott William | Lt. Colonel | TX2107 | 2/9th FA |
| White* | Alexander John Middleton | Captain | TX6074 | 2/4th CCS |
| White | Edward Rowden | Colonel | VX38992 | 10th AGH |
| White | John George Glyn | Lt. Colonel | VX21434 | Deputy Assistant Director, Medical Services, Malaya |
| White | Stanley Boyd McKellar | Captain | NX70920 | 2/12th FA |
| Woodruff | Michael Francis Addison | Captain | VX53704 | 10th AGH |
| Wright* | Reginald George | Captain | NX70664 | 10th AGH |

# Appendix B

# DOCTORS' DEATHS IN CAPTIVITY

Of the 22,000 Australian POWs in Japanese captivity, 8,000 died, while ten of the 106 medical officers in Japanese captivity died.* (This equated to a mortality rate of 36 per cent and 9.5 per cent respectively.)

This table shows the circumstances of the deaths of those ten medical officers.

| Name and rank | Age at death | Stated cause of death | Place and date of death |
| --- | --- | --- | --- |
| Major Gilbert Edgar Jose | 43 | Disease | Singapore, 18 February 1942 |
| Captain Stanley Boyd McKellar White | 26 | Executed | Ambon, 20 February 1942 |
| Captain Peter McLean Davidson | 42 | Air raid | Ambon, 15 February 1943 |
| Major William Joseph McNamara | 39 | Drowned | On Japanese transport *Tamaboko Maru*, 24 June 1944 |
| Major John Sneddon Chalmers | 33 | Drowned | On Japanese transport *Rakuyu Maru*, 14 September 1944 |
| Captain Maxwell Mansfield Brown | 32 | Drowned | On Japanese transport off Sumatra, 18 September 1944 |

| Name and rank | Age at death | Stated cause of death | Place and date of death |
|---|---|---|---|
| Captain Roderick Lionel Jeffrey | 34 | Disease | Borneo, 6 May 1945 |
| Colonel Douglas Clelland Pigdon | 53 | Disease | Manchuria, 6 July 1945 |
| Captain John Bernard Oakeshott | 44 | Disease | Borneo, 1 August 1945 |
| Captain Domenic George Picone** | 36 | Disease | Borneo, 6 August 1945 |

* These figures do not include Australian medical officers who were killed in action during the Malaya campaign: Captain G. L. Lindon, Captain K. C. Madden, Captain D. S. Shale and Captain J. F. Park. The criterion for 'died in captivity' is if a doctor died after 15 February 1942 and while a prisoner. For example, Captain Stanley Boyd McKellar White, who died 20 February 1942 (by execution) is included, while Surgeon-Lieutenant Commander Eric Mortimer Tymms is not, as he drowned on 1 March 1942 when the *HMAS Perth* was sunk, before he could be taken prisoner.

** In his service record, Captain Picone is shown as having died of illness in Borneo, but a letter enclosed in his service file suggests the Japanese may have executed him.

# ENDNOTES

**Introduction**

1. Unattributed, *'Getting on with it'—2/30th Battalion AIF*, 2/30th Battalion Association, Kingsway West NSW, 1998, p. 17.
2. Interview with Charles 'Rowley' Richards, Australians at War Film Archive, no. 1144, <www.australiansatwarfilmarchive.gov.au/aawfa/interviews/1048.aspx>, accessed 10 October 2008.
3. Joan Beaumont, ed., *The Australian Centenary History of Defence, Vol. 6, Australian defence: sources and statistics*, Oxford University Press, Oxford, 2001, p. 344.
4. John D. 'Jack' Higgs, 'Beffie and Me: Jack's Memoirs of Family, January 1991–December 2004', unpublished memoir, p. 151.
5. Albert E. Coates and Norman Rosenthal, *The Albert Coates Story: The will that found a way*, Hyland House, Melbourne, 1977, p. 110.
6. Major H. Eddey, War Crimes Trials Statement, AWM 54 1010/4/47, Australian War Memorial, Canberra.
7. Richard Reid, *In Captivity: Australian prisoners of war in the 20th century*, Commonwealth Department of Veterans' Affairs, Canberra, 1999, p. 43.

**Chapter 1    The road to captivity**

1. Stephen Due, *A Bibliography of Australian Doctors at War*, self published, Belmont Victoria, 1994, p. 6. Coates was one of ten such

doctors who saw service in both world wars. Coates, Alfred Derham, Thomas Hamilton, Bruce Hunt and Norman Eadie served as soldiers in the First AIF and another six served as AAMC medical officers: Edward R. White, Hugh Rayson, Charles Huxtable, Robert Webster, Eugene Rogers and Douglas Pigdon.

2 Commonwealth Government, *Census of the Commonwealth of Australia, 30th June, 1933*, Commonwealth Government Printer, Canberra, 1936–40, pp. 1594–5.

3 All statistics have been compiled by the author from information gathered from POW Medical Officers' service records held at Central Army Records Office, Victoria Barracks, Melbourne, and the National Archives of Australia, Canberra.

4 A sample taken from 49 British doctors who joined Australian colleagues on the Burma–Thai Railway showed similar biographical details: 57 per cent were captains, their average age was 34, and the majority had no prior military experience. Compiled from 'List of Medical Officers on Burma/Siam Railway as Obtained from our Records', WO 325/12, National Archives, London.

5 Bryan Egan, 'Understanding Medical Officers: Australian Doctors and War', unpublished manuscript, p. 8.

6 ibid., pp. 12–13.

7 Hank Nelson, 'Turning North: Australians in Southeast Asia in World War 2', *Overland*, no. 119, winter 1990, p. 31.

8 E. E. Dunlop, *The War Diaries of Weary Dunlop: Java and the Burma–Thailand Railway, 1942–1945*, Thomas Nelson, Melbourne, 1986, p. 1.

9 ibid.

10 Bryan Egan, 'Nobler than Missionaries: Australian Medical Culture, c.1880–c.1930', PhD thesis, Monash University, Melbourne, 1988, p. 225.

11 Egan, 'Understanding Medical Officers', p. 5.

12 Peter J. Morris, 'Sir Michael Woodruff', <www.rsnz.govt.nz/directory/yearbooks/2001/woodruff.php>, accessed 4 February 2003.

13 Burnett L. Clarke, *Behind the Wire: The clinical diary of Major Burnett Clarke AAMC*, Amphion Press, Brisbane, 1989, p. xiii.

14 Patricia J. Miller, *Malaria, Liverpool: An illustrated history of the Liverpool School of Tropical Medicine 1989–1998*, Liverpool School of Tropical Medicine, Liverpool, 1998, p. 9.

15 ibid., p. 27.

16 Richard Gabriel and Karen Metz, *A History of Military Medicine, Vol II: From the Renaissance through modern times*, Greenwood Press, New York, 1992, p. 216.
17 Egan, 'Nobler than Missionaries', p. 28.
18 Lionel Wigmore, *The Japanese Thrust*, Australian War Memorial, Canberra, 1957, p. 377.
19 Alan Warren, *Singapore 1942: Britain's greatest defeat*, Hardie Grant Books, Melbourne, 2002, p. 9.
20 Thelma McEachern, quoted in Ray Connolly, 'The 10th AGH—to Malacca', unpublished manuscript, p. 4.
21 Quoted in Connolly, 'The 10th AGH—to Malacca', p. 5.
22 Albert E. Coates and Norman Rosenthal, *The Albert Coates Story: The will that found a way*, Hyland House, Melbourne, 1977, p. 51.
23 Jeff Partridge, 'Alexandra Hospital: From British Military to Civilian Institution, 1938–1998', PhD thesis, National University of Singapore, <www.postcolonialweb.org/singapore/history/hospital/ah1.html>, accessed 25 February 2003.
24 Hank Nelson, *Prisoners of War: Australians under Nippon*, ABC Enterprises for the Australian Broadcasting Corporation, Sydney, 2001, p. 11.
25 Warren, *Singapore 1942*, p. 9.
26 McEachern, quoted in Connolly, 'The 10th AGH—to Malacca', p. 5.
27 John D. 'Jack' Higgs, 'Beffie and Me: Jack's Memoirs of Family, January 1991–December 2004', unpublished memoir, p. 86.
28 Harry Medlin, '2/AIF', unpublished memoir, p. 5.
29 Nelson, *Prisoners of War*, p. 12.
30 John Coates in Peter Dennis et al., *The Oxford Companion to Australian Military History*, Oxford University Press, Melbourne, 1995, p. 375.
31 Higgs, 'Beffie and Me', p. 95.
32 Richard Reid, *In Captivity: Australian prisoners of war in the 20th century*, Commonwealth Department of Veterans' Affairs, Canberra, 1999, p. 32.
33 Nelson, 'Turning North', p. 35.
34 Interview with Charles 'Rowley' Richards, Australians at War Film Archive, no. 1144, <www.australiansatwarfilmarchive.gov.au/aawfa/interviews/1048.aspx>, accessed 10 October 2008.
35 Peter Burness, 'Retracing the Malayan Campaign', *Journal of the Australian War Memorial*, no. 7, October 1985, p. 22.

36 Letter from Dr Roy Mills to Hugh Simmons, 30 October 1993, in Mills' personal papers.
37 Captain Victor Brand, 'The diary (Malaya and Singapore) of Captain Victor Brand M.C., R.M.O. 2/29th Battalion', in Robert Christie, ed., *A History of the 2/29th Battalion—8th Australian Division AIF*, 2/29th Battalion AIF Association, Melbourne, 1983, p. 65.
38 Connolly, 'The 10th AGH—to Malacca', p. 8.
39 Partridge, 'Alexandra Hospital'.
40 Nelson, *Prisoners of War*, p. 17.
41 Colonel James H. Thyer, quoted in Warren, *Singapore 1942*, p. 233.
42 ibid., p. 234.
43 Partridge, 'Alexandra Hospital'.
44 Betty Jeffrey, *White Coolies*, Angus & Robertson, Sydney, 1954, p. 3.
45 Coates and Rosenthal, *The Albert Coates Story*, p. 51.
46 Partridge, 'Alexandra Hospital'.
47 Major Hugh Rayson, personal diary, 16–21 February 1942, AWM PR00720, Australian War Memorial, Canberra.
48 Warren, *Singapore 1942*, pp. 242–3.
49 Wigmore, *The Japanese Thrust*, p. 377.
50 Higgs, *Beffie and Me*, p. 89.
51 Lieutenant Colonel C. W. Maisey, 'Courageous Acts—Military Personnel', 5 December 1945, WO 222/1391, National Archives, London.
52 Lieutenant Colonel C. W. Maisey, 'Reports on POW camps in Batavia 1942–45', 24 November 1945, WO 222/1391, National Archives, London.
53 Lieutenant Colonel C. W. Maisey, 'Report on St Vincentius P.O.W. Hospital, Batavia. August 1943–April 1945', 5 December 1945, WO 222/1391, National Archives, London.
54 Letter from Lieutenant Colonel Edward Dunlop to Brigadier Arthur S. Blackburn, 7 March 1942, in papers of Brigadier A. S. Blackburn VC, AWM EXDOC084, Australian War Memorial, Canberra.
55 Dr Peter Hendry, 'Introduction' in Ray Connolly and Bob Wilson, eds, *Medical Soldiers: 2/10 Australian Field Ambulance 8 Div. 1940–45*, 2/10th Australian Field Ambulance Association, Sydney, c. 1985, p. 11.

## Chapter 2   Changi: the beginning

1 General Gordon Bennett, OBE citation in Lieutenant Colonel John George 'Glyn' White's service record, Central Army Records Office, Victoria Barracks, Melbourne.

2  J. G. Glyn White, 'Prestige Lecture', address to Royal Women's Hospital, Melbourne, 9 November 1982, in personal papers of Bill Flowers, Melbourne, p. 3.
3  ibid.
4  John D. 'Jack' Higgs, 'Beffie and Me: Jack's Memoirs of Family, January 1991–December 2004', unpublished memoir, p. 100.
5  White, 'Prestige Lecture', p. 4.
6  Bob Goodwin and Jim Dixon, *Medicos and Memories: Further recollections of the 2/10th Field Regiment R.A.A.*, 2/10th Field Regiment Association, Rochedale Qld, 2000, p. 12.
7  Allan S. Walker, *Clinical Problems of War*, Australian War Memorial, Canberra, 1952, p. 605.
8  Lionel Wigmore, *The Japanese Thrust*, Australian War Memorial, Canberra, 1957, p. 515.
9  Stan F. Arneil, *One Man's War*, Alternative Publishing Co-operative, Sydney, 1980, p. 17.
10  H. V. Clarke, C. Burgess, and R. Braddon, *Prisoners of War*, Time-Life Books, Sydney, 1988, p. 67.
11  Roy Mills, *Doctor's Diary and Memoirs: Pond's party, F Force, Burma–Thai Railway*, self-published, New Lambton NSW, c. 1994, p. 38.
12  Major Alan Hobbs, personal diary, AWM PR85/086, Australian War Memorial, Canberra.
13  Sergeant D. Griffin, quoted in Clarke et al., *Prisoners of War*, p. 65.
14  A. J. Sweeting in Wigmore, *The Japanese Thrust*, p. 513.
15  'Medical Attendance on Prisoners of War, Report on Blakane Mati Camps, Changi, to A.D.M.S. 8th Australian Division—15th June 1942', AWM 54 481/8/1, Australian War Memorial, Canberra.
16  'The Campaign in Malaya P.O.W. Camp, Kuala Lumpur, The Campaign in Malaya P.O.W. Camp, Changi, The Campaign in Malaya P.O.W. Camp, Kranji, 1941 Dec.-1942 Feb.' WO 222/1387, National Archives, London, p. 32.
17  'Medical Attendance on Prisoners of War'.
18  White, 'Prestige Lecture', pp. 8–9.
19  ibid., p. 9.
20  Interview with Charles 'Rowley' Richards, Australians at War Film Archive, no. 1144, <www.australiansatwarfilmarchive.gov.au/aawfa/interviews/1048.aspx>, accessed 10 October 2008.
21  Mills, *Doctor's Diary and Memoirs*, p. 39.
22  Stanley Pavillard, *Bamboo Doctor*, Macmillan, London, 1960, p. 58.

23 Captain Ben Wheeler RAMC, 'Changi Annual Medical Report 16/2/44—15/2/45', RAMC 1016, Box 210, Wellcome Institute, London.
24 Correspondence between Colonel J. G. Glyn White and Allan S. Walker re Changi, 8 September 1945, AWM 54 481/8/26, Australian War Memorial, Canberra.
25 Lieutenant Colonel John Huston, quoted in Walker, *Clinical Problems of War*, p. 597.
26 Hank Nelson, *Prisoners of War: Australians under Nippon*, ABC Enterprises for the Australian Broadcasting Corporation, Sydney, 2001, p. 156.
27 White, 'Prestige Lecture', p. 4.
28 Hobbs, personal diary, 30 March 1942.
29 Wigmore, *The Japanese Thrust*, p. 515.
30 White, 'Prestige Lecture', p. 5.
31 Major Alexander Norman Thompson MBE, personal papers, AWM PR00016, Australian War Memorial, Canberra.
32 White, 'Prestige Lecture', p. 7.
33 Walker, *Clinical Problems of War*, p. 595.
34 Ray Connolly and Bob Wilson, eds, *Medical Soldiers: 2/10 Australian Field Ambulance 8 Div. 1940–45*, 2/10th Australian Field Ambulance Association, Sydney, c. 1985, p. 137.
35 Cotter Harvey, 'Medical Aspects of the Singapore Captivity', *Medical Journal of Australia*, vol. 1, 1 June 1946, p. 769.
36 Major Robert G. Orr and Captain Michael Woodruff, 'Report on Retrobulbar Neuritis with special reference to the situation in the Selarang area up to 12.12.42', 19 December 1942, AWM 54 481/8/12, Australian War Memorial, Canberra.
37 Major Heyworth Watson, 'Summary of the Clinical conditions in the mouth in Changi', 1942, in correspondence between Colonel J. G. Glyn White and Allan Walker re Changi, AWM 54 481/8/26, Australian War Memorial, Canberra.
38 Lieutenant Colonel L. Fernley, personal diary, 88/62/1, Imperial War Museum, London.
39 Interview with Charles 'Rowley' Richards, Australians at War Film Archive, no. 1144.
40 Corporal Lex Arthurson, personal papers, AWM PR91/135, Australian War Memorial, Canberra.
41 Higgs, 'Beffie and Me', p. 104.

42 *Camp Pie*, the magazine of Changi POW Hospital, Singapore, 1942, Royal Army Medical Corps 1261, Box 276, Wellcome Institute, London.
43 Lieutenant Colonel A. Dillon RAMC, 'Medical War Diary and Reports Subsequent to Capitulation of British forces in Malaya, 1942–45', WO 222/1386, National Archives, London.
44 'Medical Attendance on Prisoners of War'.
45 Letter from Major Kennedy Burnside to Colonel J. G. Glyn White, 20 August 1945, in correspondence between Colonel J. G. Glyn White and Allan Walker re Changi, AWM 54 481/8/26, Australian War Memorial, Canberra.
46 Letter from Lieutenant Colonel R. M. Oakes to Colonel J. G. Glyn White, in correspondence between Colonel J. G. Glyn White and Allan Walker re Adam Park, Bukit Timah and River Valley Road camps 1942, 20 November 1942, AWM 54 481/8/18, Australian War Memorial, Canberra.
47 Higgs, 'Beffie and Me', p. 108.
48 Major Ernest Marsden, 'Report re Bukit Timah No. 5 Camp—Reference H.Q.-AIF. memo M1080. Deficiency Diseases' 1942, in correspondence between Colonel J. G. Glyn White and Allan Walker re Adam Park, Bukit Timah and River Valley Road camps 1942, AWM 54 481/8/18, Australian War Memorial, Canberra.
49 Connolly and Wilson, *Medical Soldiers: 2/10 Australian Field Ambulance 8 Div. 1940–45*, p. 132.
50 ibid., p. 137.
51 Major Alexander Norman Thompson, his emphasis, personal diary, AWM PR00016, Australian War Memorial, Canberra.
52 Arneil, *One Man's War*, pp. 71, 155.
53 ibid., p. 49.
54 Hank Nelson, 'Travelling in memories: Australian prisoners of the Japanese, forty years after the Fall of Singapore', *Journal of the Australian War Memorial*, no. 3, October 1983, p. 21.
55 ibid.

## Chapter 3  Making bricks without straw: the Burma–Thai Railway

1 Kevin J. Fagan, 'Surgical Experiences as a Prisoner of War', *Medical Journal of Australia*, vol. 1, 1 June 1946, p. 776.
2 Lieutenant Colonel S. W. Harris, 'Report on "F" Force', WO 222/1386, National Archives, London.

3. Lieutenant Colonel A. E. Coates, War Crimes Trials Statement, 10 April 1947, AWM 54 1010/4/33, Australian War Memorial, Canberra.
4. Lieutenant Colonel T. R. Beaton, 'From both ends of the Siam–Burma Railway', *Australian Defence Force Journal*, no. 113, July/August 1995, p. 6.
5. Major Alan Hobbs, personal diary, 14 May 1942, AWM PR85/086, Australian War Memorial, Canberra.
6. Lieutenant Colonel Thomas Hamilton, 'Report on POW Hospital Camp Nakon Patom', WO 222/1389, National Archives, London.
7. Coates, War Crimes Trials Statement, 10 April 1947.
8. Hamilton, 'Report on POW Hospital Camp Nakon Patom'.
9. Lieutenant Colonel A. Dillon, 'Medical War Diary and Reports Subsequent to Capitulation of British forces in Malaya, 1942–45', WO 222/1386, National Archives, London, p. 4.
10. Unattributed, *'Getting on with it'—2/30th Battalion AIF*, 2/30th Battalion Association, Kingsway West NSW, 1998, p. 17.
11. Major Eugene Rogers in Major E. A. Marsden, 'Report of Kamburi Staging camp', AWM 54 554/17/2, Australian War Memorial, Canberra, p. 1.
12. Dillon, 'Medical War Diary and Reports', p. 7.
13. Major A. L. Dunlop, 'Brief History of Base Hospital Chungkai POW Camp, Siam. Report on diet, malnutrition, hygiene, 1942', 23 September 1945, AWM 54 554/5/2, Australian War Memorial, Canberra, p. 2.
14. Coates, War Crimes Trials Statement, 19 October 1945.
15. Major N. Courtney Lendon, 'Disease among prisoners of war', Royal Army Medical Corps 1042, Box 215, Wellcome Institute, n.d., p. 24.
16. M. Foster, 'Medico makes emotion-charged return to Hellfire Pass', *NSW Doctor*, June 1998, p. 24.
17. Stan Arneil quoted in Richard Reid, *In Captivity: Australian prisoners of war in the 20th century*, Commonwealth Department of Veterans' Affairs, Canberra, 1999, p. 41.
18. Lieutenant Colonel E. E. Dunlop, War Crimes Trials Statement, AWM 1010/4/46, Australian War Memorial, Canberra.
19. Lieutenant Colonel Albert E. Coates, 'General Report on the Medical Aspects of P.O.W. treatment by the Japanese in Burma and Thailand', 10 September 1945, Bangkok, AWM 54 554/17/3, Australian War Memorial, Canberra.
20. Colonel B. H. Anderson, War Crimes Trials Statement, 21 February 1946, AWM 54 1010/4/5, Australian War Memorial, Canberra.
21. Dunlop, War Crimes Trials Statement.

22  Lieutenant Colonel Albert Coates, 'Impressions of the Nakonpatom Hospital, written by Lt-Col Albert Ernest Coates, A.A.M.C. at the request of the I.J.A. doctor, 22.11.44', AWM 54 554/17/3, Australian War Memorial, Canberra.
23  Captain H. De Wardener, 'The Cholera Epidemic amongst British Troops in Takanun POW Camp, May–September, 1943', in the papers of Major T. M. (Max) Pemberton, Senior Medical Officer Chungkai and Tamuan POW hospitals, uncatalogued, Imperial War Museum, London.
24  A. L. Dunlop, 'Brief History of Base Hospital Chungkai POW Camp, Siam', p. 3.
25  Lendon, 'Disease among prisoners of war', p. 32.
26  Captain R. B. C. Welsh, personal diary, 13 May 1943, uncatalogued, Imperial War Museum, London.
27  Stanley Pavillard, *Bamboo Doctor*, Macmillan, London, 1960, p. 110.
28  John D. 'Jack' Higgs, 'Beffie and Me: Jack's Memoirs of Family, January 1991–December 2004', unpublished memoir, p. 123.
29  ibid., p. 124.
30  Captain Harry Silman, personal diary, 3 June 1943, IWM 66/226/1, Imperial War Museum, London, p. 14.
31  Doug Warner, quoted in Ray Connolly and Bob Wilson, eds, *Medical Soldiers: 2/10 Australian Field Ambulance 8 Div. 1940–45*, 2/10th Australian Field Ambulance Association, Sydney, c. 1985, p. 241.
32  Jack Barclay quoted in John Lack, ed., *No Lost Battalion: An oral history of the 2/29th Battalion AIF*, Slouch Hat Publications, McCrae Victoria, 2005, p. 141.
33  Harris, 'Report on "F" Force'.
34  Dillon, 'Medical War Diary and Reports Subsequent to Capitulation', p. 1.
35  Higgs, 'Beffie and Me', pp. 118–19.
36  Dillon, 'Medical War Diary and Reports Subsequent to Capitulation', p. 2.
37  Allan S. Walker, *Middle East and Far East*, Australian War Memorial, Canberra, 1953, p. 595.
38  'Getting on with it', p. 18.
39  Dillon, 'Medical War Diary and Reports Subsequent to Capitulation', p. 5.
40  Dunlop, War Crimes Trials Statement.
41  Harris, 'Report on "F" Force'.
42  J. G. Glyn White, 'Prestige Lecture', address to Royal Women's Hospital, Melbourne, 9 November 1982, in personal papers of Bill Flowers, Melbourne, p. 6.

43 Osmund E. Vickers-Bush, 'Hell and its Yellow Devils', MSS 1085, Australian War Memorial, Canberra, p. 55.
44 Major B. L. W. Clarke, War Crimes Trials Statement, 14 November 1945, AWM 54 1010/4/32, Australian War Memorial, Canberra.
45 Charles Huxtable, *From the Somme to Singapore: A medical officer in two world wars*, Kangaroo Press, Kenthurst NSW, 1987, pp. 142–3.
46 'Getting on with it', p. 13.
47 Ian L. Duncan, 'Makeshift medicine: combating disease in the Japanese prison camps', *Medical Journal of Australia*, vol. 1, 8 January 1983, p. 30.
48 A. L. Dunlop, 'Brief history of the Base Hospital—Chunkai P.W. Camp—Siam', p. 3.
49 Peter J. Morris, 'Sir Michael Woodruff', <www.rsnz.govt.nz/directory/yearbooks/2001/woodruff.php>, accessed 4 February 2003. Woodruff's notes on nutrition and deficiency diseases made during captivity were held as classified material by the Australian Government after the war, but were eventually published in the UK in 1951, under the title 'Deficiency Diseases in Japanese Prison Camps'.
50 Major A. R. Hazelton, 'Report on activities of eye clinic at Nakon Patom', 12 September 1945, WO 222/1389, National Archives, London.
51 Duncan, 'Makeshift medicine', p. 30.
52 ibid.
53 Hazelton, 'Report on activities of eye clinic at Nakon Patom'.
54 E. E. Dunlop, 'Tarsau Hospital Bulletin 3/12/43', WO 222/1389, National Archives, London. Here Dunlop is quoting Captain Cyril Vardy.
55 Rowley Richards and Marcia McEwan, *The Survival Factor*, Kangaroo Press, Kenthurst NSW, 1989, p. 76.
56 A. L. Dunlop, 'Brief history of the Base Hospital: Chunkai POW Camp, Siam', 26 September 1945, p. 1.
57 Lieutenant Colonel J. W. Malcolm, 'Report On POW Hospital Camp Nakom Paton', 11 September 1945, WO 222/1389, National Archives, London.
58 Albert Coates, 'Impressions of the Nakonpatom Hospital'.
59 See Connolly and Wilson, *Medical Soldiers*, p. 258, for an account of this use of hypnosis by Dutch medical officer, Dr Sampeman.
60 Interview with Huddleston W. Wright by Ronald Marcello, University of North Texas Oral History Program, no. 794, Denton, Texas, 2 and 14 November 1989, p. 147.

61 Interview with Colonel Ilo B. Hard by Ronald Marcello, University of North Texas Oral History Program, no. 510, Denton, Texas, 26 March 1980, p. 170.
62 Interview with Griff L. Douglas by Ronald Marcello, University of North Texas Oral History Program, no. 425, Denton, Texas, 18 April 1978, p. 104.
63 Captain C. J. van Boxtel, 'Report on Chemical and Pharmaceutical work at 55 kilo camp, Burma', AWM 54 554/2/9, Australian War Memorial, Canberra.
64 Albert E. Coates and Norman Rosenthal, *The Albert Coates Story: The will that found a way*, Hyland House, Melbourne, 1977, p. 118.
65 Van Boxtel, 'Report on Chemical and Pharmaceutical work at 55 kilo camp'.
66 ibid.
67 Bevan Warland-Browne, Australians at War Film Archive Interview, no. 0583, <www.australiansatwarfilmarchive.gov.au/aawfa/interviews/158.aspx>, accessed 8 October 2008.
68 Van Boxtel, 'Report on Chemical and Pharmaceutical work at 55 kilo camp'.
69 Duncan, 'Makeshift medicine', p. 30.
70 *'Getting on with it'*, p. 14.
71 'Medical Attendance on Prisoners of War: Memoranda on diet and treatment of various diseases by Australian Medical Officers in Japanese hands', AWM 54 481/8/9, Australian War Memorial, Canberra.
72 A. L. Dunlop, 'Brief history of the Base Hospital: Chunkai—Chunkai POW Camp, Siam', p. 3.
73 Duncan, 'Makeshift medicine', p. 31.
74 Lieutenant Colonel E. E. Dunlop, 'Chungkai Camp—Medical Report Upon Malnutrition and Diet of Prisoners of War', AWM 54 554/5/2, Australian War Memorial, Canberra.
75 M. Foster, 'Medico makes emotion-charged return to Hellfire Pass', *NSW Doctor*, June 1998, p. 24.
76 This technique using maggots is used today for the treatment of ulcers. See The Royal Free Hospital (UK) Vascular Unit, <www.freevas.demon.co.uk/alistair/maggots.htm>, accessed 21 July 2003.
77 Duncan, 'Makeshift medicine', pp. 31, 32.
78 Coates, 'General Report on the Medical Aspects of P.O.W. treatment by the Japanese in Burma and Thailand', p. 4.
79 Foster, 'Medico makes emotion-charged return to Hellfire Pass', p. 24.

80 Captain J. J. Woodward, 'Report of Service from December 1941 to September 1945 of Capt. J. J. Woodward IMC/IAMC', AWM PR83/32, Australian War Memorial, Canberra.
81 Pavillard, *Bamboo Doctor*, p. 78.
82 Lieutenant Colonel Hedley F. Summons, 'Hospital Orders No. 237 by Lieut. Colonel. Hedley F Summons O.C. Camp Hospital', 7 September 1945, in Arthurson, personal papers, AWM PR91/135.
83 Interview with Charles 'Rowley' Richards, Australians at War Film Archive, no. 1144, <www.australiansatwarfilmarchive.gov.au/aawfa/interviews/1048.aspx>, accessed 10 October 2008.
84 Captain C. S. Pitt RAMC, 'Medical Report on the Wampoy–Tavoy Road working party 19/12/44–5/6/45', WO 222/1390, National Archives, London.
85 Pavillard, *Bamboo Doctor*, p. 130.
86 Connolly and Wilson, *Medical Soldiers*, p. 204.
87 Higgs, 'Beffie and Me', pp. 125–6.
88 E. E. Dunlop, *The War Diaries of Weary Dunlop: Java and the Burma–Thailand Railway, 1942–1945*, Thomas Nelson, Melbourne, 1986, p. xv.
89 Allan S. Walker, *Clinical Problems of War*, Australian War Memorial, Canberra, 1952, p. 614. The Australian POW dentists were Captain F. W. Finch, Captain J. T. Finemore, Major D. A. Proctor, Major H. W. Park, Captain R. Mannion, Captain F. R. Reid, Major J. O. Rosson, Captain J. Scoffin, Captain S. T. Simpson, Captain J. K. Treleaven, Captain J. Throssell, Captain M. K. Winchester and Captain R. Wilkinson.

## Chapter 4   Untold stories: the other camps

1 Bob Moore and Kent Fedorowich, eds, *Prisoners of War and Their Captors in World War II*, Berg Publishers, Oxford, 1996, p. 3.
2 Hank Nelson, *Prisoners of War: Australians under Nippon*, ABC Enterprises for the Australian Broadcasting Corporation, Sydney, 2001, pp. 86, 97.
3 Joan Beaumont, review of Hugh V. Clarke, *Twilight Liberation: Australian prisoners of war between Hiroshima and home*, in *Journal of the Australian War Memorial*, no. 12, April 1988, p. 63.
4 Alexander Dandie, *The story of 'J' Force: 300, 8 Division A.I.F., Singapore to Japan P.O.W. camps with American, British and Allied troops*, A. Dandie, Sydney, 1994, pp. vi, 1.

5  Harry Leslie, 'The Lost Cause: Personal experiences of a Prisoner of War from the Taiwan War Camps', address given at Waverley Library, Bondi Junction, 26 October 1994.
6  Major Robert V. Glasgow, citation for MBE, in the service record of Captain John Finch Akeroyd VX18194, National Archives of Australia, Canberra.
7  H. F. Atkinson, 'Lest we forget', *ADA News Bulletin*, no. 22B, November 1995, p. 45.
8  Ailsa Rolley, *Survival on Ambon*, A. Rolley, Beaudesert Qld, c. 1994, p. 127. Hohl did not record the result of the amputation.
9  J. C. Collins, letter reproduced in Lieutenant Colonel R. W. Webster, 'Report on Kranji Hospital, June 1945', 10 June 1945, AWM 3DRL/3435 (2), Australian War Memorial, Canberra, p. 2.
10 Webster, 'Report on Kranji Hospital, June 1945', p. 2.
11 Major Burnett L. Clarke, War Crimes Trials Statement, 14 November 1945, AWM 54 1010/4/32, Australian War Memorial, Canberra.
12 Captain MacArthur, 'Incidence of Deficiency Disease (Mainly Vit. B2) on Camp Diet, Report submitted to IJA 1.6.45', AWM 54 554/5/2, Australian War Memorial, Canberra.
13 Ian L. Duncan, 'Final Summary of Medical Staff, 10 August 1943–28 August 1945, Fukuoka Camp, Japan', personal papers, pp. 1, 3.
14 ibid., p. 11.
15 ibid., pp. 12–13, 21.
16 ibid., p. 21.
17 'Conversation with Surg-Lt-Commander S. E. L. Stening' in 'Personal narratives of Navy Medical Officers, their experiences in action and POW camps', AWM 54 481/1/12, Australian War Memorial, Canberra.
18 Duncan, 'Final Summary of Medical Staff', pp. 14–15.
19 ibid., p. 15.
20 ibid., pp. 18, 20.
21 Allan S. Walker, *Middle East and Far East*, Australian War Memorial, Canberra, 1953, p. 654.
22 Dr Desmond Brennan, POW diary, 4 December 1942, Royal Australasian College of Physicians Library, Sydney.
23 'Dramatic struggle for lives', *NSW Doctor*, November/December 1995, p. 11.
24 ibid.

25 Captain William Aitken, 'Medical Report P.O.W. Camp, Hashio (Bakli Bay) Hainan Island', B26/82: Item M x 51467 PE 2 Miskin, National Archives of Australia, Melbourne, p. 3.
26 ibid.
27 Lieutenant Colonel C. W. Maisey, 'Report on St Vincentius P.O.W. Hospital, Batavia. August 1943–April 1945', 5 December 1945, WO 222/1391, National Archives, London.
28 ibid.
29 Aitken, 'Medical Report P.O.W. Camp, Hashio (Bakli Bay) Hainan Island', pp. 1, 8.
30 ibid., pp. 1–2.
31 Hank Nelson, 'A bowl of rice for seven camels', *Journal of the Australian War Memorial*, no. 14, April 1989, p. 37.
32 Nelson, *Prisoners of War*, p. 96.
33 Aitken, 'Medical Report P.O.W. Camp, Hashio (Bakli Bay) Hainan Island', p. 7.
34 Captain Ian Duncan, War Crimes Trials Statement, 2 September 1948, AWM 1010/4/46, Australian War Memorial, Canberra.
35 Mick Ryan, quoted in Ray Connolly and Bob Wilson, eds, *Medical Soldiers: 2/10 Australian Field Ambulance 8 Div. 1940–45*, 2/10th Australian Field Ambulance Association, Sydney, c. 1985, p. 182.
36 Brennan, POW diary, 18 November 1944.
37 Maisey, 'Report on St Vincentius P.O.W. Hospital, Batavia', p. 6.
38 ibid.
39 ibid.
40 Walker, *Middle East and Far East*, p. 655.
41 Glasgow, citation for MBE, in service record of Captain John Finch Akeroyd.
42 Richard Reid, *In Captivity: Australian prisoners of war in the 20th century*, Commonwealth Department of Veterans' Affairs, Canberra, 1999, p. 37.
43 Nelson, *Prisoners of War*, p. 156.
44 Leslie, 'The Lost Cause'.
45 J. D. C. Hammon, personal unpublished memoir of 2/3rd MG Battalion, p. 13.
46 Captain W. Aitken, War Crimes Trials Statement, 4 July 1946, AWM 54 1010/4/2, Australian War Memorial, Canberra.
47 Aitken, 'Medical Report P.O.W. Camp, Hashio (Bakli Bay) Hainan Island', p. 8.

48 Duncan, 'Final Summary of Medical Staff, 10 August 1943–28 August', p. 2.
49 Ian Duncan, 'Conditions in Japanese Coal Mines', personal papers, pp. 3, 4.
50 Duncan, 'Final Summary of Medical Staff, 10 August 1943–28 August 1945', p. 16.
51 Ken Collins, quoted in Connolly and Wilson, *Medical Soldiers*, p. 196.
52 Duncan, 'Final Summary of Medical Staff, 10 August 1943–28 August 1945', p. 16.
53 Captain A. K. Barrett, War Crimes Trials Statement, 16 January 1946, AWM 54 1010/4/10, Australian War Memorial, Canberra.
54 Rolley, *Survival on Ambon*, p. 128.
55 Aitken, 'Medical Report P.O.W. Camp, Hashio (Bakli Bay) Hainan Island', pp. 6–7.
56 Major Hugh Rayson, personal diary, 16 February 1942–21 February 1942, AWM PR00720, Australian War Memorial, Canberra.
57 Lieutenant Colonel E. E. Dunlop, 'Chungkai Camp—Medical Report Upon Malnutrition and Diet of Prisoners of War', AWM 54 554/5/2, Australian War Memorial, Canberra.
58 ibid.
59 Lieutenant Colonel Cotter Harvey, 'AIF Medical Report—Six Months at Kranji, May 28th to Nov 30th 1944', 1 December 1944, AWM 54 554/11/26, Australian War Memorial, Canberra.
60 ibid.
61 Rick Feneley, 'A-bombs "saved" 15,000 POWs', *Weekend Australian*, 18 June 1988.
62 Lieutenant Colonel Cotter Harvey, 'Notes on the use of the Red Cross Vitamin Supplies at Kranji Hospital', in personal papers of Lieutenant Colonel R. W. Webster MC, AWM 3DRL/3435(2), Australian War Memorial, Canberra.
63 Sibylla Jane Flower, 'Captors and Captives on the Burma–Thailand Railway', in Moore and Fedorowich, *Prisoners of War and Their Captors in World War II*, p. 246.
64 Major Howard Eddey, War Crimes Trials Statement, AWM 54 1010/4/47, Australian War Memorial, Canberra.
65 Major Howard Eddey, 'Prisoner-of-war camps in Borneo', *Medical Journal of Australia*, vol. 2, 21 September 1946, p. 403.
66 Rayson, personal diary.
67 ibid.
68 Eddey, War Crimes Trials Statement.

69 Rayson, personal diary.
70 Eddey, 'Prisoner-of-war camps in Borneo', p. 404.
71 Connolly and Wilson, *Medical Soldiers*, p. 263.
72 Leslie, 'The Lost Cause'.
73 Stanley Pavillard, *Bamboo Doctor*, Macmillan, London, 1960, p. 127.
74 Joan Beaumont, *Gull Force: Survival and leadership in captivity 1941–1945*, Allen & Unwin, Sydney 1988, p. 105.
75 Connolly and Wilson, *Medical Soldiers*, p. 264.
76 Maisey, 'Report on St Vincentius P.O.W. Hospital, Batavia', p. 8.
77 Duncan, 'Makeshift medicine', p. 30.
78 Maisey, 'Report on St Vincentius P.O.W. Hospital, Batavia', p. 8.
79 Interview with Charles 'Rowley' Richards, Australians at War Film Archive, no. 1144, <www.australiansatwarfilmarchive.gov.au/aawfa/interviews/1048.aspx>, accessed 10 October 2008.
80 Atkinson, 'Lest we forget', p. 47.
81 Walker, *Middle East and Far East*, p. 647.
82 Rayson, personal diary.
83 An artificial pneumothorax was a device used in the early twentieth century to inject air or a slowly absorbed gas into the pleural space to collapse the lung. This therapy was based on the idea that collapsing the section of a lung infected with tuberculosis allowed the infected area to rest and recover.
84 Dr D. J. Brennan, letter to Mr J. D. C. Bill Hammon, 5 November 1986, in personal papers of Alf Stone, Newcastle.
85 Rayson, personal diary.
86 Hank Nelson, 'Turning North: Australians in Southeast Asia in World War 2', *Overland*, no. 119, winter 1990, p. 38.
87 Laurens van der Post, 'Foreword' in E. E. Dunlop, *The War Diaries of Weary Dunlop: Java and the Burma–Thailand Railway, 1942–1945*, Thomas Nelson, Melbourne, 1986, p. xii.
88 Aitken, 'Medical Report P.O.W. Camp, Hashio (Bakli Bay) Hainan Island', p. 16.
89 Rayson, personal diary.

## Chapter 5   A complex relationship: doctors and captors

1 Major Hugh Rayson, personal diary, 16 February 1942–21 February 1942, AWM PR00720, Australian War Memorial, Canberra.

2 Unidentified Japanese Officer, 1942, quoted in A. B. Feuer, ed., *Bilibid Diary: The secret notebooks of Commander Thomas Hayes, POW, the Phillipines, 1942–45*, Archon Books, Hamden, Conn., 1987, p. 52.

3 Major Bruce Hunt, 'Notes for "F" Force Report', in papers of Major B. A. Hunt, 3DRL/3517, File 3, Australian War Memorial, Canberra, p. 2.

4 Captain I. Duncan, War Crimes Trials Statement, 2 September 1948, AWM 54 1010/4/46, Australian War Memorial, Canberra.

5 Lieutenant Colonel S. W. Harris, 'Narrative of "F" Force in Thailand, April–December, 1943', in papers of Major Bruce Hunt, 3DRL/3517, Australian War Memorial, Canberra, p. 4.

6 Lieutenant Colonel E. E. Dunlop, War Crimes Trials Statement, AWM 54 1010/4/46, Australian War Memorial, Canberra.

7 Lieutenant Colonel C. W. Maisey, 'Report on St Vincentius P.O.W. Hospital, Batavia. August 1943–April 1945', 5 December 1945, WO 222/1391, National Archives, London, p. 9.

8 Captain Newton Lee, 'Report on POW Hospital Camp Nakom Paton, by Capt Newton Lee, adjutant of hospital section of Tamakan, Chungkai and Tamuang Camps, not including Nakom Paton, January 1944–August 1945', WO 222/1389, National Archives, London.

9 Lieutenant Colonel A. Dillon RAMC, 'Medical War Diary and Reports Subsequent to Capitulation of British forces in Malaya, 1942–45', WO 222/1386, National Archives, London.

10 'A' Force reports, War Diary of 2/4 CCS, AWM 54 554/2/9, Australian War Memorial, Canberra.

11 Colonel C. A. McEachern, 'Report Conditions, Life and Work POW Burma/Siam 1942–1945', AWM 54 554/2/9, Australian War Memorial, Canberra.

12 Captain C. S. Pitt, 'Report on Kinsayok Camp, April 43–August 43', 23 October 1945, WO 222/1390, National Archives, London.

13 Red Cross Report on Far East Osaka Group Camps, WO 224/189, National Archives, London.

14 Lieutenant Colonel C. W. Maisey, 'Medical Report—Cycle camp, Batavia (No. 1 P.O.W. Camp), April–August, 1943', 5 December 1945, WO 222/1391, National Archives, London.

15 Private Albert Casey, 'Report on conditions of Prisoners of War in Thailand May to December 1943', AWM PR00701, Australian War Memorial, Canberra.

16 Lieutenant Colonel Albert Coates, 'Impressions of the Nakonpatom Hospital, written by Lt-Col Albert Ernest Coates, A.A.M.C. at the

request of the I.J.A. doctor, 22.11.44', AWM 54 554/17/3, Australian War Memorial, Canberra.
17 Lieutenant Colonel A. E. Coates, War Crimes Trials Statement, 10 April 1946, AWM 54 1010/4/33, Australian War Memorial, Canberra.
18 Lieutenant Colonel J. Huston, 'British POWs in Japanese Hands', WO 222/156, National Archives, London.
19 ibid.
20 Captain Clive Boyce, 'Medical Report', MS Box 74, Item 3, Royal Australasian College of Physicians Library.
21 Captain Osmar Julius Blau, 'Address to Toowong Boy Scouts and Cubs', 24 April 1997, AWM PR01047, Australian War Memorial, Canberra.
22 Captain J. J. Woodward, 'Report of Service from December 1941 to September 1945 of Capt. J.J. Woodward IMC/IAMC', AWM PR83/32, Australian War Memorial, Canberra.
23 Dr W. Boyd Graham, 'Articles for public information', AWM 54 773/2/5, Australian War Memorial, Canberra.
24 Captain P. P. Miskin, 'Report on Conditions on Ambon and Hainan Islands', B26/82, Item M x 51467 PE 2 Miskin, National Archives of Australia, Melbourne.
25 Woodward, 'Report of Service from December 1941 to September 1945'.
26 Captain R. W. Lennon, 'Medical Reports on a Group of Prisoners of War, Keppel Harbour Camp, Singapore, Railway Camps, Thailand 1943–44', 9 September 1945, WO 222/117, National Archives, London.
27 Major E. A. Smyth and Captain R. W. Lennon, 'POW camps in Thailand', 11 September 1945, WO 222/17, National Archives, London, p. 12.
28 Dunlop, War Crimes Trials Statement.
29 Captain A. J. N. Warrack, 'POW camps in Hong Kong and Japan', WO 222/22, National Archives, London.
30 ibid.
31 Osmund E. Vickers-Bush, 'Hell and its Yellow Devils', MSS 1085, Australian War Memorial, Canberra, p. 43.
32 Lieutenant Colonel C. W. Maisey, 'Reports on POW camps in Batavia 1942–45', 24 November 1945, WO 222/1391, National Archives, London.
33 ibid.
34 Ray Connolly and Bob Wilson, eds, *Medical Soldiers: 2/10 Australian Field Ambulance 8 Div. 1940–45*, 2/10th Australian Field Ambulance Association, Sydney, c. 1985, p. 269.

35 Captain C. R. B. Richards, 'Summary of pages from personal diary of Capt. C.R.B. Richards, Medical reports in POW Camps', AWM 54 554/2/9, Australian War Memorial, Canberra.
36 Rayson, personal diary.
37 Maisey, 'Report on St Vincentius P.O.W. Hospital, Batavia', p. 6.
38 Duncan, War Crimes Trials Statement.
39 Maisey, 'Reports on POW camps in Batavia 1942–45'.
40 Woodward, 'Report of Service from December 1941 to September 1945 of Capt. J.J. Woodward IMC/IAMC'.
41 Interview with Sam B. Moody by William J Alexander, University of North Texas Oral History Program, no. 1277, Fredericksburg, Texas, 10 October 1996, p. 18.
42 M. Arthur, 'Death was all around me for 3½ years', *Daily Mail*, 27 May 1998, p. 5.
43 Hank Nelson, *Prisoners of War: Australians under Nippon*, ABC Enterprises for the Australian Broadcasting Corporation, Sydney, 2001, p. 96.
44 Hunt, 'Notes for "F" Force Report', p. 2.
45 Yi Hak-Nae, 'A man between: A Korean guard looks back', in Gavan McCormack and Hank Nelson, eds, *The Burma–Thailand Railway: Memory and history*, Allen & Unwin, Sydney, 1993, p. 124.
46 Kasayama Yoshikichi, 'Korean Guard', in Haruko Taya Cook and Theodore F. Cook, *Japan at War: An oral history*, New Press, New York, 1992, pp. 119–20.
47 Stanley Pavillard, *Bamboo Doctor*, Macmillan, London, 1960, p. 148.
48 Interview with Captain Clark L. Taylor by Ronald Marcello, University of North Texas Oral History Program, no. 491, Denton, Texas, 14 September 1979, p. 67.
49 Lieutenant Colonel J. W. Malcolm, 'Report On POW Hospital Camp Nakom Paton', 11 September 1945, WO 222/1389, National Archives, London.
50 E. E. Dunlop, *The War Diaries of Weary Dunlop: Java and the Burma–Thailand Railway, 1942–1945*, Thomas Nelson, Melbourne, 1986, p. xv.
51 Captain B. W. Wheeler and Major J. F. Crossley, 'Prisoner of war camp Formosa, appendix to report on medical conditions', 4 November 1944, WO 222/118, National Archives, London.
52 ibid.

53  Charles G. Roland, 'Allied POWs, Japanese captors and the Geneva Convention', *War and Society*, vol. 9, no. 2, October 1991, p. 87.
54  Lieutenant Colonel S. W. Harris, 'Report on "F" Force', WO 222/1386, National Archives, London, p. 3.
55  Rayson, personal diary.
56  Major E. A. Smyth and Captain R. W. Lennon, 'POW camps in Thailand', 11 September 1945, WO 222/17, National Archives, London, p. 12.
57  Leslie Poidevin, *Samurais and Circumcisions*, self published, Burnside, SA, 1985, pp. 94–5.
58  Pavillard, *Bamboo Doctor*, p. 80.
59  Interview with Charles 'Rowley' Richards, Australians at War Film Archive, no. 1144, <www.australiansatwarfilmarchive.gov.au/aawfa/interviews/1048.aspx>, accessed 10 October 2008.
60  McEachern, 'Report Conditions, Life and Work POW Burma/Siam 1942–1945'.
61  Lieutenant Colonel A. E. Coates, War Crimes Trials Statement, 29 October 45, AWM 54 1010/4/33, Australian War Memorial, Canberra.
62  Lieutenant Colonel A. E. Coates, 'General Report on the Medical Aspects of P.O.W. treatment by the Japanese in Burma and Thailand', 10 September 1945, Bangkok, AWM 54 554/17/3, Australian War Memorial, Canberra.
63  ibid.
64  Coates, War Crimes Trials Statement, 10 April 1946.
65  Major W. E. Fisher, War Crimes Trials Statement, 29 April 1946, AWM 54 1010/4/51, Australian War Memorial, Canberra.
66  Major H. Eddey, War Crimes Trials Statement, AWM 54 1010/4/47, Australian War Memorial, Canberra.
67  Rayson, personal diary.
68  Richard Gabriel and Karen Metz, *A History of Military Medicine, Vol II: From the Renaissance through modern times*, Greenwood Press, New York, 1992, pp. 226–7, 230–1, 256.
69  Captain R. W. Lennon, 'Medical Reports on a Group of Prisoners of War'.
70  Quoted in Dr W. Boyd Graham, 'Articles for public information', AWM 54 773/2/5, Australian War Memorial, Canberra.
71  Major A. A. Moon, 'Medical Report by Major A. A. Moon, Tamarkan Prisoner of War Hospital May–December 43', 13 July 1943, AWM 54 554/17/2, Australian War Memorial, Canberra, p. 1.

72 Papers of Major T. M. (Max) Pemberton, personal papers, uncatalogued, Imperial War Museum, London.
73 Lieutenant Colonel C. W. Maisey, untitled report on Japanese Atrocities, 29 November 1945, WO 222/1391, National Archives, London.
74 Boyce, 'Medical Report'.
75 Mick Ryan, quoted in Connolly and Wilson, *Medical Soldiers*, p. 183.
76 Captain William Aitken, 'Medical Report P.O.W. Camp, Hashio (Bakli Bay) Hainan Island', B26/82: Item M x 51467 PE 2 Miskin, National Archives of Australia, Melbourne.
77 Bruce Gamble, *Darkest Hour: The true story of Lark Force at Rabaul, Australia's worst military disaster of World War II*, Zenith Press, St Paul, Michigan, 2006, p. 213.
78 McEachern, 'Report Conditions, Life and Work POW Burma/Siam 1942–1945'.
79 Interview with Captain Clark L. Taylor by Ronald Marcello, University of North Texas Oral History Program, no. 491, Denton, Texas, 14 September 1979, p. 62.
80 Interview with E. Benjamin Dunn by Ronald Marcello, University of North Texas Oral History Program, no. 1329, Denton, Texas, 16 November 1999, p. 129.
81 Pavillard, *Bamboo Doctor*, p. 123.
82 Interview with Griff L. Douglas by Ronald Marcello, University of North Texas Oral History Program, no. 425, Fort Worth, Texas, 18 April 1978, p. 132.
83 J. G. Glyn White, 'Prestige Lecture', address to Royal Women's Hospital, Melbourne, 9 November 1982, in personal papers of Bill Flowers, Melbourne, p. 12.
84 Laurens van der Post, 'Foreword' in E. E. Dunlop, *The War Diaries of Weary Dunlop: Java and the Burma–Thailand Railway, 1942–1945*, Thomas Nelson, Melbourne, 1986, p. xi.
85 Interview with Charles 'Rowley' Richards, Australians at War Film Archive, no. 1144.
86 Boyce, 'Medical Report—Cycle camp, Batavia'.
87 Maisey, 'Reports on POW camps in Batavia 1942–45'.
88 Maisey, untitled report on Japanese atrocities.
89 ibid.
90 Coates, War Crimes Trials Statement, 10 April 1946.

91 Interview with RADM Ferdinand Berley MC USN by Jan K. Herman, United States Navy Bureau of Medicine and Surgery, 7, 21 and 27 February, 6 March, 3, 10 and 24 April, and 1 May 1995, p. 29.
92 Interview with Fiske Hanley, by Ronald Marcello, University of North Texas Oral History Program, no. 1335, Denton, Texas, 13 October 1999, pp. 145–6.
93 Duncan, War Crimes Trials Statement, 2 September 1948.
94 Ikuhiko Hata, 'From Consideration to Contempt: The changing nature of Japanese military and popular perceptions of prisoners of war through the ages', in Bob Moore and Kent Fedorowich, eds, *Prisoners of War and Their Captors in World War II*, Berg Publishers, Oxford, 1996, p. 253.
95 Charles G. Roland, 'Allied POWs, Japanese captors and the Geneva Convention', *War and Society*, vol. 9, no. 2, October 1991, p. 87.
96 Daniel Yergin, *The Prize: The epic quest for oil, money and power*, Simon and Schuster, New York, 1991, p. 307.
97 Hata, 'From Consideration to Contempt', p. 255.
98 Lieutenant Yamamoto Kiyoshi, personal diary, 3DRL/8027, Australian War Memorial, Canberra, p. 40.
99 Surgeon-Lieutenant S. E. L. Stening, War Crimes Trials Statement, n.d., AWM 54 1010/4/133, Australian War Memorial, Canberra.
100 Ienaga Saburo, *The Pacific War: World War II and the Japanese, 1931–1945*, Blackwell, Oxford, 1979, p. 255.
101 Quoted in Carol Gluck, 'The Idea of Showa', in Carol Gluck and Stephen R. Graubard, eds, *Showa: The Japan of Hirohito*, Norton, New York, 1992, p. 12.
102 Y. Sugimoto, 'Clash of ideologies overshadows the struggle for Japan's soul', *Weekend Australian*, 12–13 August 1995.
103 Yoshikuni Iragashi, *Bodies of Memory: Narratives of war in postwar Japanese culture, 1945–1970*, Princeton University Press, Princeton, New Jersey, 2000, p. 4.
104 Ian Buruma, *The Wages of Guilt: Memories of war in Germany and Japan*, Farrar Straus Giroux, New York, 1994, p. 161.
105 B. K. Gordon, 'Japan's Universities: US professor recounts surprising experiences at Kobe', *Far Eastern Economic Review*, 14 January 1993, p. 35.
106 Higgs, 'Beffie and Me', p. 170.

## Chapter 6 Doctor and officer

1. Bryan Egan, 'Understanding Medical Officers: Australian Doctors and War', unpublished manuscript, p. 3.
2. P. J. N. Duckworth, 'POW Script for Broadcast to London', 12 September 1945, Papers September 1945, in papers of Major B.A. Hunt, 3DRL/3517, File 3, Australian War Memorial, Canberra.
3. Interview with Charles 'Rowley' Richards, Australians at War Film Archive, no. 1144, <www.australiansatwarfilmarchive.gov.au/aawfa/interviews/1048.aspx>, accessed 10 October 2008.
4. Major R. R. Braganza, personal diary, IWM 96/5/1, Imperial War Museum, London.
5. Egan, 'Understanding Medical Officers', p. 27.
6. Major General Cecil A. Callaghan, citation for a CBE, in service record of Lieutenant Colonel William Bye, National Archives of Australia, Canberra. Although Bye was recommended for a CBE by Calleghan, he eventually received an OBE in March 1947.
7. Egan, 'Understanding Medical Officers', p. 31.
8. Osmund E. Vickers-Bush, 'Hell and its Yellow Devils', MSS 1085, Australian War Memorial, Canberra, p. 38.
9. Lieutenant Colonel C. W. Maisey, 'Psychological Review of the Behaviour of Prisoners of War in Java from March 1942 till October 1945', WO222/1391, National Archives, London, p. 2.
10. *Bridge on the River Kwai*, Columbia Pictures, written by Pierre Boule, Carl Foreman and Michael Wilson, directed by David Lean, 1957.
11. A. Hamilton, 'Skeletons of Empire: Australians and the Burma–Thailand Railway', in Kate Darian-Smith and Paula Hamilton, eds, *Memory and History in Twentieth Century Australia*, Oxford University Press, Melbourne, 1994, p. 101.
12. Lieutenant Colonel Albert Coates, 'Impressions of the Nakonpatom Hospital, written by Lt-Col Albert Ernest Coates, A.A.M.C. at the request of the I.J.A. doctor, 22.11.44', AWM 54 554/17/3, Australian War Memorial, Canberra.
13. J. G. Glyn White, 'Prestige Lecture', address to Royal Women's Hospital, Melbourne, 9 November 1982, in personal papers of Bill Flowers, Melbourne, p. 6.
14. Maisey, 'Psychological Review of the Behaviour of Prisoners of War', p. 3.

15 Joan Beaumont, *Gull Force: Survival and leadership in captivity 1941–1945*, Allen & Unwin, Sydney 1988, pp. 182–3.
16 Rowley Richards and Marcia McEwan, *The Survival Factor*, Kangaroo Press, Kenthurst NSW, 1989, pp. 157–8.
17 Major Hugh Rayson, personal diary, AWM PR00720, Australian War Memorial, Canberra.
18 Hank Nelson, *Prisoners of War: Australians under Nippon*, ABC Enterprises for the Australian Broadcasting Corporation, Sydney, 2001, p. 24–5.
19 Brigadier A. S. Blackburn VC, personal papers, AWM EXDOC084, Australian War Memorial, Canberra.
20 Alan Warren, *Singapore 1942: Britain's greatest defeat*, Hardie Grant Books, Melbourne, 2002, p. 242.
21 Hank Nelson, 'A bowl of rice for seven camels', *Journal of the Australian War Memorial*, no. 14, April 1989, p. 38.
22 Major J. W. D. Bull, transcript of conversation between Major Bull and Mrs Piers Mackesy, 26 March 1986, in personal papers, IWM 87/50/1, Imperial War Museum, London.
23 Joan Beaumont, 'Rank, Privilege and Prisoners of War', *War and Society*, vol. 1, no. 1, May 1983, p. 67.
24 Nelson, 'A bowl of rice for seven camels', p. 36.
25 Ailsa Rolley, *Survival on Ambon*, A. Rolley, Beaudesert Qld, c. 1994, pp. 111–13.
26 Vickers-Bush, 'Hell and its Yellow Devils', p. 41.
27 Nelson, *Prisoners of War*, p. 59.
28 Nelson, 'A bowl of rice for seven camels', p. 36.
29 Beaumont, 'Rank, Privilege and Prisoners of War', p. 78.
30 Interview with Colonel Ilo B. Hard by Ronald Marcello, University of North Texas Oral History Program, no. 510, Denton, Texas, 26 March 1980, p. 154.
31 ibid.
32 Sibylla Jane Flower, 'Captors and Captives on the Burma–Thailand Railway', in Bob Moore and Kent Fedorowich, eds, *Prisoners of War and their captors in World War II*, Berg Publishers, Oxford, 1996, p. 227.
33 Dr Roy Mills, '"F" Force, Thailand', in Ray Connolly and Bob Wilson, eds, *Medical Soldiers: 2/10 Australian Field Ambulance 8 Div. 1940–45*, 2/10th Australian Field Ambulance Association, Sydney, c. 1985, pp. 229–30.

34 Interview with Huddleston W. Wright by Ronald Marcello, University of North Texas Oral History Program, no. 794, Denton, Texas, 2 and 14 November 1989, p. 140.
35 Brigadier A. L. Varley, 'Extracts from Recommendations by Brig. A. L. Varley', Thailand, March 1944, in papers of Colonel G. E. Ramsay, AWM PR00079, Australian War Memorial, Canberra.
36 ibid.
37 Captain Cyril Vardy, personal papers, IWM 67/166/1, Imperial War Museum, London, pp. 199–200.
38 White, 'Prestige Lecture', p. 11.
39 Sue Ebury, *Weary: The life of Sir Edward Dunlop*, Viking, Melbourne, 1994, p. 158.
40 White, 'Prestige Lecture', p. 10.
41 ibid., p. 13.
42 Nelson, *Prisoners of War*, p. 65.
43 ibid., p. 64.
44 Harry Medlin, '2/AIF', unpublished memoir, p. 8.
45 Richards and McEwan, *The Survival Factor*, p. 220.
46 Interview with Chaplain Robert Taylor by Ronald Marcello, University of North Texas Oral History Program, no. 255, Arlington, Texas, 2 November 1974, p. 160.
47 Interview with Frank H. Bigelow by Ronald Marcello, University of North Texas Oral History Program, no. 1464, San Antonio, Texas, 12 June 2002, p. 60.
48 Interview with Horace Chumley by Ronald Marcello, University of North Texas Oral History Program, no. 199, Decatur, Texas, 3 April 1974, p. 61.
49 Interview with Luther Prunty by Ronald Marcello, University of North Texas Oral History Program, no. 689, Denton, Texas, 20 and 27 October 1986, p. 87.
50 Interview with Colonel Ilo B. Hard, University of North Texas Oral History Program, pp. 131–3.
51 Interview with Otto C. Schwarz by Ronald Marcello, University of North Texas Oral History Program, no. 497, Granbury, Texas, 7 September 1979, p. 81.
52 Interview with Martin Chambers by Ronald Marcello, University of North Texas Oral History Program, no. 575, location unspecified, 8 April 1982, pp. 63–4.
53 ibid.

54 Beaumont, *Gull Force*, p. 100.
55 ibid., p. 183.
56 Duncan, War Crimes Trials Statement, 22 February 1947, AWM 54 1010/4/46, Australian War Memorial, Canberra.
57 Colonel James H. Thyer, 'Leadership', address delivered to officers, warrant officers and senior NCOs, Changi, 18 June 1942, Royal Australian Corps of Signals Museum, Simpson Barracks, Melbourne.
58 *'Getting on with it'—2/30th Battalion AIF*, 2/30th Battalion Association, Kingsway West NSW, 1998, p. 5.
59 Rayson, personal diary.
60 F. V. B. Dumoulin [sic], private diary, IWM 97/6/1, Imperial War Museum, London.
61 ibid.
62 Lieutenant Colonel A. Dillon RAMC, 'Medical War Diary and Reports Subsequent to Capitulation of British forces in Malaya, 1942–45', WO 222/1386, National Archives, London.
63 Richards and McEwan, *The Survival Factor*, p. 15.
64 Maisey, 'Psychological Review of the Behaviour of Prisoners of War', p. 3.
65 ibid., p. 2.
66 Lieutenant Colonel C. W. Maisey, 'Reports on POW camps in Batavia 1942–45', 24 November 1945, WO 222/1391, National Archives, London.
67 Major N. Courtney Lendon, 'Disease among prisoners of war', Royal Army Medical Corps 1042, Box 215, Wellcome Institute, n.d., p. 24.
68 R. B. C. Welsh, personal diary, 13 May 1943, uncatalogued, Imperial War Museum, London, pp. 59–60, 110.
69 Major D. W. Gillies, personal diary, 21 May 1944, IWM 84/18/1, Imperial War Museum, London.
70 Bull, transcript of conversation between Major Bull and Mrs Piers Mackesy.
71 Gillies, personal diary, 23 May 1942.
72 Welsh, personal diary, p. 163.
73 Reports on Malaya POW Camps, Jan 42–Aug 1945, WO 222/1388, National Archives, London.
74 A. N. H. Peach, in Maisey, 'Reports on POW camps in Batavia 1942–45'.
75 Maisey, 'Psychological Review of the Behaviour of Prisoners of War', p. 4.

76 Maisey, 'Psychological Review of the Behaviour of Prisoners of War', pp. 3–4.
77 Letter from Dr Bloomsma, Dutch Section, Red Cross Hospital, Bangkok to SMO (Lt-Col Thomas Hamilton) 2/4 CCS, 20 September 1945, AWM 54 554/2/9, Australian War Memorial, Canberra.
78 Joan Beaumont, ed., *The Australian Centenary History of Defence, Vol. 6, Australian defence: sources and statistics*, Oxford University Press, Oxford, 2001, p. 344.
79 John D. 'Jack' Higgs, 'Beffie and Me: Jack's Memoirs of Family, January 1991–December 2004', unpublished memoir, p. 130.
80 ibid., p. 133.

## Chapter 7  Beyond the call: coping in captivity

1 Ailsa Rolley, *Survival on Ambon*, self published, Beaudesert Qld, c. 1994, p. 128.
2 Ian Duncan, 'Conditions in Japanese Coal Mines', personal papers, p. 6.
3 Dr Thomas Hewlett, 'Di Ju Nana Bunshyo—Nightmare—Revisited', paper presented to 'Survivors of Bataan-Corregidor' reunion, August 1978, in personal papers of Dr Ian Duncan, pp. 6, 17–18.
4 Lieutenant Colonel C. W. Maisey, 'Report on Tanjong Priok Camp, May 42–Apr 43', 7 December 1945, WO 222/1391, National Archives, London.
5 M. Foster, 'Medico makes emotion-charged return to Hellfire Pass', *NSW Doctor*, June 1998, p. 24.
6 Captain Cyril Vardy, personal diary, IWM 67/166/1, Imperial War Museum, London, p. 164.
7 Interview with Bevan Warland-Browne, Australians at War Film Archive, no. 0583, <www.australiansatwarfilmarchive.gov.au/aawfa/interviews/158.aspx>, accessed 8 October 2008.
8 Ian L. Duncan, 'Makeshift medicine: combating disease in the Japanese prison camps', *Medical Journal of Australia*, vol. 1, 8 January 1983, pp. 29–32.
9 'Dramatic struggle for lives', *NSW Doctor*, November/December 1995, p. 13.
10 Stanley Pavillard, *Bamboo Doctor*, Macmillan, London, 1960, p. 85.
11 Hewlett, 'Di Ju Nana Bunshyo—Nightmare—Revisited', p. 1.
12 G. Gill, 'Disease and Death on the Burma–Thai Railway', *Medical Historian*, no. 8, 1995/1996, p. 59.

13 Gilbert Edward Brooke, *Medico-Tropical Practice: A handbook for medical practioners and students,* 2nd edn, C. Griffin, London, 1920, pp. 283, 312.
14 Driver Walter Cobden, War Crimes Trials Statement, 5 April 1946, AWM 54 1010/4/33, Australian War Memorial, Canberra.
15 Warland-Browne, Australians at War Film Archive, no. 0583.
16 Pavillard, *Bamboo Doctor,* p. 102.
17 Frank Nankervis quoted in John Lack, ed., *No Lost Battalion: An oral history of the 2/29th Battalion AIF,* Slouch Hat Publications, McCrae Victoria, 2005, p. 174.
18 R. J. Armstrong, unpublished memoir, pp. 187, 189.
19 Captain J. R. Goding, War Crimes Trials Statement, 14 May 1946, AWM 54 1010/4/59, Australian War Memorial, Canberra.
20 Richard Reid, *In Captivity: Australian prisoners of war in the 20th century,* Commonwealth Department of Veterans' Affairs, Canberra, 1999, p. 43.
21 Pavillard, *Bamboo Doctor,* p. 66.
22 Ian Duncan, quoted in Nikki Barrowclough et al., 'My war', Good Weekend Magazine, *Sydney Morning Herald,* 26 August 1989, p. 53.
23 Hank Nelson, review of *Last Stop Nagasaki* by Hugh Clarke in *Journal of the Australian War Memorial,* no. 7, October 1985, p. 50.
24 Interview with Charles 'Rowley' Richards, Australians at War Film Archive, no. 1144, <www.australiansatwarfilmarchive.gov.au/aawfa/interviews/1048.aspx>, accessed 10 October 2008.
25 Captain H. Churchill, personal unpublished memoir, IWM 67/158/1, Imperial War Museum, London.
26 'Medical Attendance on Prisoners of War Report "M" Services, Changi, March 1945', AWM 54 481/8/4, Australian War Memorial, Canberra.
27 Pavillard, *Bamboo Doctor,* p. 118.
28 Vardy, personal diary, p. 217.
29 Pavillard, *Bamboo Doctor,* pp. 84–5.
30 Osmund E. Vickers-Bush, 'Hell and its Yellow Devils', MSS 1085, Australian War Memorial, Canberra, p. 52.
31 Pavillard, *Bamboo Doctor,* p. 108.
32 Vickers-Bush, 'Hell and its Yellow Devils', pp. 45–6.
33 Pavillard, *Bamboo Doctor,* p. 120.
34 Lieutenant Colonel Thomas Hamilton, 'Report on POW Hospital Nakom Paton', WO 222/1389, National Archives, London.
35 Maisey, 'Report on Tanjong Priok Camp'.

36 Ray Connolly and Bob Wilson, eds, *Medical Soldiers: 2/10 Australian Field Ambulance 8 Div. 1940–45*, 2/10th Australian Field Ambulance Association, Sydney, c. 1985, p. 215.
37 Rowley Richards and Marcia McEwan, *The Survival Factor*, Kangaroo Press, Kenthurst NSW, 1989, p. 188.
38 ibid., p. 152.
39 Pavillard, *Bamboo Doctor*, p. 47.
40 Duncan in Barrowclough et al, 'My war', p. 53.
41 Captain William Aitken, 'Medical Report P.O.W. Camp, Hashio (Bakli Bay) Hainan Island', B26/82: Item M x 51467 PE 2 Miskin, National Archives of Australia, Melbourne, p. 2.
42 Captain Desmond Brennan, POW diary, 24 November 1942, Royal Australasian College of Physicians Library, Sydney.
43 Richards and McEwan, *The Survival Factor*, p. 156.
44 Interview with Charles 'Rowley' Richards, Australians at War Film Archive, no. 1144.
45 Major D. W. Gillies, personal diary, 21 May 1944, IWM 84/18/1, Imperial War Museum, London.
46 Interview with Charles 'Rowley' Richards, Australians at War Film Archive, no. 1144.
47 Duncan in Barrowclough et al, 'My war', p. 53.
48 Gillies, personal diary, 8 November 1942.
49 Richards and McEwan, *The Survival Factor*, p. 114.
50 Pavillard, *Bamboo Doctor*, p. 81.
51 Armstrong, unpublished memoir, p. 186.
52 Interview with Captain P. G. Seed by Anne Wheeler, IWM 91/35/1, Imperial War Museum, London, p. 25.
53 Hank Nelson, 'A bowl of rice for seven camels', *Journal of the Australian War Memorial*, no. 14, April 1989, p. 33.
54 Interview with Chaplain Robert Taylor by Ronald Marcello, University of North Texas Oral History Program, no. 255, Arlington, Texas, 2 November 1974, p. 170.
55 Major Alan Hazelton, personal papers, AWM PR00230, Australian War Memorial, Canberra.
56 Lieutenant Colonel E. E. Dunlop, Report 'The Surgical treatment of Dysentery lesions of the bowel amongst Allied Prisoners of War, Burma and Thailand', Bangkok, 8 September 1945, WO 222/1389, National Archives, London.

57 Lieutenant Colonel Albert Coates, 'Impressions of the Nakonpatom Hospital, written by Lt-Col Albert Ernest Coates, A.A.M.C. at the request of the I.J.A. doctor, 22.11.44', AWM 54 554/17/3, Australian War Memorial, Canberra.
58 'Conversation with Surg-Lt-Commander S. E. L. Stening' in 'Personal narratives of Navy Medical Officers, their experiences in action and POW camps', AWM 54 481/1/12, Australian War Memorial, Canberra.
59 Red Cross reports on Camp 3, Formosa, 4 June 1944, WO 224/187, National Archives, London.
60 Coates, 'Impressions of the Nakompaton Hospital'.
61 Joan Beaumont, 'Gull Force comes home: the aftermath of captivity', *Journal of the Australian War Memorial*, vol. 14, April 1989, p. 43.
62 Duncan, 'Makeshift Medicine', p. 32.
63 Hank Nelson, *Prisoners of War: Australians under Nippon*, ABC Enterprises for the Australian Broadcasting Corporation, Sydney, 2001, p. 90.
64 Major Alan Hobbs, personal diary, February 1942, AWM PR85/86, Australian War Memorial, Canberra.
65 John Waterford, quoted in 'Former Burma POW doctor an inspiration', *Sydney Morning Herald*, 20 June 1992.
66 Pavillard, *Bamboo Doctor*, p. 107.

## Chapter 8    The long shadow: after the war

1 Reproduced in Albert E. Coates and Norman Rosenthal, *The Albert Coates Story: The will that found a way*, Hyland House, Melbourne, 1977, p. 110.
2 Osmund E. Vickers-Bush, 'Hell and its Yellow Devils', MSS 1085, Australian War Memorial, Canberra, p. 67.
3 G. Cooke, 'On the track of the fallen', Panorama, *Canberra Times*, 25 April 1998, p. 13.
4 Transcript of Memorial Service, Omuta Japan, 16 August 1945, in personal papers of Dr Ian Duncan.
5 Allan S. Walker, *Middle East and Far East*, Australian War Memorial, Canberra, 1953, p. 673.
6 Harry Leslie, 'The Lost Cause: Personal experiences of a Prisoner of War from the Taiwan War Camps', address given at Waverley Library, Bondi Junction, 26 October 1994.

# ENDNOTES

7  '"B"—Treatment of medical conditions peculiar to ex Ps W. experiences in Malaya', n.d., AWM 54 779/6/2, Australian War Memorial, Canberra, p. 1.
8  Colonel G. T. Gibson, 'Descriptive Report of the work of the Medical Services', 2nd Australian Prisoner of War Group, Singapore, August–November 1945, 30 October 1945, AWM 54 554/11/5, Australian War Memorial, Canberra, p. 3.
9  'Advice to Officers interviewing returned PW for Historical purposes', n.d, AWM 54 779/6/2, Australian War Memorial, Canberra.
10 ibid.
11 Colonel G. T. Gibson, 'Medical Appreciation concerning Australian R.P's W Now Concentrating in Singapore', AWM 54 838/3/12, Australian War Memorial, Canberra, p. 2.
12 Colonel G. T. Gibson, 'Notes for Medical historian On Medical Task of 2 Aust PW Reception Group Singapore Period August–September, 1945', 28 September 1945, AWM 54 838/3/12, 28/9/45, Australian War Memorial, Canberra.
13 ibid.
14 'Conduct of recovered JPOWs, 102 Aust. Convalescent Depot—Medical Reports and interrogatory statements, April–Oct 1945', AWM 54 779/6/2, Australian War Memorial, Canberra.
15 Lieutenant Colonel Jackson, 'Australian Military Forces 102 Aust Con Depot weekly report—Convalescent P.W.', 8 October 1945, AWM 54 779/6/2, Australian War Memorial, Canberra.
16 Dr Roy Mills, 'The after years' in Ray Connolly and Bob Wilson, eds, *Medical Soldiers: 2/10 Australian Field Ambulance 8 Div. 1940-45*, 2/10th Australian Field Ambulance Association, Sydney, c. 1985, p. 273.
17 'Discipline of AMF Ex prisoners of war on arrival in Australia', 9 August 1945, AWM 54 779/6/2, Australian War Memorial, Canberra.
18 ibid.
19 Lieutenant Colonel Jackson, 'Report on Ps.O.W (8th Div) draft which arrived at 102 Aust Con Depot on 24 Mar 45', 12 April 1945, AWM 54 779/6/2, Australian War Memorial, Canberra, p. 1.
20 'Con Depot Treatment for Ex Ps. OW', 5 July 1945, AWM 54 779/6/2, Australian War Memorial, Canberra.
21 Jackson, 'Report on Ps.O.W (8th Div) draft which arrived at 102 Aust Con Depot on 24 Mar 45', pp. 1–2.
22 'Medical Report on Ex. Japanese P.O.W.'s' 11 April 1945, AWM 54 779/6/2, Australian War Memorial, Canberra, pp. 2–3.

23 'Report of the Repatriation Committee on Repatriated Prisoners of War', 4 July 1947, AWM 54 838/3/12, Australian War Memorial, Canberra, p. 2.
24 Hank Nelson, 'Travelling in memories: Australian prisoners of the Japanese, forty years after the Fall of Singapore', *Journal of the Australian War Memorial*, no. 3, October 1983, p. 22.
25 Michael McKernan, *This War Never Ends: The pain of separation and return*, University of Queensland Press, Brisbane, 2001, p. 127.
26 Bob Rolls, quoted in John Lack, ed., *No Lost Battalion: An Oral History of the 2/29th Battalion AIF*, Slouch Hat Publications, McCrae Victoria, 2005, p. 242.
27 ibid., p. 127.
28 Roy Whitecross in *Every inch of the way*, directed by Aviva Ziegler, produced for the Department of Veterans' Affairs by Film Australia, Sydney, 1990.
29 'Data on rehabilitation: Method of handling repatriated Prisoners of War, 1945. Medical procedure on demobilization', AWM 54 838/3/12, Australian War Memorial, Canberra.
30 John D. 'Jack' Higgs, 'Beffie and Me: Jack's Memoirs of Family, January 1991–December 2004', unpublished memoir, p. 164.
31 McKernan, *This War Never Ends*, p. 127.
32 Joan Beaumont, 'Gull Force comes home: the aftermath of captivity', *Journal of the Australian War Memorial*, vol. 14, April 1989, p. 48.
33 ibid., pp. 48–9.
34 Charles Roland, 'Human Vivisection: The Intoxication of Limitless Power in Wartime', in Bob Moore and Kent Fedorowich, eds, *Prisoners of war and their captors in World War II*, Berg Publishers, Oxford, 1996, p. 149.
35 Dr Ian Duncan, quoted in Hank Nelson, *Prisoners of War: Australians under Nippon*, ABC Enterprises for the Australian Broadcasting Corporation, Sydney, 2001, p. 216.
36 'Report of the Repatriation Committee on Repatriated Prisoners of War', p. 4.
37 E. E. Dunlop, 'Repatriation Committee on Repatriated Prisoners of War' in papers of Lieutenant Colonel R. M. W Webster, AWM 3DRL/3435, Australian War Memorial, Canberra.
38 Beaumont, 'Gull Force comes home', p. 51.

39 G. Freed and P. B. Stringer, 'Comparative Mortality Experience 1946–1963', *Australian Repatriation Department Medical Research Bulletin*, no. 2, 1968.
40 G. Gill, 'Disease and Death on the Burma–Thai Railway', p. 63; G. Gill and D. Bell, 'Persisting tropical diseases amongst former prisoners of war of the Japanese', *The Practitioner*, vol. 224, August 1980, p. 801.
41 G. Gill and D. Bell, 'Persisting nutritional neuropathy amongst former war prisoners', *Journal of Neurology, Neurosurgery and Psychiatry*, vol. 45, 1982, p. 861.
42 G. Gill and D. Bell, 'The health of former prisoners of war of the Japanese', *The Practitioner*, vol. 225, April 1981, pp. 534, 536.
43 I. L. Duncan et al., *Morbidity in ex-prisoners of war*, New South Wales POW Association of Australia, 1985.
44 Vickers-Bush, 'Hell and its Yellow Devils', p. 39.
45 Major Burnett L. Clarke, War Crimes Trials Statement, 14 November 1945, AWM 54 1010/4/32, Australian War Memorial, Canberra.
46 F. E. de W Cayley, personal papers, IWM 98/19/1, Imperial War Museum, London.
47 Dunlop, 'Repatriation Committee on Repatriated Prisoners of War', p. 1.
48 Higgs, 'Beffie and Me', p. 165.
49 Interview with Granville T. Summerlin by Ronald Marcello, University of North Texas Oral History Program, no. 543, Denton, Texas, 9 June 1981, p. 129.
50 McKernan, *This War Never Ends*, p. 156.
51 Dunlop, 'Repatriation Committee on Repatriated Prisoners of War', p. 2.
52 Lieutenant Colonel R. M. W. Webster, 'Evidence given before the Committee of Repatriation Commission on Repatriated prisoners of War', AWM 3DRL/3435, Australian War Memorial, Canberra. See also E. E. Dunlop, 'Repatriation Committee on Repatriated Prisoners of War' in papers of Lieutenant Colonel R. M. W. Webster, AWM 3DRL/3435, Australian War Memorial, Canberra.
53 Beaumont, 'Gull Force comes home', p. 49.
54 M. Arthur, 'Death was all around me for 3½ years', *Daily Mail*, 27 May 1998, p. 5.
55 'Report of the Repatriation Committee on Repatriated Prisoners of War', p. 7.

56 Repatriation Commission, 'Some aspects of Medical Investigation and Treatment', Commonwealth of Australia, Melbourne, 1947, p. 19.
57 Megan Howe, 'Living with war's leftover horrors', *Telegraph Mirror*, 19 April 1993, p. 10.
58 'Report of the Repatriation Committee on Repatriated Prisoners of War', p. 5.
59 ibid.
60 Department of Veterans' Affairs, *Lifelong Captives: The medical legacy of POWs of the Japanese*, Commonwealth of Australia, Canberra, 1990.
61 G. Jacobsen, 'POWs rebuffed by Tokyo court', *Sydney Morning Herald*, 27 November 1998.
62 Department of Veterans' Affairs, 'Budget Facts' available at <www.dva.gov.au/media/aboutus/budget/budget01/facts_PoW.htm>, accessed 6 March 2002.
63 E. E. Dunlop, *The War Diaries of Weary Dunlop: Java and the Burma–Thailand Railway, 1942–1945*, Thomas Nelson, Melbourne, 1986, p. 218.
64 ibid., p. xvi.
65 Duncan, quoted in *Lifelong Captives*, p. 2.
66 'Report of the Repatriation Committee on Repatriated Prisoners of War', p. 2.
67 ibid.
68 Repatriation Commission, 'Some aspects of Medical Investigation and Treatment', p. 3.
69 Gill and Bell, 'The health of former prisoners of war of the Japanese', pp. 531–3.
70 ibid., p. 533.
71 ibid.
72 Duncan et al., *Morbidity in ex-prisoners of war*, p. 1.
73 *Lifelong Captives*, p. 2.
74 Bevan Warland-Browne, Australians at War Film Archive Interview, no. 0583, <www.australiansatwarfilmarchive.gov.au/aawfa/interviews/158.aspx>, accessed 8 October 2008.
75 Higgs, 'Beffie and Me', p. 137.
76 Interview with Griff L. Douglas by Ronald Marcello, University of North Texas Oral History Program, no. 425, Fort Worth, Texas, 18 April 1978, p. 129.
77 Christopher Tennant, Kerry Goulston and Owen Dent, 'Australian Prisoners of War of the Japanese: Post-war psychiatric hospitalisation

and psychological morbidity', *Australian and New Zealand Journal of Psychiatry*, no. 20, 1986, pp. 334, 338–9.
78  R. J. Armstrong, unpublished memoir, p. 185.
79  Duncan et al., *Morbidity in ex-prisoners of war*.
80  Howe, 'Living with war's leftover horrors', p. 10.
81  *Lifelong Captives*, p. 6.
82  Mills, 'The after years' in Connolly and Wilson, *Medical Soldiers*, p. 274.
83  Beaumont, 'Gull Force comes home', p. 51.
84  R. Ong, letter to P. Millard, 4 June 1986, personal papers of P. Millard.
85  J. D. C. Hammon, personal unpublished memoir of 2/3rd MG Battalion, p. 13.
86  Harry Medlin, '2/AIF', unpublished memoir.
87  Angela Gunn, 'Reflections', in Carolyn Newman, ed., *Legacies of our fathers*, Thomas C. Lothian, South Melbourne, 2005, p. 98.
88  H. F. Atkinson, 'Lest we forget', *ADA News Bulletin*, no. 22B, November 1995, p. 47.
89  Howe, 'Living with war's leftover horrors', p. 10.
90  Dr Roy Mills, letter to author, 15 March 1999.
91  Allan S. Walker, *Clinical Problems of War*, Australian War Memorial, Canberra, 1952, p. 712.
92  Beaumont, 'Gull Force comes home', p. 47.
93  Pat Nossiter in *Every Inch of the Way*.
94  Cayley, personal papers.
95  Dr Rowley Richards, letter to the author, 5 October 1998.
96  Quoted in 'Book Excerpt: *Conduct under Fire: Four American doctors and their fight for life as prisoners of the Japanese, 1941–1945*', *American Medical News*, 14 August 2006, p. 9.
97  Bob Goodwin and Jim Dixon, *Medicos and Memories: Further recollections of the 2/10th Field Regiment R.A.A.*, 2/10th Field Regiment Association, Rochedale Qld, 2000, p. 127.
98  Peter J. Morris, 'Sir Michael Woodruff', <www.rsnz.govt.nz/directory/yearbooks/2001/woodruff.php>, accessed 4 February 2003.
99  Mental Health Services, 'John Cade Unit Opens', available at <www.health.vic.gov.au/mentalhealth/mhupdate/2000feb/cade.htm>, accessed 15 March 2003. Lithium is still widely used for treating bipolar affective disorder.
100 Letter from B. Hunt to W. Kent Hughes, 31 January 1948, in private papers of Mrs Kevin Fagan.
101 Letter to Dr Kevin Fagan from Commonwealth Investigation Services, in private papers of Mrs Kevin Fagan, n.d.

102 Robin Gerster, 'Wasted lives, wasted words', Spectrum, *Sydney Morning Herald,* 22 April 1995, p. 10A.
103 Denise Higgins, *Weary Dunlop: Doctor, diplomat and saviour,* Cardigan Street, Melbourne, 1996.
104 McKernan, *This War Never Ends,* p. 175.
105 Robert D. Marshall, 'Weary Dunlop: Surgeon', *Australia and New Zealand Journal of Surgery,* no. 64, 1994, p. 26.
106 John Howard, speech given to Gladesville RSL Club, 19 February 1998, <www.pm.gov.au/news/speeches/1998/gladsvll.htm>, accessed 23 August 2002.
107 Laurens van der Post, foreword in Dunlop, *War Diaries,* p. x.
108 Lieutenant Colonel F. G. Galleghan, 'Command AIF troops from Java', letter to Dunlop, 11 January 1943, in papers of Brigadier F. G. Galleghan, 'collection of correspondence, special orders etc, 1941–1945', AWM 54 749 [2313], part 2, Australian War Memorial, Canberra.
109 Sue Ebury, *Weary: The life of Sir Edward Dunlop,* Penguin Books, Ringwood Vic, 2001, p. 494.
110 Designed by Peter Corlett, a replica also stands in the grounds of the Australian War Memorial, Canberra.
111 S. F. Denning, 'Memoirs of QX 12605 Private Denning SF', MSS 1542, Australian War Memorial, Canberra, p. 54.
112 *Hellfire Pass: A journey back in time,* directed by Graham Chase, Film Australia, Sydney, 1988.
113 Ebury, *Weary,* p. xiii.
114 Citation for MBE, in service record of Captain John Finch Akeroyd.
115 Frank Nankervis quoted in *No Lost Battalion,* p. 178.
116 Norman Derrington, quoted in Begbie, 'Little wonder these doctors were revered', Panorama, *Canberra Times,* 11 July 1998, p. 9.
117 Higgs, 'Beffie and Me', p. 118.
118 Bryan Egan, 'Understanding Medical Officers: Australian doctors and war', unpublished manuscript, p. 40.
119 *Lifelong Captives,* p. 2.
120 Dr Kevin Fagan, quoted in Richard Reid, *In Captivity: Australian prisoners of war in the 20th century,* Commonwealth Department of Veterans' Affairs, Canberra, 1999, p. 1.
121 Desmond Brennan, 'When I was a lad', *Radius: Newsletter of the University of Sydney Medical Graduates' Association,* vol. 12, no. 1, March 1999, p. 13.

# BIBLIOGRAPHY

## INTERVIEWS

| | |
|---|---|
| Dr Claude Anderson | Taped interview with author, Perth, WA, 12 November 1998. |
| Mr Dick Armstrong | Taped interview with author, Bonnells Bay, NSW, 2 February 1999. |
| Mr Ken Astill | Taped interview with author, Cessnock, NSW, 5 October 1998. |
| Dr Victor Brand | Taped interview with author, Melbourne, Vic, 16 April 1999. |
| Dr Desmond Brennan | Taped interview with author, Sydney, NSW, 30 June 1998. |
| Dr Lloyd Cahill | Taped interview with author, Sydney, NSW, 7 October 1998. |
| Dr David Christison | Taped interview with author, Glasgow, UK, 6 July 1999. |
| Mr Ray Connolly | Taped interview with author, Belmont, NSW, 8 October 1998. |
| Dr William Donaldson | Taped interview with author, Edinburgh, UK, 7 July 1999. |
| Mrs Joyce Duncan | Taped interview with author, Sydney, NSW, 3 October 1998. |

| | |
|---|---|
| Mr Hal Finkelstein | Taped interview with author, Perth, WA, 13 November 1998. |
| Mr Bill Flowers | Taped interview with author, Melbourne, Vic, 18 September 1998. |
| Dr Geoffrey Gill | Conversation with author, Liverpool, UK, 16 June 1999. |
| Mr Bill Hammon | Taped interview with author, Cessnock, NSW, 5 October 1998. |
| Dr Alan Hazelton | Taped interview with author, Goulburn, NSW, 5 July 1998. |
| Dr Peter Hendry | Taped interview with author, Newcastle, NSW, 6 July 1998. |
| Dr Bill Hetreed | Taped interviews with author, Coombe Keynes, Dorset, UK, 28–30 June 1999. |
| Mrs Laurie Hobbs | Taped interview with author, Adelaide, SA, 6 November 1998. |
| Dr Colin Juttner | Taped interview with author, Adelaide, SA, 4 November 1998. |
| Dr Max Mayrhofer | Taped interview with author, Perth, WA, 11 November 1998. |
| Dr Bob McInerney | Taped interview with author, Sydney, NSW, 18 May 1997. |
| Dr Philip Millard | Taped interview with author, Sydney, NSW, 19 October 1998. |
| Dr Roy Mills | Taped interview with author, Newcastle, NSW, 4 March 1999. |
| Mr Gordon Nichols | Taped interview with author, Sydney, NSW, 4 February 1998. |
| Dr Leslie Poidevin | Taped interview with author, Adelaide, SA, 3 November 1998. |
| Dr Robert Pufflett | Taped interview with author, Sydney, NSW, 7 July 1998. |
| Dr Rowley Richards | Taped interview with author, Sydney, NSW, 1 October 1998. |
| Mr Douglas Skippen | Taped interview with author, Ipswich, UK, 2 June 1999. |

| | |
|---|---|
| Mrs Vivien Statham | Taped interview with author, Perth, WA, 17 November 1998. |
| Mr Alf Stone | Taped interview with author, Newcastle, NSW, 15 April 1998. |
| Mr Bob Wilson | Taped interview with author, Sydney, NSW, 6 October 1998. |

**University of North Texas Oral History Program, Denton, Texas**

Interview with Frank H. Bigelow by Ronald Marcello, University of North Texas Oral History Program, no. 1464, San Antonio, Texas, 12 June 2002.

Interview with Martin Chambers by Ronald Marcello, University of North Texas Oral History Program, no. 575, location unspecified, 8 April 1982.

Interview with Horace Chumley by Ronald Marcello, University of North Texas Oral History Program, no. 199, Decatur, Texas, 3 April 1974.

Interview with Griff L. Douglas by Ronald Marcello, University of North Texas Oral History Program, no. 425, Fort Worth, Texas, 18 April 1978.

Interview with E. Benjamin Dunn by Ronald Marcello, University of North Texas Oral History Program, no. 1329, Denton, Texas, 16 November 1999.

Interview with Colonel Ilo B. Hard by Ronald Marcello, University of North Texas Oral History Program, no. 510, Denton, Texas, 26 March 1980.

Interview with Luther Prunty by Ronald Marcello, University of North Texas Oral History Program, no. 689, Denton, Texas, 20 and 27 October 1986.

Interview with Otto C. Schwarz by Ronald Marcello, University of North Texas Oral History Program, no. 497, Granbury, Texas, 7 September 1979.

Interview with Granville T. Summerlin by Ronald Marcello, University of North Texas Oral History Program, no. 543, Denton, Texas, 9 June 1981.

Interview with Captain Clark L. Taylor by Ronald Marcello, University of North Texas Oral History Program, no. 491, Denton, Texas, 14 September 1979.

Interview with Chaplain Robert Taylor by Ronald Marcello, University of North Texas Oral History Program, no. 255, Arlington, Texas, 2 November 1974.

Interview with Huddleston W. Wright by Ronald Marcello, University of North Texas Oral History Program, no. 794, Denton, Texas, 2 and 14 November 1989.

## ARCHIVES
### National Archives of Australia, Canberra
*World War II service records of:*
NX34905 Captain Robert Bradley Speirs
NX70505 Colonel Thomas Hamilton
NX70506 Major Walter Edward Fisher
NX70920 Captain Stanley Boyd McKellar White
NX76223 Captain John Bernard Oakeshott
QX23518 Captain Clive Rodney Boyce
SX10761 Major Alan Hobbs
SX11028 Major Gilbert Edgar Jose
VX18194 Captain John Finch Akeroyd
VX39198 Lieutenant Colonel Albert Ernest Coates
VX39275 Colonel Douglas Clelland Pigdon
VX39702 Captain Francis Joseph Cahill
WX11177 Major Bruce Attlee Hunt

### Australian War Memorial, Canberra
*War Crimes and Trials—Affidavits and Sworn Statements (catalogued in alphabetical order by surname):*
AWM 54 1010/4/2: Capt W. Aitken; Major F. J. [sic] Akeroyd
AWM 54 1010/4/4 Part 1: Captain C. L.W. Clarke
AWM 54 1010/4/5: Major B. H. Anderson
AWM 54 1010/4/5: Major H. L. Andrews
AWM 54 1010/4/10: Captain A. K. Barrett
AWM 54 1010/4/20: Captain D. J. Brennan
AWM 54 1010/4/32: Major B. L. W. Clarke
AWM 54 1010/4/33: Lieutenant Colonel A. E. Coates; Pte W. E. McEwan Cobden
AWM 54 1010/4/40: Major G. F. S. Davies
AWM 54 1010/4/45: Captain E. B. Drevermann
AWM 54 1010/4/46: Captain I. L. Duncan; Lieutenant Colonel E. E. Dunlop
AWM 54 1010/4/47: Lieutenant Colonel N. M. Eadie; Major H. H. Eddey
AWM 54 1010/4/51: Major W. E. Fisher
AWM 54 1010/4/55: Captain J. L. Frew
AWM 54 1010/4/59: Captain J. R. Goding; Captain T. Godlee
AWM 54 1010/4/104: Major F. H. Mills
AWM 54 1010/4/121: Captain C. R. B. Richards
AWM 54 1010/4/133: Surgeon-Lieutenant S. E. L. Stening

*Official records:*

AWM 54 351/5/2: [Food—for sick:] Nutrition in Rice-Eating Populations, Lecture delivered to Changi Medical Society by Major Burgess, Royal Australian Division, June 1942.

AWM 54 417/1/7: Diary of L/Sgt D. G. P. Foley.

AWM 54 481/1/12: Personal narratives of Navy Medical Officers, their experiences in action and POW camps.

AWM 54 481/8/1: Report on Blakane Mati Camp Changi, to ADMS 8 Australian Division, June 1942.

AWM 54 481/8/2: 2 reports on conditions of working party at Pulan Bakom, July 1942 by Capt. Robert Pufflett, 12 July 1942 and 24 July 1942.

AWM 54 481/8/3: Medical attendance on Prisoner of War Report on State of health, Changi June 1944.

AWM 54 481/8/4: Report 'M' Services, Changi, March 1945.

AWM 54 481/8/8: Guiding principles, treatment of medical conditions peculiar to ex Prisoners of War—Guide for Medical Officers on transport, by Lieutenant Colonel WL Neal, IMS DDMS, PsW Camps experiences as a P.O.W. of the Japanese. Medical arrangements on the Thai-Burma railway.

AWM 54 481/8/9: Memoranda on diet and treatment of various diseases by Australian Medical Officers in Japanese hands, March 1943.

AWM 54 481/8/11: 'Medical appreciation of position as affecting Australian Ps.W. at Singapore' 1 September 1945, Lt Col Glyn White.

AWM 54 481/8/12: Reports, data and narratives prepared by Medical Officers in captivity in relation to food and nutritional diseases, Singapore.

AWM 54 481/8/18: Medical records and returns handed in by Lt Col J E Glyn White, No 1 Camp, Adam Park, Changi, No 5 Camp, Bukit Timah HQ Camp 'B' AIF River Valley Working Party, October–November 1942.

AWM 54 481/8/22: Medical Reports on Prisoners of War, New Guinea Force Prisoners of War reception unit, recovered P.Ws admitted to 107 General Hospital, Darwin.

AWM 54 481/8/26: Part of medical returns and correspondence handed to medical historian by Lt Col J G Glyn White (Includes: Officers AAMC, AIF Malaya; POW Camp Changi; Rations average daily issues by months; Death AIF personnel).

AWM 54 481/8/31: Correspondence to Lt Col Glyn White, from Bruce Hunt, C H Wilson and L H Stevens, regarding medical affairs, POW Camps, Malaya.

AWM 54 481/8/33: Report on reception and treatment of Prisoners of War at Ambon, 24 September 1945, by Surg-Lt I C Galbraith RANR.

AWM 54 481/8/35: Charts of food etc from Hainan Island, compiled, recorded and kept by Sgt WP Foley.

AWM 54 554/2/9: Report on chemical and pharmaceutical work at 55 Kilo Hospital Camps, Burma—Conditions, life and work of POW Burma Siam, 1942/45 by C A McEachern, Brigadier RAA—Extracts from War Diary Lieutenant Colonel N M Eadie AAMC, War Diary 2/4 Australian Casualty Clearing Station—Summary of Medical reports in POW Camps by Captain CRB Richards.

AWM 54 554/5/2: Brief History of Base Hospital Chungkai POW Camp, Siam. Report on diet, malnutrition, hygiene, 1942.

AWM 54 554/5/3: Reports of Red Cross Medical supplies 1943–45, notes from meetings of Chungkai POW Hospital Finance Committee.

AWM 54 554/11/5: Descriptive report of the work of the Medical Services, 2nd Aust POW Group, Singapore, August–November 1945.

AWM 54 554/11/26: Kranji Prisoner of War Camp Medical Reports and Activities—Lt Col Glyn White, Lt Col Harvey Cotter.

AWM 54 554/12/4: Medical reports by Capt CRB Richards, Sakata, Japan, 3 October 1944–15 August 1945.

AWM 54 554/15/1: Diary by Capt CR Boyce, Medical records 'J' Force, 1943–45, written 13 January 1945.

AWM 54 554/17/2: Report 'Base Hospital Kanchanaburi' by Lt Col JW Malcolm RAMC.

AWM 54 554/17/3: Reports by Lt Col A. E. Coates, Impressions of the Nakom Pakon [sic] Hospital, written at the request of the Japanese Imperial Army. Experience as a POW in Burma and Thailand, general report on medical aspects of POWs' treatment by Japanese, 1944.

AWM 54 554/18/2: Medical Case Histories of Australian Prisoners-of-War compiled by Dutch doctor on Ambon.

AWM 54 749 [2313], part 2: Papers of Brigadier F. G. Galleghan, Collection of correspondence, special orders etc, 1941–1945.

AWM 54 773/2/5: Articles for public information by W. Boyd Graham. Broadcast by Lieutenant Colonel Coates experiences as a POW of the Japanese. Medical arrangements on the Burma–Thai railway.

AWM 54 779/3/97: Various reports—'Allied PW in Borneo', 9 August 1945.

AWM 54 779/6/2: A file of papers dealing mainly with conduct of recovered POW's of the Japanese, on their return to Australia [Medical reports, and interrogation statements] March–October 1945.

AWM 54 838/3/12: Data on rehabilitation—Method of handling repatriated Prisoners of War, 1945. Medical procedure on demobilisation.

AWM 127/79: Admission and discharge book of Changi POW Hospital 29 March–19 July 1945.

*Private records:*

AWM 3DRL/3435 (2): Papers of Lieutenant Colonel Robert M W Webster MC, AAMC and POW, Changi.
AWM 3DRL/3517: Papers of Hunt, Bruce Atlee (Major, b.1899), MBE.
AWM 3DRL/8027: Papers of Yamamoto Kiyoshi (Japanese medical officer with 5 Yokosuka SNLF).
AWM EXDOC084: Papers of Brigadier Arthur Seaforth Blackburn, VC, CMG, CBE, ED.
AWM PR00014: World War I POW diary of Brigadier Arthur Seaforth Blackburn VC.
AWM PR00016: Papers of Major Alexander Norman Thompson, MBE.
AWM PR00079: Papers of Colonel George Ernest Ramsay, ED, 1899–1981.
AWM PR00230: Papers of Major Alan Richard Hazelton (b. 1915).
AWM PR00701: Papers of Pte W. S. (Bill) Cameron.
AWM PR00720: Papers of Rayson MC, Hugh (Major, 2/10 Australian Field Ambulance b: 1891, d: 1961).
AWM PR00788: Papers of Dr Ernest P. Hodgkin.
AWM PR00860: Papers of Pte W. S. (Bill) Cameron.
AWM PR01047: Papers of Blau, Osmar Julius (Captain, b: 1913).
AWM PR84/99: Papers of Sir Edward 'Weary' Dunlop AC CMG OBE KStJ.
AWM PR85/086: Papers of Major Alan Frank Hobbs MID.
AWM PR86/276: Papers of Captain I. L. Duncan.
AWM PR87/154: Papers of Sir Edward 'Weary' Dunlop AC CMG OBE KStJ.
AWM PR90/043: Papers of Lieutenant Colonel N. M. Eadie.
AWM PR91/135: Papers of Corp Lex Arthurson, 13 AGH.
MSS 1085: Manuscript: 'Hell and its Yellow Devils' by Osmund E. Vickers-Bush.
MSS 1542: Manuscript of Private Stanley Francis Denning.

## Central Army Records Office, Victoria Barracks, Melbourne
*World War II service records of:*
N/A Surgeon-Lieutenant Samuel Edward Lees Stening
NX 455 Major Arthur Alexander Moon
NX34665 Lieutenant Colonel Edmund MacArthur Sheppard
NX34706 Major Hugh Rayson
NX34761 Captain Roderick Lionel Jeffrey

NX34949 Captain John Perceval Higgin
NX350 Major Ewan Lawrie Corlette
NX35101 Captain Sandy Edwin John Robertson
NX35102 Captain Alex Keith Barrett
NX35134 Major Alan Richard Hazelton
NX35135 Captain Ian Lovell Duncan
NX35139 Captain Roy Markham Mills
NX35147 Captain Peter Ian Alexander Hendry
NX35149 Captain Richard Lloyd Cahill
NX70158 Major Reginald Errol Maffey
NX70273 Captain Charles Rowland Bromley Richards
NX70378 Captain Robert Delmont Pufflett
NX70385 Captain Gordon David Cumming
NX70489 Major Patrick Francis Murphy
NX70516 Major Carl Russell Furner
NX70579 Major Francis Patrick Christopher Claffy
NX70581 Lieutenant Colonel William Alick Bye
NX70643 Major Kevin James Fagan
NX70664 Captain Reginald George Wright
NX70668 Lieutenant Colonel William Cotter Burnell Harvey
NX70671 Major Frank Harland Mills
NX70674 Major Ernest Ambrose Marsden
NX70970 Major Robert Dick
NX71018 Major William Joseph McNamara
NX71022 Captain Desmond James Brennan
NX71114 Captain Leslie Oswyn Sheridan Poidevin
NX71143 Captain Richard Grey Vernon Parker
NX76180 Captain Thomas Le Gay Brereton
NX76302 Captain David Clive Critchley Hinder
NX76351 Major Geoffrey Francis Seymour Davies
NX76360 Captain Douglas Neil Gillies
NX76511 Captain Philip Thornton Millard
NX76596 Major Carl Ernest Mitchelmore Gunther
NX77245 Captain Alan Frederick Smith
NX79453 Captain John Lindsay Taylor
QX19079 Major Clive Wentworth Uhr
QX22801 Captain Charles Reginald Ralston Huxtable
QX22806 Major Burnett Leslie Woodburn Clarke
QX6380 Captain Domenic George Picone

# BIBLIOGRAPHY

QX6476 Captain Peter McLean Davidson
SX13978 Major Sydney Krantz
SX14044 Captain Colin Percival Juttner
TX2107 Lieutenant Colonel Robert Marriott William Webster
TX2109 Captain Maxwell Mansfield Brown
TX2150 Major John Sneddon Chalmers
TX2185 Captain Tulloch Graham Heuze Hogg
TX2199 Major Eugene Augustine Rogers
TX6071 Captain Gavin Murray Crabbe
TX6074 Captain Alexander John Middleton White
VX 47449 Major Bruce Hunter Anderson
VX13486 Colonel Alfred Plumley Derham
VX14845 Lieutenant Colonel Norman Basil Menzies Eadie
VX14906 Captain James Russell Goding
VX21434 Lieutenant Colonel John George Glyn White
VX259 Lieutenant Colonel Ernest Edward Dunlop
VX31470 Captain William Aitken
VX38992 Colonel Edward Rowden White
VX39043 Major Roy Halford Stevens
VX39055 Major Henry Anthony Phillips
VX39059 Captain Ronald Wellesley Greville
VX39085 Captain Victor Brand
VX39095 Captain Horace Finn Tucker
VX39181 Captain John Lewtas Frew
VX39183 Captain Patrick Neil O'Donnell
VX39223 Captain John Pelham Catchlove
VX39258 Captain Ian Conrad Heinz
VX39316 Major Howard Lyell Andrews
VX39436 Captain Vincent George Bristow
VX39972 Captain Victor Alexander Conlon
VX40219 Lieutenant Colonel Hedley Francis Summons
VX42966 Lieutenant Colonel Charles Harwood Osborn
VX45001 Major John Frederick Joseph Cade
VX45273 Major Julian Johnstone Searby
VX45320 Major Kennedy Byron Burnside
VX46174 Major Roy Bryant Maynard
VX47129 Major Ian Thomas Cameron
VX53704 Captain Michael Francis Addison Woodruff
VX57546 Captain Frank Robertson Vincent

VX60748 Major Robert Graeme Orr
VX61260 Captain Ernest Barclay Drevermann
VX61356 Major Howard Hadfield Eddey
VX62081 Major Thomas Pilkington Crankshaw
VX66657 Major Heyworth Alexander Wigglesworth Watson
W17 Captain Claude Leonard Anderson
WX11015 Major Adrian Ward Farmer
WX11067 Captain Theodore Godlee
WX11151 Major Arthur Robinson Home
WX11168 Major Bertram William Nairn

**Imperial War Museum, London**
*Private papers of:*
IWM 66/226/1 Captain Harry Silman
IWM 66/226/1 Captain Robert S. Hardie
IWM 67/158/1 Captain H. Churchill
IWM 67/166/1 Captain E. Cyril Vardy
IWM 67/202/1 Dr Stanley Pavillard
IWM 80/49/1 Major R. J. Bower
IWM 83/48/1 Dr Rudi Springer
IWM 84/18/1 Major D. W. Gillies
IWM 86/67/1 Colonel Horace Claude Benson
IWM 87/50/1 Flight Lieutenant F. R. Philps
IWM 88/62/1 Lieutenant Colonel L. Fernley
IWM 91/35/1 Captain P. G. Seed, interview by Anne Wheeler
IWM 92/4/1 Arthur Frederick Gibbs
IWM 96/19/1 Dr O. E. Fisher
IWM 96/19/1 Dr R. A. Pallister
IWM 96/41/1 W. Simpson
IWM 96/6/1 D. S. Cave
IWM 97/32/1-2 Lieutenant Colonel Sir Treffry O. Thompson
IWM 97/6/1 Frans V. B. Dumoulin
IWM 98/19/1 Dr F. E. de W Cayley
IWM 98/7/1 Dr G. F. West
Uncatalogued: Papers of Major T. M. (Max) Pemberton, SMO, Chungkai and Tamuan POW hospitals, IWM.
Uncatalogued: Personal diary Captain R. B. C. Welsh, personal diary, 13 May 1943, uncatalogued, IWM.
Uncatalogued: Papers of Captain Ian Mackay.

Uncatalogued: Papers of Captain R. B. C. Welsh.
Uncatalogued: Papers of Professor Hugh De Wardener.
Uncatalogued: Papers of Professor T. Wilson.

**National Archives, London**

*Official records:*

FO 916/446: Atrocities in Thailand—reports 1942.

FO 916/1059: Prisoners of war camps in Japan—reports January—March 1944.

WO 222/117: Prisoner of war camps in Thailand, reports by Major E. A. Smyth and Capt. R. W. Lennon, 1942–1945.

WO 222/118: Prisoner of war camp Formosa, appendix to report on medical conditions by Major J. F. Crossley 1942–1943.

WO 222/156: British prisoners of war in Japanese hands, reports by Lt. Col. J. Huston, R.A.M.C. 1943–1945.

WO 222/218: Morale, Discipline and Mental Fitness: Circular to M.O.s.

WO 222/22: POW camps in Hong Kong and Japan, by Capt. AJN Warrack RAMC.

WO 222/245: Account of 500 British wounded POWs June 1940–June 1941.

WO 222/252: Training of medical officers in tropical medicine, by Lt Col Drew, Professor of Tropical Medicine, RAMC College, Millbank.

WO 222/256: Impressions of the Malaya Campaign, by Major L. E. C. Davies RAMC.

WO 222/257: Experiences as a POW in Italy, by Lt Col JM Steel and Lt Col JT Lewis RAMC, 1942–43.

WO 222/1386: Diary and reports—Malaya area 1942–1945.

WO 222/1387: The Campaign in Malaya P.O.W. Camp, Kuala Lumpur, The Campaign in Malaya P.O.W. Camp, Changi, The Campaign in Malaya P.O.W. Camp, Kranji, 1941 December–1942 February.

WO 222/1388: P.O.W. Camp, Malaya, January 1942–August 1945.

WO 222/1389: P.O.W. Camp, Nakompaton 1942–1945.

WO 222/1390: Report on POW camps: Thailand and Saigon, Tamuan and Kanburi, Chungkai, Tamuang, Takanum.

WO 222/1391: Reports on POW camps in Batavia 1942–45, by Lt Col CW Maisey, written 5 December 1945.

WO 222/1393: Report on Chemical and Pharmaceutical work at 55 Kilo hospital camp, by Capt C J v. Boxtel.

WO 224/180: POW Hospitals (Italy) Inspection and Visit Reports 1943–44.

WO 224/187: Formosa: P.O.W. camps and hospitals.

WO 224/188: Red Cross Reports—Hong Kong.
WO 224/189: Japan, Osaka group: P.O.W. camps and hospitals. Undated.
WO 224/197: Red Cross Reports—Far East—Manchuria.
WO 224/200: Red Cross Red X Reports, Far East—Thailand.
WO 325/12: 'List of Medical Officers on Burma/Siam Railway as Obtained from our Records'.

**Wellcome Institute, London**
RAMC 1016, Box 210
RAMC 1042, Box 215
RAMC 1261, Box 276

**Royal Australasian College of Physicians, Sydney**
MS Box 2
MS Box 74, Item 1–3
Captain Desmond Brennan—POW diary, uncatalogued

**Unpublished papers, memoirs and manuscripts, in possession of authors:**
Mr R. J. Armstrong, unpublished memoir, Bonnells Bay, NSW.
Dr Lloyd Cahill, POW diary, Sydney.
Mr Ray Connolly, 'The 10th AGH—to Malacca', unpublished manuscript, Belmont, NSW.
Dr Ian Duncan, personal papers, in possession of Mrs Joyce Duncan, Sydney.
Dr Bryan Egan, 'Understanding Medical Officers: Australian Doctors and War', unpublished manuscript, Melbourne.
Dr Kevin Fagan, private papers, in possession of Mrs Kevin Fagan.
Mr Bill Hammon, unpublished memoir of 2/3 MG Battalion, Cessnock, NSW.
Dr Peter Hendry, POW diary, Newcastle.
John D. 'Jack' Higgs, *Beffie and Me—Jack's Memoirs of Family, January 1991–December 2004*, unpublished memoir, Malvern, Vic.
Dr Harry Medlin, '2/AIF', unpublished memoir, Adelaide.
Dr Philip Millard, personal papers, Sydney.
Dr Roy Mills, personal papers, Newcastle.
Mr Douglas Skippen, *My World War II Travels*, unpublished memoir, Ipswich UK, 1997.
Mr Alf Stone, POW diary and personal papers, Newcastle.

## Speeches

Hewlett, Dr Thomas, 'Di Ju Nana Bunshyo—Nightmare—Revisited', paper presented to Survivors of Bataan–Corregidor Reunion, August 1978.

Thyer, Colonel James H., 'Leadership', address delivered to officers, warrant officers and senior NCOs, Changi, 18 June 1942, Royal Australian Corps of Signals Museum, Simpson Barracks, Melbourne.

White, J. G. Glyn, 'Prestige Lecture', address to Royal Women's Hospital, Melbourne, 9 November 1982, in personal papers of Bill Flowers, Melbourne.

## Books

Arneil, Stan F., *One Man's War*, Alternative Publishing Co-operative, Sydney, 1980.

——*Black Jack: The life and times of Brigadier Sir Frederick Galleghan*, Macmillan, Melbourne, 1983.

Beaumont, Joan, *Gull Force: Survival and leadership in captivity 1941–1945*, Allen & Unwin, Sydney, 1988.

Beaumont, Joan, ed., *The Australian Centenary History of Defence, Vol. 6, Australian Defence: Sources and Statistics*, Oxford University Press, Oxford, 2001.

Bellair, J., *From Snow to Jungle: A history of the 2/3rd Australian Machine Gun Battalion*, Allen & Unwin, Sydney, 1987.

Blair, John S. G., *In Arduis Fidelis: Centenary history of the Royal Army Medical Corps*, Scottish Academic Press, Edinburgh, 1998.

Braddon, Russell, *The Naked Island*, Penguin, Melbourne, 1993.

Brodziak, Innes, *Proudly We Served: Stories of the 2/5 Australian General Hospital at war with Germany, behind German lines, and at war with Japan in the Pacific*, 2/5 Australian General Hospital Association, Sydney, 1980.

Brooke, Gilbert Edward, *Medico-Tropical Practice: A handbook for medical practitioners and students*, 2nd edn, C. Griffin, London, 1920.

Buruma, Ian, *The Wages of Guilt: Memories of war in Germany and Japan*, Farrar Straus Giroux, New York, 1994.

Butler, Arthur G., *Official History of the Australian Army Medical Services in the War of 1914–1918*, vol. 3, Australian War Memorial, Melbourne 1943.

Christie, Robert, ed., *A History of the 2/29th Battalion—8th Australian Division AIF*, 2/29th Battalion AIF Association, Melbourne, 1983.

Clarke, Burnett L., *Behind the Wire: The clinical diary of Major Burnett Clarke AAMC*, Amphion Press, Brisbane, 1989.

Clarke, H. V., *Twilight Liberation: Australian prisoners of war between Hiroshima and home*, Allen & Unwin, Sydney, 1985.

Clarke, H. V., and Burgess, C., *Barbed Wire and Bamboo: Australian POWs in Europe, North Africa, Singapore, Thailand and Japan*, Allen & Unwin, Sydney, 1992.

Coates, Albert E., and Rosenthal, Norman, *The Albert Coates Story: The will that found a way*, Hyland House, Melbourne, 1977.

Connolly, Ray, and Wilson, Bob, eds, *Medical Soldiers: 2/10 Australian Field Ambulance 8 Div. 1940–45*, 2/10 Australian Field Ambulance Association, Sydney, c. 1985.

Cook, Haruko Taya, and Cook, Theodore F., *Japan at War: An oral history*, New Press, New York, 1992.

Dandie, Alexander, *The story of 'J' Force: 300, 8 Division A.I.F., Singapore to Japan P.O.W. camps with American, British and Allied troops*, A. Dandie, Sydney, 1994.

Darian-Smith, Kate, and Hamilton, Paula, eds, *Memory and History in Twentieth Century Australia*, Oxford University Press, Melbourne, 1994.

Daws, Gavan, *Prisoners of the Japanese: POWs of World War II in the Pacific*, William Morris, New York, 1994.

Dennis, Peter, et al, *The Oxford Companion to Australian Military History*, Oxford University Press, Melbourne, 1995.

Department of Veterans' Affairs, *Lifelong Captives: The medical legacy of POWs of the Japanese*, Commonwealth of Australia, Canberra, 1990.

——'The Australian P.O.W. Story—Courage and Mateship in Adversity', *Australia Remembers 1945–1995 Series*, Department of Veterans' Affairs, Canberra, 1995.

——*Stolen Years: Australian prisoners of war*, Commonwealth of Australia, Canberra, 2002.

Douglas, S., *Prison Camp Doctor*, Horwitz, London, 1963.

Dower, John, *Japan in War and Peace: Essays on history, culture and race*, HarperCollins, London, 1995.

Due, Stephen, *A Bibliography of Australian Doctors at War*, self published, Belmont Vic., 1994.

Duncan I. L., et al., *Morbidity in ex-prisoners of war*, P.O.W. Association of Australia, NSW, 1985.

Dunlop, E. E., *The War Diaries of Weary Dunlop: Java and the Burma–Thailand Railway, 1942–1945*, Thomas Nelson, Melbourne, 1986.

Ebury, Sue, *Weary: The life of Sir Edward Dunlop*, Penguin Books, Ringwood Vic., 2001.

Elphick, Peter, *Singapore: The pregnable fortress: A study in deception, discord and desertion*, Hodder & Stoughton, London, 1995.

Feuer, A. B., ed., *Bilibid Diary: The secret notebooks of Commander Thomas Hayes, POW, the Philippines, 1942–45*, Archon Books, Hamden Conn., 1987.

Firkins, Peter, *Borneo Surgeon: A reluctant hero: The life and times of Dr James Patrick Taylor, OBE, MB, CH.M*, Hesperian Press, Perth, 1995.

Gabriel, Richard and Metz, Karen, *A History of Military Medicine, Vol II: From the Renaissance through modern times*, Greenwood Press, New York, 1992.

Gamble, Bruce, *Darkest Hour: The true story of Lark Force at Rabaul, Australia's worst military disaster of World War II*, Zenith Press, St Paul MN, 2006.

Gandevia, B., et al., *An Annotated Bibliography of the History of Medicine and Health in Australia*, Royal Australasian College of Physicians, Sydney, 1984.

Gerster, Robin, *Big-Noting: The heroic theme in Australian war writing*, Melbourne University Press, Carlton Vic., 1987.

*'Getting on with it'—2/30th Battalion AIF*, The 2/30th Battalion Association, Kingsway West NSW, 1998.

Goodwin, Bob and Dixon, Jim, *Medicos and memories: further recollections of the 2/10th Field Regiment R.A.A.*, 2/10th Field Regiment Association, Rochedale Qld, 2000.

Griffin, Murray, *Changi*, Edmund and Alexander, Sydney, 1992.

Gurner J., *The Origins of the Royal Australian Army Medical Corps*, Hawthorn Press, Melbourne, 1970.

Hamilton, T., *Soldier Surgeon in Malaya*, Angus & Robertson, Sydney, 1957.

Hardie, R., *Burma–Siam Railway*, Collins, Sydney, 1983.

Hoff, Gordon, *The Rise, Fall and Regeneration of the 2/7th Australian Field Ambulance, A.I.F. in World War II*, Peacock Publications, Norwood SA, 1995.

Huxtable, Charles, *From the Somme to Singapore: A medical officer in two world wars*, Kangaroo Press, Kenthurst NSW, 1987.

*Instructions for Medical Officers (Australia) 1942*, D. W. Paterson, Melbourne, 1942.

Iragashi, Yoshikuni, *Bodies of Memory: Narratives of war in postwar Japanese culture, 1945–1970*, Princeton University Press, Princeton NJ, 2000.

Kell, Derwent, *A Doctor's Borneo*, Boolarong, Brisbane, 1984.

Lack, John, ed., *No Lost Battalion: An oral history of the 2/29th Battalion AIF*, Slouch Hat Publications, McCrae Vic., 2005.

McCormack, Gavan and Nelson, Hank, eds, *The Burma–Thailand Railway: Memory and history*, Allen & Unwin, St Leonards NSW, 1993.

McKernan, Michael, *This War Never Ends: The pain of separation and return*, University of Queensland Press, St Lucia Qld, 2001.

Miller, Patricia J., *'Malaria, Liverpool': An illustrated history of the Liverpool School of Tropical Medicine 1989–1998*, Liverpool School of Tropical Medicine, Liverpool, 1998.

Mills, Roy, *Doctor's Diary and Memoirs: Pond's party, F Force, Burma–Thai railway*, R. M. Mills, New Lambton NSW, c. 1994.

Moore, Bob and Fedorowich, Kent, eds, *Prisoners of War and Their Captors in World War II*, Berg Publishers, Oxford, 1996.

Nelson, Hank, *Prisoners of War: Australians under Nippon*, ABC Enterprises for the Australian Broadcasting Corporation, Sydney, 2001.

Newman, Carolyn, ed., *Legacies of our Fathers*, Thomas C. Lothian, South Melbourne, 2005.

Pavillard, Stanley, *Bamboo Doctor*, MacMillan, London, 1960.

Poidevin, Leslie, *Samurais and Circumcisions*, self published, Burnside SA, 1985.

Reid, Richard, *The Burma–Thai Railway 1942–1943*, Commonwealth Department of Veterans' Affairs, Canberra, 1998.

——*In Captivity: Australian prisoners of war in the 20th century*, Commonwealth Department of Veterans' Affairs, Canberra, 1999.

——*Laden, Fevered, Starved: The POWs of Sandakan North Borneo, 1945*, Commonwealth Department of Veterans' Affairs, Canberra, 1999.

Repatriation Commission, *Some Aspects of Medical Investigation and Treatment*, Commonwealth of Australia, Melbourne, 1947.

Repatriation Department, *Medical research bulletin*, no. 2, Repatriation Department, Canberra, 1965–1980.

Richards, Rowley, *A Doctor's War*, HarperCollins, Pymble NSW, 2006.

Richards, Rowley and McEwan, Marcia, *The Survival Factor*, Kangaroo Press, Kenthurst NSW, 1989.

Rivett, Rohan, *Behind Bamboo: An inside story of the Japanese prison camps*, Angus & Robertson, Sydney, 1946.

Saburo, Ienaga, *The Pacific War: World War II and the Japanese, 1931–1945*, Blackwell, Oxford, 1979.

Smith, D. A. and Woodruff, M. F. A., *Deficiency Diseases in Japanese Prison Camps*, H.M.S.O., London, 1951.

Sommers, Stan, *Arthritis, Alcoholism, Visual, Ulcer, Varicose Veins, Skin, Impotency, Brain Damage, Tuberculosis, etc: After-effects of imprisonment*, American Ex-prisoners of War, National Medical Research Committee, Marshfield WI, 1980.

——*Stresses of Incarceration: After-effects of extreme stress: psychological, neurological, residual nervous conditions*, American Ex-prisoners of War, National Medical Research Committee, Marshfield WI, 1982.

Steward, Henry Devenish, *Recollections of a Regimental Medical Officer*, Melbourne University Press, Carlton Vic., 1983.

*Their Service, Our Heritage: The story of the medicos 1885–1998*, Westpac Sub-Branch of the RSL, Sydney, 1998.

Thelen, David, ed., *Memory and American History*, Indiana University Press, Bloomington, 1990.

Towle, Philip, Kosuge, N. Margaret and Kibata, Yoichi, eds, *Japanese Prisoners of War*, Hambledon Press, London, 2000.

Walker, Allan S., *Australia in the War of 1939–1945*, series 5 (Medical), vols. I–IV, Australian War Memorial, Canberra, 1952–1961.

Wall, D., *Singapore and Beyond: The story of the men of the 2/20 Battalion told by the survivors*, 2/20 Battalion Association, East Hills NSW, 1985.

——*Heroes of F Force*, self published, Mona Vale, NSW, c. 1993.

Warren, Alan, *Singapore 1942: Britain's greatest defeat*, Hardie Grant Books, South Yarra Vic., 2002.

Wigmore, Lionel, *The Japanese Thrust*, Australian War Memorial, Canberra, 1957.

## Journal and newspaper articles

'A call to the medical profession', *Medical Journal of Australia*, vol. 2, 4 November 1939, pp. 691–2.

'Australian doctors and the war', editorial, *Medical Journal of Australia*, vol. 1, 3 May 1941, pp. 553–4.

'Dramatic struggle for lives', *NSW Doctor*, November/December 1995, pp. 10–13.

'Ex-POW doctor had courage', *The Listening Post*, vol. 43, no. 8, December 1964, p. 13.

'The Development of the Australian Repatriation System', *Medical Journal of Australia*, vol. 1, 19 February 1966, pp. 309–10.

'When our POWs return: Will they be different and difficult?' *Mufti*, 9, no. 5, 1 May 1944, pp. 16–17.

Beaton, T. R., 'From both ends of the Siam–Burma Railway', *Australian Defence Force Journal*, no. 113, July/August 1995, pp. 5–16.

Beaumont, Joan, 'Rank, Privilege and Prisoners of War', *War and Society*, vol. 1, no. 1, May 1983, p. 67.

——'Gull Force comes home: the aftermath of captivity', *Journal of the Australian War Memorial*, no. 14, April 1989, pp. 43–52.

Beebe, G. W., 'Follow up Studies of World War II and Korean War Prisoners', *American Journal of Epidemiology*, vol. 101, no. 5, May 1975, pp. 400–22.

Begbie, Richard, 'Little wonder these doctors were revered', Panorama, *Canberra Times*, 11 July 1998, p. 9.

Boyce, C. R., 'A Report on the Psychopathic States of the Australian Imperial Force in the Malayan Campaign', *Medical Journal of Australia*, vol. 2, 7 September 1946, pp. 339–45.

Brennan, D. J., 'Malaya and Singapore Revisited', *Medical Journal of Australia*, vol. 2, 26 December 1970, pp. 1257–8.

——'When I was a lad', *Radius: Newsletter of the University of Sydney Medical Graduates' Association*, vol. 12, no. 1, March 1999, p. 13.

Burness, Peter, 'Retracing the Malayan Campaign', *Journal of the Australian War Memorial*, no. 7, October 1985, pp. 18–23.

Caplan, J. P., 'Medical Memorandum: Creeping Eruption and Intestinal Strongyloidiasis', *British Medical Journal*, 5 March 1949, p. 396.

Coates, Albert E., 'An Address', *Medical Journal of Australia*, vol. 1, 17 January 1942, pp. 63–7.

——'The doctor in the jungle prison camps', *Speculum*, vol. 150, 1946, pp. 26–8.

——'Fundamental principles in medical practice', *Medical Journal of Australia*, vol. 2, 30 November 1946, pp. 757–63.

——'Clinical Lessons from Prisoner of War Hospitals in the Far East (Burma and Siam)', *Medical Journal of Australia*, vol. 1, 1 June 1946, pp. 753–61.

——'Surgery in Japanese prison camps', *Australian and New Zealand Journal of Surgery*, vol. 15, no. 3, 1946, pp. 147–58.

Dent, Owen et al., 'Postwar Mortality among Australian World War II Prisoners of the Japanese', *Medical Journal of Australia*, vol. 150, 3 April 1989, pp. 378–82.

Derham, A. P., 'Singapore and After: A Brief Historical Survey of the Activities of the Australian Army Medical Corps in Malaya', *Medical Journal of Australia*, vol. 2, 21 September 1946, pp. 397–401.

Downes, R. M., 'The medical profession and the war', *Medical Journal of Australia*, vol. 1, 15 June 1940, pp. 841–4.

Duncan, Ian L., 'Life in a Japanese prisoner-of-war camp', *Medical Journal of Australia*, vol. 1, 3 April 1982, pp. 302–6.

——'Makeshift medicine: combating disease in the Japanese prison camps', *Medical Journal of Australia*, vol. 1, 8 January 1983, pp. 29–32.

Dunlop, E. E., 'Clinical Lessons from Prisoner of War Hospitals in the Far East', *Medical Journal of Australia*, vol. 1, 1 June 1946, pp. 761–6.

——'Medical experiences in Japanese captivity', *British Medical Journal*, vol. 2, 5 October 1946, pp. 481–6.

Eddey, H. D., 'Prisoner-of-war camps in Borneo', *Medical Journal of Australia*, vol. 2, 21 September 1946, pp. 403–4.

Fagan, Kevin J., 'Surgical Experiences as a Prisoner of War', *Medical Journal of Australia*, vol. 1, 1 June 1946, pp. 775–6.

Foster, M., 'Medico makes emotion-charged return to Hellfire Pass', *NSW Doctor*, June 1998, pp. 24–5.

Gill, Geoffrey, 'Disease & death on the Burma–Thai Railway', *Medical Historian*, no. 8, 1995/1996, pp. 55–63.

——'Strongyloides stercoralis infection in former Far East prisoners of war', *British Medical Journal*, vol. 2, 1979, pp. 572–4.

Gill, Geoffrey and Bell, Dion, 'Strongyloides stercoralis infection in former Far East prisoners of war', *British Medical Journal*, vol. 2, 1979, pp. 572–4.

——'Chronic cardiac beriberi in a former prisoner of the Japanese', *British Journal of Nutrition*, vol. 44, 1980, pp. 273–5.

——'Persisting tropical diseases amongst former prisoners of war of the Japanese', *The Practitioner*, vol. 224, August 1980, pp. 801–3.

——'The health of former prisoners of war of the Japanese', *The Practitioner*, vol. 225, April 1981, pp. 531–8.

——'Longstanding Tropical Infections Amongst Former War Prisoners of the Japanese', *Lancet*, 24 April 1982, pp. 958–9.

——'Persisting nutritional neuropathy amongst former war prisoners', *Journal of Neurology, Neurosurgery and Psychiatry*, vol. 45, 1982, pp. 861–5.

Harvey, Cotter, 'Medical Aspects of the Singapore Captivity', *Medical Journal of Australia*, vol. 1, 1 June 1946, pp. 769–72.

Hinder, D. C. C., 'Prisoners of war: long term effects', *Medical Journal of Australia*, vol. 1, 30 May 1981, pp. 565–6.

Hurley, Victor, 'The role of the medical services in modern warfare, with a review of some of the special medical problems of the present world war', *Medical Journal of Australia*, vol. 2, 9 September 1944, pp. 265–73.

Huxtable, C., 'Australian doctors and the war', *Medical Journal of Australia*, vol. 1, 31 May 1941, pp. 690–1.

Marsden, A. T. H., 'Observations by a pathologist during three and a half years as a prisoner of war in Malaya and Thailand', *Medical Journal of Australia*, vol. 1, 1 June 1946, pp. 766–9.

McCormack, Gavan, 'Remembering and Forgetting: the War 1945–1995', *Journal of the Australian War Memorial*, no. 27, October 1985, pp. 5–14.

McWhae, D. M., 'The Medical Profession of Australia and the War', *Medical Journal of Australia*, vol. 2, 25 September 1948, pp. 337–42.

Nefzger, M. D., 'Follow up studies of World War II and Korean War Prisoners', *American Journal of Epidemiology*, vol. 91, 1970, pp. 123–38.

Nelson, Hank, 'Travelling in memories: Australian prisoners of the Japanese, forty years after the fall of Singapore', *Journal of the Australian War Memorial*, no. 3, October 1983, pp. 13–25.

—— 'A bowl of rice for seven camels', *Journal of the Australian War Memorial*, no. 14, April 1989, pp. 33–42.

Noad, Kenneth, 'Bruce Hunt Memorial Oration—1969', *Medical Journal of Australia*, vol. 1, 20 January 1973, pp. 134–8.

Pearn, John H., 'Murray Griffin and his Changi clinical paintings', *Medical Journal of Australia*, vol. 156, 2 December 1991, pp. 775–7.

Roland, Charles G., 'Allied POWs, Japanese captors and the Geneva Convention', *War and Society*, vol. 9, no. 2, October 1991, p. 87.

Rose, N. H., 'Some Medical experiences as a Prisoner of War', *Medical Journal of Australia*, vol. 1, 1 June 1946, pp. 772–3.

Smith, I. C., Patterson, F. and Goulston, K., 'Evidence of hepatitis virus infection among Australian prisoners of war during World War 2', *Medical Journal of Australia*, vol. 147, 7 September 1987, pp. 229–30.

Stanley, Peter, '"Sniffing the ground": Australians and Borneo—1945, 1994', *Journal of the Australian War Memorial*, no. 25, October 1994, p. 40.

Stening, S. E. L., 'Experiences as a Prisoner of War in Japan', *Medical Journal of Australia*, vol. 1, 1 June 1946, pp. 773–5.

Tennant, Christopher, Goulston, Kerry and Dent, Owen, 'Australian Prisoners of War of the Japanese: Post-war psychiatric hospitalisation and psychological morbidity', *Australian and New Zealand Journal of Psychiatry*, vol. 20, 1986, pp. 334–40.

Venables G. S. et al., 'Clinical and subclinical nutritional neurological damage in former war prisoners of the Japanese', *Transaction of the Royal Society of Tropical Medicine and Hygiene*, vol. 79, 1985, pp. 412–14.

Walker, Allan S., 'The impact of two world wars on medicine in Australia', *Medical Journal of Australia*, vol. 1, 1951, pp. 32–5.

Walter, J. H., 'Neurological Disease Due to Malnutrition', *Transactions of the Royal Society of Tropical Medicine and Hygiene*, vol. 60, 4 February 1966, pp. 128–35.

Watson, Ian B., 'Post-traumatic disorder in Australian prisoners of the Japanese: A clinical study', *Australian and New Zealand Journal of Psychiatry*, vol. 27, no. 1, March 1993, pp. 20–9.

Webb, R., 'Sir Albert Coates KB, OBE, LLD (HON), MD MS, FRCS (HON), FRACS, 1895–1977', *Australian and New Zealand Journal of Surgery*, vol. 58, 1988, pp. 419–22.

White, Glyn, 'Administrative and clinical problems in Australian and British prisoner-of-war camps in Singapore, 1942–1945', *Medical Journal of Australia*, vol. 2, 21 September 1946, pp. 401–3.

## Theses

Egan, Bryan, '"Nobler than Missionaries": Australian Medical Culture, c.1880–c.1930', PhD history thesis, Monash University, Melbourne, 1988.

Gill, Geoffrey, 'Long term health effects in former prisoners of war of the Japanese: a survey of morbidity patterns in a group of British World War II prisoners of the Japanese, studied some 30 years after release', MD thesis, University of Newcastle-upon-Tyne, January 1980.

# ACKNOWLEDGEMENTS

I have been very fortunate in the people who have helped me along my journey from PhD thesis to book.

I began this study at the University of New South Wales under the supervision of Dr Bruce Scates, whose early energy and enthusiasm were extremely valuable.

At the University of Melbourne, Associate Professor John Lack, the son of a POW of the Japanese from the 2/29th Battalion, showed me endless patience and support. I could not have asked for a better supervisor, mentor and friend. Thanks also to the wonderful Sue Lack.

My associate supervisor Dr Charles Schencking's expert knowledge about Japan and its people, sharp eye for detail and skill in making and assessing arguments taught me a great deal for which I am extremely grateful.

Several colleagues and friends have helped me over the past years. I would like to express my sincere gratitude to the Australian War Memorial's Military History Section, particularly Dr Peter Stanley who has been a steady mentor and friend since I began my interest in military history. Great appreciation goes to the staff of the Australian War Memorial Research Centre, particularly Geoff Brewster and Ian Smith; Brenda Heagney at the Royal Australasian College of Physicians; Professor

Hank Nelson and Professor Joan Beaumont for their helpful advice and encouragement; General John Pearn; Professor John Hilton; the Australian Military Medicine Association; Jim Allen at the Central Army Records Office, Melbourne; Michael Caulfield; and the staff of Australian Archives in Canberra and Melbourne. A special thanks to former POWs Alf Stone, Bill Flowers, and Tom Morris for starting me in the right direction.

For his continuous kindness and assistance, and for his advice about 'seamless webs', I am extremely grateful to Dr Bryan Egan. As both a historian and medical doctor, his insightful studies of Australian medical culture and Australian medical officers in war were inspirational.

Beyond Australia, I would like to thank Dr Kent Fedorowich, Dr Geoffrey Gill and Dr Yoshikuni Iragashi for their helpful expertise and interest in my work. Due to a John Treloar Travelling Grant from the Australian War Memorial, I was able to extend my research to Thailand and Britain. I owe a great debt of thanks to Rod Suddaby at the Imperial War Museum; Captain Peter Starling at the Royal Army Medical Corps Archives; and the staff at the National Archives, the Wellcome Institute of Medicine, and the Library of the Royal College of Surgeons. Special thanks to former British POW Doug Skippen for his kindness.

My gratitude also goes to the Australian Fulbright Commission for sending me to the USA on a post-doctoral fellowship for a year to continue my research. I would particularly like to thank Professor Ron Numbers at the University of Wisconsin–Madison and Professor John Lynn of the University of Illinois at Urbana–Champaign for giving me unique perspectives on my work and the best of American hospitality and friendship.

Also in the United States, my thanks go to Michelle Mears at the Oral History Program Archives at the University of North Texas, Denton, and to staff of the National Archives in College Park, Maryland. I am grateful to André B. Sobocinski of the US Navy Bureau of Medicine and Surgery and the staff of the National Museum of Health and Medicine Archives at the Walter Reed Army Medical Center, Washington DC, for their patient advice and assistance. I was particularly fortunate to interview Ambassador Charles A. Ray, Deputy Assistant Secretary of

## ACKNOWLEDGEMENTS

Defense (Prisoner of War/Missing Personnel Affairs), and am grateful for his expert insights. Much love to Hillary Caruthers, Mikkel Heuck, Feline Freier, and Ben Dewberry for many happy days of fun and 'inspiration' during my American stay.

Years of friendship and support have been provided by Dr Catherine Barnhart, Dr Andrea Bendrups, David Blanken, John Brownell, Dr Jennifer Conn, Dr John Connor and Karen Costello, Dr Martin Crotty and Amy Hyslop, Dr Wayne Geerling, Daniel Flitton and Emma Hines, Adam Gescheit, Melissa Jennings, Corey Jensen, James Johnston, Meredith Law, Dr David Liebowitz, Michele Martyn, Josh Mehlman, Amanda Mulligan, Dr Joshua Newman, Natasha Norton, Amanda Perry, Associate Professor David Philips, Leigh Richards, Hannah Robert, Elizabeth Rowan and Travis Chandler, Cameron Solnordal and Heidi Orr, Dr Richard Trembath, Simon Ward and last but not least, Michelle Lippey. Special thanks to Dr Garth Pratten for his long and generous friendship as well as endless advice on military protocol.

I would not have been able to do any of this without the considerable support (including financial) of my parents, Jeremy and Dr Kay Hearder, who read endless drafts, shared both historical and medical knowledge, and provided daily encouragement and wisdom. I also thank my siblings Michael, Jenny, Susie and Dixon, their partners and gorgeous children and the fabulous Barnes family. My sincerest gratitude goes to the late, great Brigadier Sir Frederick Chilton for his life-long inspiration and affection.

I could not ask for a better partner through life than Ryan Wick. His constant love, support, humour and superlative culinary skills have sustained me through many difficult days.

For many years I have been the fortunate recipient of the wisdom and counsel of Dr Michael McKernan, who led me to Ian Bowring, Jane Bowring, Aziza Kuypers and Katri Hilden at Allen & Unwin. Many thanks to them all for their encouragement and incredible efforts in making this book happen.

Most importantly, I would like to thank all the former POWs and their family members—Australian, American and British—who have taken me into their homes and shared their memories. They talked to me, showed me their private papers, and trusted that a young woman would understand the uniqueness of their life stories. It has been my honour and privilege to know them, and I hope they feel this book does them justice.

A final tribute goes to those former Australian POWs and medical officers whom I could not meet, but who left their voices and stories through official papers, letters and diaries. Most were written in a time of crisis, but with the firm belief that what was being recorded was important for posterity. This book is for them.

Rosalind Hearder
Canberra 2009

# INDEX

'A' Force 103
Adam Park camp 32, 144
Aitken, Captain William 69, 76, 82, 90, 114, 131, 168, 177, 211
Akeroyd, Captain John Finch 17, 72, 80, 209
Alexandra Military Hospital 8, 13, 15
Allied doctors
  captivity, in 149–54
Allied Mobile Bacteriological Unit 29
Allied nationalities, differences between 139–49
Allied Nutritional Advisory Committee 30
Allied POWs
  repatriation of 180–6
  transportation of 33
Ambon POW camp xiv, 69, 72, 78, 83, 87, 104, 181
Anderson, Captain Claude 14, 23

Anderson, Colonel Bruce 45
Anderson, Lieutenant Colonel Charles G. W. 132, 137
Anzac Day 139
Aonuma, Lieutenant Takeo 117
Armstrong, Dick 144, 145, 160, 163, 171, 197
Arneil, Sergeant Stan 22, 35, 44
Astill, Ken 66
'Australia Remembers' campaign 207
Australian army
  rank differentiation 132–9
  rescue teams 182
Australian Imperial Force hospitals 19
Australian medical personnel
  relationship with captors 92–123
Australian military hierarchy 127
Azuarma (Kim Yung Duk) 116

'B' Force 80
Bakri 10

Bandoeng camp 69
Barclay, Private John 'Jack' 51
Barrett, Captain Alex 83
Batavian hospital camps 77
Beadnell, Major 16
Beattie, Rod 206
Beaumont, Joan 70, 134, 142, 201
Bell, Dr Dion 189
Bennett, Major-General H. Gordon 16, 19, 133
Berley, Ferdinand 117
Bicycle Camp 97, 115
Bigelow, Frank H. 141
Blackburn, Brigadier Arthur S. 17, 133
Blau, Captain Osmar J. 99
Bloemsma, Dr 152
Boon Pong 61
Boyce, Captain Clive 70, 99, 114, 116
Bradman, Don 209
Braganza, Major R. R. 126
Brand, Captain Will 8
Brand, Dr Victor 5, 10, 11, 36, 50, 134, 149, 169
Brennan, Dr Des 3, 4, 9, 13, 70, 76, 79, 89, 90, 157, 168, 171, 203
Brereton, Captain Thomas Le Gay 166
British, attitude of 8–9, 139–49
British military structure 140
Bukit Timah camp 32, 33
Bull, Major John W. D. 15, 133, 150
Burma–Thai Railway xiv, 26, 34–5, 38–67, 69, 70
Buruma, Ian 122
Bye, Lieutenant Colonel William 127

Cade, Dr John 204
Cahill, Dr Lloyd 3, 4, 31, 39, 110, 127–8, 146, 158, 166, 171, 210
Callaghan, Major General Cecil A. 127
camp command 104–6
captivity
  allied doctors in 149–54
  Australian military in 125–39
  British military in 139–49
  careers after 201–6
  coping in 155–78
  road to 1–7
captors see Japanese
careers, postwar 201–6
Casey, Private Albert 98
Cayley, Dr F. E. 190, 202
Changi 35
Changi camp 18–37, 70, 71, 126
'Changi Concert Party' 179
Changi gardens 28
Changi Medical Society 30
'Changi piano' 179
'Changi University' 31
chaplains 172
Chikumi, Dr 114
cholera outbreak 47–9, 159–60
Christison, Captain David 106, 148
Chumley, Horace 141
Chungkai hospital camp 42, 47, 61, 71, 84
Churchill, Captain H. 163
Churchill, Winston 15
Clarke, Dr Burnett 5, 73, 190, 205
climate effects 74–7
Clipton, Major 129
Coates, Lieutenant Colonel Albert xvii, 8, 15, 39, 57, 62, 63, 98,

111, 117, 130, 153, 157, 175–6, 179, 203, 205, 209
Cobden, Walter McEwan 159
Cole, Neil 204
Collins, Lieutenant Colonel John C. 73
Collins, Private Ken 83
'Command Rubber Factory' 29
Connolly, Private Ray 31, 65, 87, 159, 166
cultural differences 118–23

Davidson, Captain Peter M. 72
Deakin, Corporal Arthur 87
deficiency diseases 29, 74–6
dentists 66
Depression, The 5
Derham, Colonel Alfred 5
Derrington, Norman 210
dietary deficiency 22–7, 71
Dillon, Lieutenant Colonel Andrew 52, 96
disease 22–7, 74–6
Dixon, Jim 204
*Dr Cade* 204
doctors
  enlistment of 1–7
  psychological impact on 198–201
Douglas, Griff 116, 196
Doyle, John 35
Du Moulin, Dr Frans V. B. 146
Duckworth, Noel 124
Duncan, Captain Ian 54, 74, 78, 82, 94, 103, 117–18, 143, 155, 161, 168, 176, 187, 191, 193, 195–7, 200
Dunlop, Major A. L. 43, 47, 55
Dunlop, Sir Edward 'Weary' xviii, 2, 17, 45, 53, 56, 62, 84, 90, 94,
101, 106–7, 138, 175–6, 188, 190–4, 206–12
Dutch medical personnel 57, 151–2
'Dutch Ointment' 58

'E' force 80
Ebury, Sue 207, 209
Eddey, Major Howard xvii, 86, 89, 112, 174
Egan, Bryan 124, 211
8th Division 7
Ehlhart, Captain J. H. 72–3, 155
Empire Day 2
ethical dilemmas 161–5
EPOWs
  JPOWs, comparison with 184

'F' Force 50–4, 128, 152, 210
Fagan, Major Kevin 163, 177, 204, 205–6, 210, 213
Fernley, Lieutenant Colonel L. 30
55 Kilo camp 117
Finkelstein, Hal 109
Fisher, Major Walter 85, 111
Flower, Jane 136
Flowers, Bill 4, 13, 31, 125, 194
foods
  lack of familiarity with 24
  utilisation of 28–9, 56, 60
Formosa POW camps 81, 175
Fukuda, Lieutenant 108
Fukahara, Lieutenant 79, 94
Fukuoka Camp No 17 74, 75, 78, 82, 83, 87

Galleghan, Lieutenant Colonel F. G. 'Black Jack' 27, 138, 143, 205, 208
Gemas, action at 10

Geneva Convention *see* 1929 Geneva Convention
Gibson, Lieutenant Colonel George T. 182
Gibson, Staff Sergeant Alan 66
Gill, Dr Geoffrey 158, 189, 195
Gillies, Major D. W. 149, 150, 169, 170
Glasgow, Major Robert V. 72
Glusman, Dr Murray 203
Goding, Captain James 160
Gonlag, Dr 161
Goodwin, Lieutenant Bob 204
grass extract 29
Gray, John 114
'Great World' camp 32
Gull Force 69, 89, 186, 201

'H' force 152, 205
Hague Convention 146
Hainan POW camp xiv, 69, 76, 78, 83
Haito camp 81, 87
Hak-Nae, Yi 105
Hakensho camp 70
Hamilton, Lieutenant Colonel Thomas 152, 166
Hammon, Captain Bill 81, 199
Hanley, Fiske 117
'happy feet' 25
Hard, Colonel Ilo B. 135, 141
Harris, Lieutenant Colonel S. W. 38, 94, 108
Harris, Roy 177
Harvey, Lieutenant Colonel Cotter 29, 84
Hayakawa, Colonel 45
Hazelton, Major Alan 55, 56, 173
Heidelberg Repatriation Hospital 197

'Hellfire Pass' Museum 206
Hendry, Captain Peter 9, 11, 17, 30, 60, 170, 171, 173, 186, 202, 204
Hetreed, Captain Bill 65, 119, 121, 128, 139, 203
Hewlett, Dr Thomas 156, 158
Heysteck, Dr 151
Higgs, Sergeant John 'Jack' xvi, 9, 10, 16, 31, 33, 48, 51–2, 122, 153, 186, 191, 196, 210
Higuchi, Dr 86, 98, 111
Hindati camp 163
Hiroshima 180, 189
Hirota, Lieutenant 53
Hobbs, Major Alan 23, 40, 152, 177
Hohl, Les 73, 134
Holmes, Colonel E. B. 27
Hoshijima, Lieutenant 103
Hoshiko, Cadet Officer 117
Howard, John 207
Hughes, William Kent 205
Hunt, Major Bruce 94, 106, 128, 145, 158, 171, 191, 205, 210
Huston, Lieutenant Colonel John 26, 99
Huxtable, Captain Charles 54

Ienaga, Saburo 119
ileostomies 62
Indian Medical Service 63
individual approaches 62–4
ingenuity 54–7, 88–91
interpersonal relationships 124–54
Iragashi, Yoshikuni 122
isolation 71–3

'J' force 70
Japanese
  administration 20, 93–8

camp guards 104–6
culture 119
enemy, communication with
    106–8
medical personnel 110–15
POW doctors, and 108–10
schoolchildren 122
secret police Kempeitai 117
sympathetic to POWs 115–18
ultra-nationalism 119
Western-based medical profession
    112
Japanese home island camps 70, 89
JPOWs
    EPOWs, comparison with 184
Japanese War Crimes trials 186
Jeffrey, Betty 14
joining up, reasons for 1–7
Jones, Ralph 165
Jose, Major Gilbert 177
*Journey's End* 140
Juttner, Captain Colin xvi, 3, 8, 50,
    54, 66, 157, 160, 167–8, 200

Kakuchi, Dr 114
Kami Songkurai camp 153
Kanchanaburi base hospital 57
Kelly, Ned 209
Keppel Harbour camp 32, 73
King, Lieutenant Colonel 166
Kinsayok camp 115
Kirkpatrick, John 'Simpson' 207
Kishi, Nobusuke 122
Kobe camp 70, 114
Korean guards 115–16
Kota Bahru 10
Kranji hospital camp 71, 73, 84, 85,
    163
Kuching camp 83, 86, 134

Labuan cemetery 80
Lark Force 69, 80
Lee, Captain Newton 95
legacies, postwar 212–14
Lendon, Major N. Courtney 148
Lennon, Captain R. W. 100, 113
Leslie, Private Harry 81, 87, 181
liberation 180–6
*Lifelong Captives* 193
Lillie, Flight Lieutenant J. 148
limits, pushing 158–61
Liverpool School of Tropical
    Medicine 6, 188
Lumpkin, Hugh 57–8

McEachern, Colonel Cranston 110
McGregor, Captain Ian 23
McKernan, Michael 186
Maisey, Lieutenant Colonel C. W.
    16, 77, 79, 88, 97–8, 104, 114,
    116–17, 129, 131, 147–8, 151,
    156, 166
malaria 6, 10, 25–6, 46, 69, 70, 75,
    81, 85, 94
Malaya campaign, The 7–17
Malcolm, Lieutenant Colonel J. W.
    57, 106
malnutrition 10, 73–7
Manchurian camps xiv, 70, 72, 81
Markowitz, Captain Jacob 55, 174
Marsden, Major Ernest 33
Marshall, Captain Gordon C. 72, 88,
    200
*Martindale's Pharmacopeia* 159
Maxwell, Lieutenant Colonel
    Duncan 3, 14, 133
*Medical Journal of Australia* 173,
    176
medical officers relationships 125–39

*Medico-Tropical practice: A handbook for medical practitioners and students* 158–9
Medlin, Lieutenant Harry 140, 199
Mergui Road camp 121
Millard, Dr Philip 4, 46, 60, 198–9
Mills, Captain Roy Markham xvi, 5, 11, 13, 23, 50, 136, 149, 183, 190, 193, 201–3, 205
Miskin, Captain Philip P. 100
Mitsufutsi, Dr 116–17
*Montevideo Maru* 80
Moody, Sam 104
Moon, Major Arthur 113
Morris, Tom 132, 181
mortality rates 152–3, 167
Muar River 10
Mukden camp 70, 81, 90, 157
Murao, Dr 117

Nagasaki 180, 189
'Nakom Paton Medical Society' 174–5
Nakon Patom hospital camp 42, 55, 71, 84, 98, 106
Nankervis, Lieutenant Frank 160, 210
nationalities
  mortality rate of 152–3
  working with doctors of different 149–54
Nazism 5
Nebuzawa, Dr 74
necessity, mother of invention 28–32
Nefzger, Dr M. D. 195
Nelson, Hank 89, 162
Nichols, Gordon 4, 34, 46, 47, 49, 147, 204
Nicholson, Colonel 129

nicknames 107
Niki camp 159
1929 Geneva Convention 119, 135, 155
1933 Australian population census 1
Nong Pladuk camp 87, 100–1
Nossiter, Reg 201

Oakeshott, Captain John Bernard 84
O'Donnell, Captain Patrick 87, 175
Oeyama camp 120
Ofuna camp 80
Ohashi, Dr 117
Omuta camp 103, 156, 181
102 Australian Convalescent Depot 183, 184
105 Transport Company 159
Ong, Russell 198–9
orderlies 15, 64–7
*Our Nation's Path* 122

Paisho camp 72
Pavillard, Dr Stanley 25, 48, 64, 65, 87, 105, 109, 115, 158, 159, 161, 164, 165, 166, 168, 170, 177–8
Peach, Flight-Lieutenant A. N. H. 151
Peach, Lieutenant F. Stuart 190
Pearl Harbor 7
Pemberton, Major T. M. (Max) 113
Percival, Lieutenant-General Arthur 14, 15
personal tolls 165–72
Phar Lap 209
physical abuse 99–104
physical health *see* postwar physical health
Picone, Captain Domenic George 84
Pigdon, Colonel Douglas C. 70

Pitt, Captain C. S. 65, 96
pneumonia 74–6
Poidevin, Dr Leslie 2, 4, 6, 50, 88, 109, 161, 169
Pond, Lieutenant Colonel Samuel F. 136
post traumatic stress disorder *see* postwar psychological problems
postwar careers 201–6
postwar legacies 212–14
postwar physical health 187–94
postwar psychological problems 195–8
POW camps, map of xv
*Prince of Wales* 7
professional dedication 172–8
professional frustration 156–8
Prunty, Luther 141
psychological problems *see* postwar psychological problems
Pufflett, Captain Robert 11, 13, 16, 24, 26, 46, 71, 127, 129, 163, 165, 170, 199–200

raison d'être 172–8
Ramsay, Lieutenant Colonel G. E. 137
Rayson, Major Hugh 15, 83, 89, 91, 92, 103, 108, 112, 132, 144
Read, Major 149
Red Cross 24, 73, 95–8, 108–9
repatriation 180–6
Repatriation Commission 185, 187–8, 190–3, 195
*Repulse* 7
resourcefulness 57–62
Richards, Dr Rowley xiii, 11, 24, 44, 62, 63, 88, 103, 109, 116, 125, 132–3, 140–1, 157, 162, 167, 168–70, 174, 200, 202, 203
River Valley Road camp 32
Roberts Hospital 151
Robinson, Private Frank 26, 81
Rogers, Major Eugene 42
Rolls, Bob 185
Royal Melbourne Hospital 204
Ryan, Private Mick 79, 114

St Andrew's Anglican Cathedral 13, 20
St Vincentius Hospital 97, 160
St Vincent's Hospital 3, 202
Sandakan camp 80
Sandakan death marches 34, 80
Schmidt, Dr 95
Schwartz, Otto 142
Scott, Lieutenant Colonel William J. R. 131, 142–3
2/3rd Motor Ambulance convoy 4
2/10th Field Ambulance 5, 11
2/19th Battalion 3, 15
2/21st Battalion 69
2/29th Battalion 135, 136
Seed, Captain P. G. 172
Sekiguchi, C. L. 20
Selarang Barracks 21
Serangoon camp 33
7th Division 69
Sharpe, John 104, 192
Sheedy, Redmond 204
Sheppard, Colonel Edmund M. 34
Shimo Songkurai camp 51
Silman, Captain Harry 49
Sime Road camp xvi
Simpson, Captain Stuart T. 152
Sinatra, Frank 180
Singapore 7, 11, 15

Sitwell, General 133
6th Division 69
skin complaints 25, 71, 76
Skippen, Corporal Doug 32, 145, 152
Smith, Harry 'Happy' 179
Smyth, Major E. A. 100
Sone, Lieutenant 161
Songkurai camp 153, 171
Sparrow Force 69
Stening, Surgeon-Lieutenant Samuel 75, 80, 120, 129, 175, 208
Stringer, Brigadier C. H. 14
Sumatra railway 80–1
Summerlin, Granville 191
Summons, Lieutenant Colonel Hedley 20, 64, 116, 205
surgery 75–6

Takanun camp 47, 99
Tan Tui camp 69, 87
Tanbaya POW hospital 153
Tarsau hospital camp 56, 157, 198
Tatiyama 116
Taylor, Captain Clark 106
Taylor, Chaplain Robert 141, 172
Taylor, Dr James P. 89
10th Australian General Hospital (AGH) 13
ter Laag, Dr 79
Thanbyuzayat 40
*The Bridge on the River Kwai* 129
13th Australian General Hospital 8
Thompson, Major Alexander N. 28
Thyer, Lieutenant Colonel James H. 14, 143
time, passage of 83–8
Toheda, Captain 101
Tol Plantation 80
tropical ulcers 49, 62, 69, 175–6

Ubon camp 100–1
University of Melbourne 204
Uren, Tom 194

van Boxtel, Captain Christoffel 58
van der Post, Colonel Laurens 116, 208
Vardy, Captain E. Cyril 137, 157, 164
Varley, Brigadier Arthur L. 136–7
Vaughan, Acting Sergeant 55
Veterans' Affairs, Department of *see* Repatriation Commission
Vickers-Bush, Osmund 53, 102, 128, 134, 164, 165, 189
Vincent, Captain Frank 'Joe' xvi
visual problems, alleviation of 55, 63

Walker, Allan 21, 182
war crimes 186–7
Warland-Browne, Bevan 59, 157, 159, 196
Warrack, Captain A. J. N. 101–2
Warren, Alan 133
'Weary' Dunlop Boon Pong Exchange Fellowship 211
*Weary: The Life of Sir Edward Dunlop* 207
Webster, Colonel Robert 85
Welsh, Captain R. B. C. 148, 150
Wheeler, Captain Ben 25, 107
White, Colonel Edward Rowden xvi
White, Colonel John 'Glyn' 5, 19, 26, 28, 53, 116, 130, 138, 205
Whitecross, Roy 185
Whitlam government 193–4
Williamson, George 78
Wilson, Bob 34
Wolf, Dr Pat 144

Woodlands camp 71
Woodruff, Dr Michael 5, 55, 204
Woodward, Captain J. J. 63, 99, 104
workload 77–83
World War II
  last months of 83–8
worm infestations 71
Wright, Huddleston 57, 136

Yamamoto, Lieutenant 112, 120
Yamani, Dr 114
yeast brew 28
Yoshikichi, Kasayama 105
Yung Duk, Kim *see* Azuarma

Zaadnordijk, Major 88
Zentsuji camp 70